A-level Study Guide

English Language and Literature

Alan Gardiner

Revision Express

Acknowledgements

Alan Gardiner would like to thank the staff and students of St John Rigby College, Wigan, who have contributed in many ways to the writing of this book.

The publishers are grateful to the following for permission to reproduce copyright material: easyJet for an extract from an advertisement for employment published in *In-flight Magazine* October 2003; Faber & Faber Limited for extracts from *Translations* by Brian Friel and an extract from 'The Trees' from *Collected Poems* by Philip Larkin; Guardian Newspaper Services Limited for 'Inquiries? Now the accent is on profit' by Stephen Khan published in *The Observer*, 24th August 2003 (© Observer), 'It ain't what you do it's the way you say it' by Colin Cottell published in *The Guardian*, 20th December 2003 (© Colin Cottell) and 'Kilroy Silk is an ass. So is the BBC' published in *The Observer*, 11th January 2004 (© Observer); The Labour Party for Tony Blair's speech to the Labour Party Conference 2001 and an extract from Neil Kinnock's 1987 General Election speech at Llandudno; Macmillan Books Limited for an extract from *Bridget Jones's Diary* by Helen Fielding; Methuen Publishing Limited for an extract from *Glengarry Glen Ross* by David Mamet and an extract from *Our Day Out* by Willy Russell; and Mirrorpix/Daily Mirror for an extract from 'Don't give sick Kilroy a platform' published in *The Daily Mirror*, 10th January 2004.

In some instances we have been unable to trace the owners of copyright material and we would appreciate any information that would enable us to do so.

Series Consultants: Geoff Black and Stuart Wall

Pearson Education Limited
Edinburgh Gate, Harlow
Essex CM20 2JE, England
and Associated Companies throughout the world
www.pearsoned.co.uk

© Pearson Education Limited 2005

The right of Alan Gardiner to be identified as author of this work has been asserted by him in accordance with the Copyright, Designs and Patents Act 1988.

British Library Cataloguing-in-Publication Data
A catalogue entry for this title is available from the British Library.

ISBN 1-405-82367-4
First published 2005

10 9 8 7 6 5 4 3 2 1
09 08 07 06 05

Set by 35 in Univers, Cheltenham
Printed by Ashford Colour Press, Gosport, Hants

Language terms and concepts

One of the main differences you'll find between your AS/A2 English course and GCSE English is that you're required to look at texts more analytically, and to use more technical terms in doing this. This applies to all the texts that you study, whether it's a Shakespeare play, a transcript of a conversation or an advertisement for a holiday in Ibiza. Students often lose marks in exams because they do not include enough terminology, so you need to develop a familiarity with all the important terms, including – to name a few random examples – 'syndetic listing', 'imperative sentences' and 'ellipsis'. Although these terms often sound difficult, what they actually mean is usually fairly straightforward, so it's really just a case of learning the terms and getting used to using them in your answers.

Another way marks are lost is to name a feature that is in a text (writing something like 'The poet uses a metaphor in line 3'), but to then say nothing about the effect the feature has, or why it is there. So beware of 'feature spotting' – remember you should always add a comment on how the feature relates to the meaning and effect of the text.

This chapter also includes sections on language change. You'll be studying texts from different historical periods, and need to show you can recognise how language has altered over the centuries.

Exam themes

➔ Language features (lexis, grammar etc.).

➔ How language has changed over time.

Topic checklist

○ AS ● A2	OCR	EDEXCEL	AQA A	AQA B	WJEC
Word classes	○●	○●	○●	○●	○●
Lexis and semantics 1	○●	○●	○●	○●	○●
Lexis and semantics 2	○●	○●	○●	○●	○●
Grammar and syntax 1	○●	○●	○●	○●	○●
Grammar and syntax 2	○●	○●	○●	○●	○●
Phonology, discourse and graphology	○●	○●	○●	○●	○●
Dialects and registers	○●	○●	○●	○●	○●
Language change	○●	○●	○●	○●	○●
Analysing texts from the past	○●	○●	○●	○●	○●

Word classes

You were probably taught **word classes** before you started your AS course (possibly even at primary school!), but you may well have forgotten them. Try to learn them early in the course and get into the habit of using them regularly.

Nouns

Nouns are naming words. They are words that give names to people, objects, places, feelings etc. These words all are nouns: *woman*, *pencil*, *Liverpool*, *excitement*.

The main **types of noun** include:

→ **Proper nouns**   These usually begin with a capital letter and refer to specific people, places, occasions etc.: *Italy*, *Olivia*, *Saturday*.
→ **Common nouns**   These are not so specific and refer to types of people, objects, feelings etc.: *student*, *city*, *disappointment*. Most nouns are common nouns, which can be subdivided further into:
  → **Concrete nouns**, which refer to things that physically exist: *house*, *tree*, *table*.
  → **Abstract nouns**, which refer to feelings, ideas, qualities etc. (things that do not physically exist): *freedom*, *friendship*, *strength*.
  → **Collective nouns**, which are names given to groups of people, animals, objects: *team*, *flock*, *herd*.

Adjectives

Adjectives are words used to describe nouns: *an <u>expensive</u> car*, *a <u>tall</u> man*. Words such as *colder* and *bigger* are known as **comparative adjectives** (or simply **comparatives**). Words such as *coldest* and *biggest* are **superlative adjectives** (or simply **superlatives**).

Verbs

Many **verbs** refer to physical actions: *run*, *jump*, *walk* etc. However, they can also refer to 'mental actions' (*think*, *feel*, *imagine*) and to 'states' (*The house <u>stands</u> on a hill*, *That <u>seems</u> fair*). It is also important to remember that *to be* is a verb, as are all its forms (*is*, *was*, *are*, *were* etc.).

The **main verb** in a clause or sentence is a single verb that expresses the main meaning. **Auxiliary verbs** are 'helping' verbs placed in front of main verbs: *I <u>must have been</u> going in the wrong direction*. Here *going* is the main verb. *Must*, *have* and *been* are all being used as auxiliary verbs.

Verbs can also be **active** or **passive**. When a verb is used actively, the person or thing performing the action is emphasised as the subject of the verb: *The teacher <u>spoke</u> to the student*. If the passive voice is used, the emphasis shifts to the object of the verb (the person or thing to which something has been done): *The student <u>was spoken to</u> by the teacher*.

Checkpoint 1

The same word can be a different word class if it is used in different ways. What word class is the word *paint* in each of the following?
→ *She likes to <u>paint</u> in the evening.*
→ *He bought a tin of <u>paint</u>.*

The jargon

Words that clearly refer to actions (*push*, *throw* etc.) are known as **dynamic verbs**. Verbs that refer to states or processes (e.g. *believe*, *know*) are **stative verbs**.

Take note

Primary verbs are verbs that can act as auxiliary verbs and also as main verbs. There are only three of them: *be*, *have* and *do*. For example, *have* is used as a main verb in the sentence *I have a new coat*. **Modal auxiliaries** are only ever used alongside a main verb. There are nine of them: *can*, *could*, *will*, *would*, *shall*, *should*, *may*, *might*, *must*.

Adverbs

Adverbs usually give us more information about verbs, describing verbs in rather the same way that adjectives describe nouns: *She felt better*, *He laughed loudly*. Many adverbs are formed by adding *-ly* to the end of adjectives.

Pronouns

Pronouns are words that take the place of nouns. If the sentence *John gave his telephone number to Laura* is changed to *He gave it to her*, three pronouns take the place of nouns. Many pronouns are **personal pronouns** (pronouns which replace the subject or object of a sentence). They include: *I, me, we, us* (all **first person** pronouns); *you* (**second person**); *he, she, it, him, her, they, them* (**third person**). Other pronouns include such words as *mine, ours, yourself, who, whose, someone, anything*.

Conjunctions

Conjunctions are joining words, used to connect the different parts of a sentence. **Co-ordinating conjunctions** are used when the parts of a sentence are of equal value. The most common are *and*, *but* and *or* (e.g. *I went to the shop and bought some chocolate*). **Subordinating conjunctions** link a subordinate clause (see page 12) to a main clause. Examples include *because, although, unless, until*.

Prepositions

Prepositions usually indicate in some way how one thing is related to something else. Examples include prepositions relating to position (*on, under, above*), direction (*towards, past, to*) and time (*before, during, after*).

Determiners

Determiners are placed in front of nouns to indicate quantity or identify the noun in some way. The most common are the words *a*, *an* and *the*. Other examples include *some* (*some money*), *that* (*that car*) and *one, two, three* etc. Most determiners are also a kind of adjective.

Take note

Tense is another important aspect of verbs. Verbs can be **present** (*I am watching* television, *I watch* television frequently) or **past** (*I watched* television last night). The term *tense* refers to verb endings, which means that strictly speaking English does not have a **future tense** (because we do not attach special endings to verbs to give them a future meaning). Instead we use other kinds of constructions to refer to the future, the most common of which is adding the modal auxiliary *will* or *shall* to the infinitive form of the verb (*I will watch* less television once term starts).

Checkpoint 2

An **intensifier** is a particular kind of adverb. Do you know what this term means, and can you give any examples?

The jargon

Relative pronouns are like other pronouns in that they refer to nouns, but they do not actually take the place of them. They act as linking words in a sentence and are always placed immediately after the noun they refer to: *the man who robbed the bank*, *a house that has many attractive features*.

Exam preparation (10 minutes) answer: page 22

Find ten verbs in the following extract from the novel *Wuthering Heights*:

> On that bleak hill-top the earth was hard with a black frost, and the air made me shiver through every limb. Being unable to remove the chain, I jumped over, and, running up the flagged causeway bordered with straggling gooseberry bushes, knocked vainly for admittance, till my knuckles tingled and the dogs howled.

Lexis and semantics 1

The next two sections look at words and their meanings. **Lexis** is another term for **vocabulary**. The study of word meanings is called **semantics**.

Denotation and connotation

Denotation refers to the straightforward, objective meaning of a word – the kind of meaning we might expect to find if we looked the word up in a dictionary. The word *summer*, for example, denotes the season between spring and autumn.

The **connotations** of a word are the *associations* that a word has – the emotions and attitudes that are aroused by it. These can be **positive** or **negative**. In the case of *summer*, the connotations are generally positive – most people associate summer with long, sunny days, holidays and so on.

Connotations are very important when analysing texts. Writers choose their words carefully, and you need to think about the feelings and ideas conveyed by particular words. You should also look for patterns in the lexis that is used. Are there groups of words with similar connotations? For example, if words such as *gloomy*, *miserable* and *dark* appear close together in a text, you would note that these words have similar associations and therefore reinforce each other.

Figurative and literal language

The term **figurative language** usually refers to the use of **metaphor**. A metaphor is a comparison that describes a person, object or situation as if it were something else. What is said is not literally true. Take these two sentences:

> The heavy rain turned the river into a raging torrent.
> He responded to her criticism with a torrent of abuse.

In the first sentence, *torrent* is used **literally**, to refer to a rushing stream of water. In the second sentence, *torrent* is a **metaphor**, used figuratively to describe the man's aggressive response.

Metaphors are firmly embedded in our everyday language, and we often use them without thinking: *under the weather*, *over the top*, *get to the point* and so on. When you are analysing texts, you are more likely to comment on the use of the writer's use of unusual and original metaphors. Explain what is conveyed by the comparison: how is the writer's perception of the thing being described made sharper, clearer or more powerful by comparing it to something else?

Be careful not to confuse metaphors and **similes**. A simile is a comparison that uses the words *like* or *as*. Again, many similes are in everyday use (e.g. *He had a face like thunder*).

Other types of comparison include **personification** (see page 57) and **pathetic fallacy** (see page 76).

Imagery is a term used for figurative language in literary texts. Later in the book there are sections on imagery in poetry (pages 56–57) and prose fiction (pages 84–85).

The jargon

Metaphorical expressions that are so familiar that they are no longer thought of as metaphors are known as **dead metaphors**.

Checkpoint 1

Do you know what an **extended metaphor** is?

Semantic fields

Semantics is the study of word meanings. A **semantic field** (also known as a **lexical field**) is a group of words with associated meanings and uses. The semantic field of football, for example, includes words such as *goal*, *penalty*, *referee*, *touchline*, *tackle* and so on. Vocabulary that is relevant to a particular field or topic is also known as **field-specific lexis** (an alternative term is **subject-specific lexis**).

Hypernyms and hyponyms

A **hypernym** is a general word that describes a category or group, within which there are more specific words. These more specific words are called **hyponyms**. An example of a hypernym is the word *clothes*. Some of the hyponyms of clothes are shown in the diagram below:

```
           clothes                    hypernym
          / |  |  | \
         /  |  |  |  \
  jacket skirt trousers top coat      hyponyms
```

A word can be a hypernym in one context and a hyponym in another. *Jacket* is listed above as a hyponym of clothes, but it is itself a hypernym in relation to *blazer*, *sports jacket*, *leather jacket* and so on.

Synonyms and antonyms

Synonyms are words that are similar in meaning. Examples are the words *start/begin/commence* and *finish/conclude/end*. Synonyms may be used in a text in order to avoid repetition. Alternatively, a writer's or speaker's **lexical choice** (choice of words) might for example be influenced by the relative **formality** or **informality** of particular words.

Antonyms are words whose meanings are in some way opposite to each other. *Start/finish*, *fat/thin*, *old/new* are examples.

The jargon

Another term sometimes used for a group of words linked in meaning is **lexical set**.

Checkpoint 2

The word *poem* can be a hypernym. List some hyponyms of this word.

Links

For more on **formal** and **informal lexis**, see page 8.

Exam preparation (10 minutes)   answer: page 22

The words below all refer to parts of the body. Make up two sentences for each word, one sentence using the word literally, the other using the word figuratively.

foot	eye	face	leg
mouth	stomach	shoulder	heart
chin	thumb	head	neck

Take note

For each of these words there are many metaphorical expressions in everyday use.

Lexis and semantics 2

This second section on lexis and semantics identifies some other areas to consider when you are examining the vocabulary of a text.

Formal and informal lexis

Formal lexis is serious and impersonal, and is generally more likely to be written than spoken. **Informal lexis** is relaxed and conversational, and is more likely to be spoken than written, though it is also found in many written texts. Formal words are often **complex** and **polysyllabic** (having three or more syllables), whereas informal words are often **simple** and **monosyllabic** (containing only one syllable). The word *automobile*, for example, is more formal than *car*.

There is not a simple division between formal and informal lexis. It is true that some words are obviously formal, while others are obviously informal, but with many words it depends on the context. Using the above example, *car* appears relatively informal when compared with *automobile*. However, it becomes a more formal word if we compare it with *banger*. This is what is meant by **levels of formality**. Some words are at opposite ends of the spectrum, but many words fall somewhere in between.

If you are analysing a text and want to describe it as 'formal' or 'informal', try to develop this observation by asking yourself such questions as:

→ Where exactly is the formality/informality evident? Refer to specific words and phrases.
→ Is the same level of formality present throughout the text?
→ Why has this level of formality been chosen by the writer, and what effect does it have?

If you are comparing texts, you may well find that one is more formal than the other, and you should consider why this is. For example, the texts might be aimed at different audiences, or one text might be written while the other is a transcript of spontaneous speech.

In your own writing, you should consider the nature of the task and the identity of your audience and try to adopt an appropriate level of formality.

Ambiguity

Ambiguous language has more than one possible meaning. In the final chapter of Charles Dickens's *Great Expectations*, the narrator, Pip, describes meeting Estella, the woman he loves, after several years apart from her. As the chapter closes, they are walking hand in hand, and the novel's last words are *I saw no shadow of another parting from her*. Are we to interpret this optimistically and assume Pip and Estella remained together? Or does it imply that perhaps they did part, but Pip did not 'see' (anticipate) that this would happen? This ambiguity is probably intentional: rather than simply offering us a neat, happy ending, Dickens is more realistic and suggests that the couple's future is not necessarily certain. Ambiguity is a common feature of literary texts.

Watch out!

Formal words are not all polysyllabic, and informal words are not all monosyllabic. *Thus* is a monosyllabic formal word. *Malarkey* is a polysyllabic informal word.

Take note

Informal lexis often involves the use of **colloquial** (conversational) words and expressions – e.g. *give it a rest, all my eye*.

Links

Using an appropriate level of formality is an important element in choosing a suitable **register**. For more on registers, see page 17.

Related terms include:

→ **Irony**   In its most straightforward sense, irony means saying or writing the opposite of what is actually meant (used in this way, it is similar to sarcasm). It is also used to refer to an event having consequences that are the opposite of those expected or intended (e.g. *He told her he forgave her, but ironically this only made her feel even more guilty.*). Another kind of irony is **dramatic irony**, which occurs when something said in a play has a deeper meaning or significance, which is understood by the audience but not by the characters.

→ **Pun**   This is a humorous play on words that depends on a word or phrase having a double meaning. Puns are especially common in newspaper headlines. A headline about a trade dispute over butter read *Butter Battle Spreads*.

→ **Oxymoron**   This occurs when contradictory words or phrases are brought together, as in the expression *bitter sweet*.

Links

For more on **dramatic irony**, see page 103.

Checkpoint 1

Explain the play on words in *Butter Battle Spreads*, and identify another linguistic feature in this headline.

Emotive language   ●●●

Language that is intended to produce an emotional response in the reader or listener is described as **emotive**. Words such as *distressing, harrowing, heartwarming* and *uplifting* are obvious examples. It can also be contrasted with **referential language**, which is neutral, factual and objective.

Moments in plays and novels that arouse strong feelings of pity and grief are said to have **pathos**.

Taboo language   ●●●

Taboo language is a term for words that are avoided because they are considered offensive, embarrassing, obscene or unpleasant. Often the context influences whether a word is taboo or not: swear words are usually considered taboo, but in some social situations the people present may consider swearing perfectly acceptable. Some taboo expressions are objected to because they are **politically incorrect** – that is, they express or imply prejudice against another social group (on the grounds of race or gender, for example).

Checkpoint 2

Do you know what the term **bathos** means?

Exam preparation (10 minutes)   answer: page 22

Sort the twenty words below into ten pairs. The words in each pair should be similar in meaning, but one word should be less formal than the other.

Chopper, beverage, scarper, quiz, impecunious, occupation, drink, cop, barrister, chat, retreat, helicopter, police officer, brief, interrogate, broke, binmen, job, converse, refuse collectors

Grammar and syntax 1

Links

For this section you need to know about **word classes** (see pages 4–5).

Grammar is a broad term for the rules and systems that govern how we use English. **Syntax** (which is an aspect of grammar) refers more specifically to the ways in which words are put together to form sentences.

Phrases

A **phrase** is one or more words, functioning as a unit in a sentence, usually containing a **head word** and accompanying **modifiers**. The **head word** is the main word used in a phrase. **Modifiers** are words that describe the head word or give us more information about it. If they come before the head word they are called **pre-modifiers**. If they come after the head word they are known as **post-modifiers**.

If the head word is a verb, the phrase is a **verb phrase**; if the head word is an adjective, the phrase is an **adjective phrase**, and so on. Looking in more detail at **noun phrases** will help you to understand how phrases work.

Noun phrases

Most sentences have one or more **noun phrases**. A noun phrase usually has a noun or pronoun as its head word. These are all noun phrases:

the house   the old house   the beautiful old house
the house over there   the house across the road

The head word in all of these examples is *house*, in each case preceded by a pre-modifying determiner (*the*). Many noun phrases also have adjectives that act as **pre-modifiers**. In two of the above examples, *old* and *beautiful old* are used in this way. The last two examples have **post-modifiers** (*over there* and *across the road*).

Noun phrases can be very short (a single noun or pronoun), or quite lengthy if several pre-modifiers and post-modifiers are used to describe the head word: *the beautiful old house at the far end of our street* is a single noun phrase.

Take note

Pre-modifiers and post-modifiers can be very important in a text. As well as providing descriptive detail, they can suggest attitudes and viewpoints. Think about the **connotations** of the modifiers that are used (see page 6). Often it is also helpful to consider whether the modifiers are **positive** or **negative**.

Clauses

Phrases can be combined to form **clauses**. A clause has to contain a verb phrase, and usually consists of a verb phrase and one or more other types of phrase. Rather like noun phrases, a verb phrase can be a single word (e.g. *go*), or a few words if auxiliary verbs are added to the main verb (e.g. *might go, will go, should have gone*).

There are five elements that can be combined in various ways to form clauses. All five are present in this example:

Checkpoint 1

Explain the differences between a **main verb** and an **auxiliary verb**.

A visitor/called/the old house/a ruin/yesterday.

1 The **subject** of a clause performs the action that is described, so it usually comes before the verb. It is normally a noun phrase, as in this example (*A visitor*).

2 The **verb** (*called*) is the second element.

3 The **object** (*the old house*) normally follows the verb, providing an answer to the question 'Who or what has something been done to?' In this case, it is the old house that has been called something. As with the subject, the object in a clause is usually a noun phrase.

4 The **complement** (*a ruin*) gives more information about the subject or (as in this case) more information about the object.

5 The **adverbial** (*yesterday*) is usually a kind of optional extra in a sentence. It normally provides information of the following kinds:

→ **Time** (when or how often something happened) *He met her last night*.

→ **Place** (where something happened) *He met her in the park*.

→ **Manner** (how something happened) *He met her secretly*.

Checkpoint 2

Do these five clause elements always have to be in this order?

Most clauses contain a subject and a verb. Depending on the type of clause, the other elements can be present in a variety of combinations. There are seven main clause types, shown in the list below (S = subject, V = verb, O = object, C = complement, A = adverbial).

S+V	She/smiled
S+V+O	He/closed/his eyes
S+V+O+O	John/handed/Mark/a key
S+V+C	Paula/was feeling/tired
S+V+O+C	The crowd/made/her/angry
S+V+A	Leaves/were falling/from the trees
S+V+O+A	Fiona/put/the money/in her purse

Each of the above clause types makes sense on its own and can stand alone as a **sentence**. As explained in the next section (page 12), a sentence that consists of a single clause is known as a **simple sentence**.

Ellipsis occurs when elements are missing from a clause or a sentence. Ellipsis is especially common in conversation. Take the following exchange:

A: Off out tonight?

B: Not sure.

Each of these utterances is **elliptical**. This is because in each case there is no subject and no verb. The utterances would be grammatically complete if A asked, *Are you off out tonight?* and B replied, *I am not sure.*

Take note

You can usually test if a sentence is complete by asking yourself, *Does it make sense on its own?* You should then try to work out which clause elements are missing.

The jargon

Sentences which are grammatically incomplete are also known as **minor sentences**.

Links

Ellipsis is also common in newspaper headlines. See pages 140–141.

Exam preparation (10 minutes)   answer: page 22

Look again at the examples of the seven clause types above. Identify the noun phrase, or noun phrases, in each case. Where it is possible, add pre-modifiers or post-modifiers of your own to lengthen each noun phrase.

Grammar and syntax 2

This section looks more closely at sentences, and also at how the arrangement of words in a sentence can be used by writers and speakers to achieve specific effects.

Simple, compound and complex sentences

A **simple sentence** has only one clause. In other words it has one main verb and a combination of some or all of the other clause elements.

A **compound sentence** consists of two simple sentences joined together by a coordinating conjunction (*and*, *but* or *so*):

> He had 60 driving lessons but he failed his test.

If the conjunction (*but*) is removed, this becomes two simple sentences (*He had 60 driving lessons. He failed his test.*). In changing two simple sentences into a single sentence, words are sometimes left out (a process known as **ellipsis**). In this case, the second *he* could be omitted (*He had 60 driving lessons but failed his test*).

Sentences such as this are still considered compound sentences. In a compound sentence, the two 'halves' of the sentence (that is the two clauses) are of equal importance. In a **complex sentence**, one or more of the clauses is of lesser importance than the main clause. These lesser clauses are called **subordinate clauses**. Unlike main clauses, a subordinate clause cannot stand on its own and make sense. One way of spotting subordinate clauses is to look for the subordinating conjunctions that often introduce them. These include such words as *because*, *when*, *who*, *after*, *although*, *as*, *except* and such expressions as *in order to*, *so that*, *as though* and *rather than*. In these examples the subordinate clause is in italics:

> His mother, *who grew up in Glasgow*, had a Scottish accent.
> The driver swerved violently *in order to avoid an oncoming car*.

Sentence moods

Another way of classifying sentences is to identify their functions or **moods**. Looking at sentences in this way, we can identify four types:

→ **Declarative sentences** make statements or give information. Most sentences are declarative sentences: *Helen is 18. She starts university next month*.
→ **Interrogative sentences** ask questions: *Where have you been?*
→ **Imperative sentences** issue commands, advice, instructions etc. They usually begin with the verb and omit the subject: *Close the door please. Sit down and listen carefully to what I am going to tell you.*
→ **Exclamatory sentences** are emphatic sentences, which in written texts are indicated by the use of an exclamation mark: *I don't believe it!*

Links

The **clause elements** in sentences are explained on pages 10–11.

Links

For more on **ellipsis**, see page 11.

Take note

Long sentences, with two or more subordinate clauses, are especially likely to occur in more complex texts. A large number of simple sentences may mean that an effort has been made to make the text accessible and easy to understand. Short, simple sentences can also have a variety of other effects. For example, they may be used to create a sense of speed or tension.

Examiner's secrets

In both of these examples, if the subordinate clause is removed what is left would make a perfectly acceptable sentence. This is a good way of testing whether part of a sentence is a subordinate clause.

Checkpoint 1

Is the sentence *I told you to keep quiet* an imperative or a declarative sentence?

Word order

Word order in sentences can be used by writers to achieve particular effects. **Foregrounding** occurs when the usual word order of a sentence is changed in order to draw attention to a particular part of the sentence (often the beginning). In this example from E.M. Foster's *A Passage to India*, the word *Dead* is foregrounded by placing it at the start of the sentence:

> Dead she was – committed to the deep while still on the southward track...

Parallelism

This occurs when parts of a sentence (or complete sentences) have a similar grammatical structure. This sentence is from *After the Race*, a short story in James Joyce's *Dubliners*. It describes a crowd watching a car race in Dublin, in which many European cars are taking part:

> At the crest of a hill at Inchicare sightseers had gathered in clumps to watch the cars careering homeward and through this channel of poverty and inaction the Continent sped its wealth and industry.

The parallel parts of this sentence are *poverty and inaction* and *wealth and industry*, where the grammatical sequence *noun–conjunction–noun* is repeated. The effect in this case is to point up the contrast between Ireland's poverty and economic stagnation on the one hand and the wealth and commercial success of its European neighbours on the other.

Syndetic and asyndetic listing

If a sentence contains a list, and within the list there are one or more conjunctions, this is known as **syndetic listing**. A sentence such as the following, which uses several conjunctions, is heavily syndetic (the sentence is from *The Dead*, another Joyce story):

> The raisins and almonds and figs and apples and oranges and chocolate and sweets were passed about the table and Aunt Julia invited all the guests to have either port or sherry.

If items are listed without the presence of any conjunctions, this is called **asyndetic listing**.

The jargon

Reversing the usual order of words in a grammatical construction, as in the example here (*Dead she was* instead of *she was dead*), is known as **inversion**.

The jargon

End-focus occurs when the arrangement of words places particular emphasis on the end of a sentence. In the last line of a poem by Philip Larkin, the word order stresses the word *love*: *What will survive of us is love*.

Links

Parallelism is common in public speeches. See page 38.

The jargon

When structural patterns are apparent in sentences, this is also known as **patterning**.

Checkpoint 2

What is the effect of the heavily syndetic listing in this sentence?

Exam preparation (30 minutes)   answer: page 22

Write the first 150 words of a short story, making sure you use the following kinds of sentence: simple, complex, declarative, interrogative, imperative and exclamatory. To accompany what you have written, write a short commentary explaining the effects achieved by the different kinds of sentences you have used.

Phonology, discourse and graphology

Apart from lexis and grammar, the other main aspects (or **frameworks**) of language that are usually relevant when analysing texts are **phonology**, **discourse structure** and **graphology**. As explained below, material related to these topics can also be found in later chapters of the book, but this section offers a brief overview.

Phonology

Phonology is the study of the system of **sounds** in a language. It is relevant to both written and spoken texts. In the case of written texts, an examination of phonology would mainly focus on stylistic techniques, such as **onomatopoeia**, **alliteration**, **rhyme** and so on. These devices are especially common in poetry (see the section *Sound in poetry*, pages 64–65). In spoken language, **prosodic** features such as **pace**, **intonation** and **stress** are important. Again, these are covered later in the book (*Phonological aspects of speech*, pages 30–31).

Discourse structure

Discourse structure means the overall organisation and structure of a text (the term **discourse** usually refers to a set of sentences making up a complete text). If you are analysing this aspect of a text, you should think about how the text begins, develops and ends, and the use of structural devices such as **paragraphs** and **stanzas**. The organisation of a poem may correspond to the conventions of a particular **poetic form**, such as the sonnet. For more on this, see *Poetic form and structure* in the chapter on poetry, pages 54–55. Discourse structure is important in spoken as well as written texts (see *Elements of conversation*, pages 32–33).

Cohesion

Cohesion is a term for the techniques and devices used to connect different parts of a text with each other. The more cohesion a text has, the more structured it is likely to be. For this reason, cohesion is especially important in texts that present complex information or a carefully developed argument. Some of the techniques used to achieve cohesion are outlined below.

→ **Repetition** If a word or phrase is repeated, it forms a link between different sentences or different parts of a text. Sometimes the word itself is not repeated. Instead a **synonym** is used:

> The government's decision will have *consequences*. The first *result* will be that street crime will undoubtedly increase.

→ **Anaphoric reference** This occurs when a word or phrase refers back to something mentioned earlier in the text. Often this involves the use of pronouns: *the reason for this, soon after that* etc.

→ **Cataphoric references** are references forward, as in *The following items were stolen from the house.*

Take note

Examination papers and specifications sometimes refer to language **frameworks**.

Checkpoint 1

Explain the difference between **onomatopoeia** and **alliteration**.

Checkpoint 2

Synonyms are words that are similar in meaning. What are words with opposite meanings called?

The jargon

Other kinds of reference include:
→ **Exophoric reference** These are references to the wider situation or context, to things *outside* the text.
→ **Intertextual reference** This occurs when a text makes an implied or explicit reference to *another text*.

→ **Conjunctions** The purpose of conjunctions is to link together different parts of a sentence. They also indicate the relationship between ideas in a text. The conjunction *because*, for example, indicates a cause and effect relationship between ideas or events:

> Spurs defeated Arsenal *because* their play was more inventive.

Most texts will contain simple conjunctions such as *and*, *or* and *but*. More complex texts are likely to use a wider range of conjunctions: *although*, *therefore*, *however* and so on.

Graphology

The **graphological features** of a text are its visual elements. With many literary texts (novels, plays etc.) graphology is irrelevant, but it is often a significant feature in such texts as advertisements and newspaper articles. If you are examining the graphology of a text, here are some of the things to look for:

→ **Layout** Is there a lot of dense text, or is the text broken up – if so, how? Are parts of the text separated from the rest by use of such devices as boxed sections and speech bubbles? Is there a reason for this? Are visual symbols such as asterisks and bullet points used to organise, or draw attention to, parts of the text?

→ **Typeface** Look for the use of bold print, italics, upper-case letters and underlining, usually to highlight elements of the text. Font styles can be significant – they may be chosen to appear elegant, sophisticated, zany or unconventional.

→ **Illustrations** These can take the form of photographs, cartoons, diagrams etc. Focus on the relationship between the illustrations and the written text. What do the illustrations convey, and how do they reinforce what is said in the main text?

Watch out!

When analysing a text, be careful not to spend too much time on graphology. The bulk of your answer should focus on the language of the text.

Examiner's secrets

As with other aspects of a text, remember you should always try to explain the *effects* of graphological features.

Exam preparation (15 minutes)   answer: page 22

The paragraphs below are the closing part of a speech made by Nelson Mandela at his trial in South Africa in 1964. He was charged with acts of resistance against the apartheid regime. Identify and explain the cohesive devices present in the text.

> This then is what the ANC is fighting. Our struggle is a truly national one. It is a struggle of the African people, inspired by our own suffering and our own experience. It is a struggle for the right to live.
>
> During my lifetime I have dedicated my life to this struggle of the African people. I have fought against white domination, and I have fought against black domination. I have cherished the ideal of a democratic and free society in which all persons live together in harmony with equal opportunities. It is an ideal which I hope to live for, and to see realised. But my lord, if needs be, it is an ideal for which I am prepared to die.

Take note

The *ANC* is the African National Congress, a political organisation to which Mandela belonged.

Dialects and registers

Previous sections have looked at specific elements of language, such as lexis and grammar. **Dialect** and **register** are broader terms for the kinds of language different people might use in different situations.

Dialects

Dialect is a term used for a form of language with distinctive features of vocabulary, grammar and punctuation. It is most commonly used in connection with **regional dialects** – that is, different varieties of a language spoken in different geographical regions. In the case of English, these include the Scouse dialect, the Cockney dialect and so on.

Examples of **dialect vocabulary** are the use in Liverpool of *bizzies* to refer to police, and *kecks* to mean trousers. **Dialect grammar** usually involves the use of **non-standard** forms, such as *I seen him last week* instead of *I saw him last week*.

As dialect refers to vocabulary, grammar and pronunciation, it is a broader term than **accent**, which refers only to pronunciation. (To avoid confusion between the two, dialect is sometimes used to refer only to vocabulary and grammar.)

Often one of the dialects of a language will come to be accepted as the 'standard' variety. This means that it has more social prestige than other dialects, is more generally accepted and is the dialect usually favoured in education and in most forms of written communication. In Britain, this 'prestige' variety is known as **Standard English**, originally a dialect spoken in south-east England.

Sociolects

A **sociolect** is a social dialect – that is, a variety of language associated with a particular social group. An example is the language used by teenagers, whose vocabulary is characterised by a large and ever-changing collection of slang words and expressions. As with other sociolects, this vocabulary strengthens their identity as a social group, separating them from the world of adults.

Some sociolects are based on occupation (these are also known as **occupational dialects**). Any trade or profession – builders, estate agents, lawyers etc. – will have its own specialist vocabulary. This is likely to be made up of technical terms associated with the particular occupation (**jargon**), as well as more informal slang expressions. There may also be distinctive grammatical features. In legal documents, for example, sentences are often lengthy and complex, with many subordinate clauses.

Idiolect

An **idiolect** is the language used by a single individual. No two people use language in exactly the same way. Every individual's spoken and written language is a kind of linguistic fingerprint – a unique combination of social, regional, educational and other influences.

When you are studying literary texts, you should look for the ways in which writers try to give different characters distinctive ways of speaking.

Register

A **register** is a form of language appropriate to a particular situation or context. Registers can be spoken or written. In the course of a single day, we are all likely to use several different registers: one kind of language with friends, another when speaking to strangers, another when writing a letter or an essay and so on. Each of these situations requires us to use language in a different way. When you are writing texts, you should take care to adopt an appropriate register. When you are analysing texts, it is often relevant to comment on the kind of register the writer or speaker is using, the features of language that characterise the register, and the appropriateness of the register to the text's context.

The main influence on register is usually the **audience**. Writers and speakers adjust their language according to the people they are addressing: children, adults, authority figures and so on. In particular, different audiences often require us to adopt different **levels of formality** – one of the main ways we are usually able to distinguish between different registers.

Another important influence is **genre**. The registers used in tabloid and broadsheet newspaper articles, for instance, have different conventions and characteristics.

Checkpoint 2

Explain some of the ways in which the registers used in these different contexts might differ from each other.

Links

Levels of formality are explained on page 8.

Links

For more on the linguistic features of tabloid and broadsheet newspaper articles, see pages 140–141.

Exam preparation (15 minutes)   answer: page 23

Imagine that someone has been asked to write a dialogue between two friends, making it as realistic as possible, and has written the script below. Has the writer succeeded in capturing the register of natural, everyday conversation? If not, why not? Comment closely on the language of the text in order to justify your answer.

John: Did you hear about Southampton's shock FA Cup exit last week?

Susan: Yes. Plucky Tranmere overturned a three-goal deficit and added yet another Premiership scalp to their collection.

John: A seven-goal thriller that was the stuff of FA Cup legend. Tranmere's performance confounded their critics and belied their lowly league placing. Now they face high-flying Liverpool – their Merseyside neighbours – in the next round.

Susan: Of course, they've triumphed in one derby clash already – they eliminated Everton earlier in the competition.

John: Even so, the in-form Reds should cruise through to the semis.

Susan: I'm not so sure. Terrific Tranmere could cause another Cup upset. I've a hunch they're going to KO the Kop Kings.

Language change

During your AS/A2 course you will study texts from several different periods of English. You need to be able to comment on how the language of a text reflects the time when it was written. This section helps to prepare you for this by identifying some of the key stages in the development of English.

Old English (400–1150)

English developed from the speech of the Angles, Saxons and Jutes – tribes who invaded England from northern Germany and southern Denmark in the fifth century. From the time of these invasions through to around 1150 is known as the **Old English** period.

England had earlier been occupied by Celtic tribes, but the Germanic invasions drove the Celts to the fringes of Britain. Welsh, Irish Gaelic and Scots Gaelic are all **Celtic** languages. In England itself, the Celtic language was almost completely overtaken by **Anglo-Saxon** (another term for Old English).

The next group of invaders were the Vikings, who began arriving from Scandinavia towards the end of the eighth century. Their **Old Norse** language resembled that of the Anglo-Saxon invaders, and much of its vocabulary was absorbed into Old English.

Middle English (1150–1450)

The next period in the history of English was triggered by another invasion: that of the Norman French in 1066. Their influence on the language was not felt immediately, and the beginning of the **Middle English** period is usually said to be around 1150. During the long period of French rule (England did not have an English-speaking king for over 300 years), **French** became the language of the royal court and of government and the law. English survived as a language but was enormously influenced by French. It has been estimated that as many as 10,000 French words were added to our vocabulary. The mixture of Old English and French that resulted is known as **Middle English**. Words of French origin tend to be more elegant and refined than their Old English equivalents. They also often have connotations of authority and status. Examples include the words *crown*, *government*, *parliament*, *court*, *palace*, *mansion* and *castle*.

The main change to **grammar** during the Middle English period was the loss of a large number of **inflections**. These are word endings that serve a grammatical function. Examples are adding *-s* to the end of a noun to make it a plural (*book/books*), and adding *-ed* to the end of a verb to make it past tense (*lift/lifted*). As these examples show, inflections still exist in English, but there used to be many more. The existence of so many inflections meant that meaning was less dependent on **word order** than in contemporary English, so the construction of Old and Middle English sentences was looser and more flexible.

Early Modern English (1450–1700)

During the **Early Modern English** period English became increasingly **standardised**. William Caxton introduced printing to England in 1476, and this was a crucial factor in the emergence of an accepted 'standard' English. During the Middle English period there were five main regional dialects, each very different from the other. Caxton chose to use the **East Midland dialect** for the texts that he printed (the East Midland area included London, Oxford and Cambridge), and this became established as the most prestigious form of English.

With the arrival of printing, **spelling** and **punctuation** slowly became more standardised. For most of its history English has not had a single, agreed system of spelling. During the Early Modern English period inconsistencies of spelling remained, but gradually became fewer. Most modern punctuation marks entered English after the invention of printing, though it wasn't until the end of this period that something resembling the modern punctuation system began to emerge.

Latin was a strong influence on English **vocabulary** during the 16th and 17th centuries. English had been taking words from Latin for centuries, but during the Renaissance there was an intense interest among scholars in classical texts and authors.

The **grammar** of Early Modern English reflected the fact that this was a time of transition between Middle English and the English we use today. The language of Shakespeare's plays is still marked by unusual **word order**, **archaic inflections** such as -*est* and -*eth*, and the **archaic pronouns** *thou*, *thee* and *thy*.

Late Modern English (1700–present)

The changes to English since the beginning of the **Late Modern English** period have not been as far reaching as those that occurred in the centuries before. The movement towards a stable, standardised language has continued. Many of the rules of **grammar** that we observe today began life in the 18th century, when several influential textbooks of grammar were written. The first great dictionary of English, compiled by Samuel Johnson, was published in 1755. This made an important contribution to the standardisation of **word meanings** and **spellings**. **Regional differences** in the way language is used have also lessened.

New words have continued to pour into the language. Industrial and technological development, **borrowings** from overseas (especially in recent years from the USA) and changing social and political ideas and attitudes have been the main sources for the additions to our vocabulary.

Links

Standard English (see page 16) evolved from the East Midland dialect.

Take note

The main **phonological** development during the Early Modern English period was the **great vowel shift** of the 15th and 16th centuries, when the pronunciation of long vowel sounds was transformed and became similar to the pronunciation we have today.

Take note

If Latin words that entered the language via French are included, more than half of our modern English vocabulary can be said to be derived from Latin. Latin words are often quite lengthy, and **Latinate vocabulary** tends to sound weighty and learned. Examples include *magnificent*, *ambiguous* and *ultimate*.

Links

For more on Shakespeare's language, see pages 120–125.

Checkpoint 1

Can you think of three reasons why regional differences in language use have decreased?

Checkpoint 2

List some examples to illustrate how these factors have brought new words and expressions into English.

Exam preparation (15 minutes)   answer: page 23

With the help of a good dictionary, investigate the origins of the following words: *courtesy, exaggerate, citizen, amusement, anger, ill, romance, belittle, quotation, movie.*

Analysing texts from the past

This section offers advice on analysing short texts from the past (such as poems and prose extracts), though many of the points are also relevant to longer texts. It focuses on linguistic features, but remember that as with all parts of the course your primary concern should always be the **meaning** of a text, and what the writer or speaker is trying to convey.

Periods of English

Remember the periods of English: **Old English** (400–1150); **Middle English** (1150–1450); **Early Modern English** (1450–1700); **Late Modern English** (1700–present).

Identifying the period a text comes from is a useful way to begin an analysis of it. You might also be able to recognise in the text features that are characteristic of the period (see pages 18–19).

Spelling

This may not be relevant to all texts because the spelling may have been modernised, or the text may not be old enough for the spelling to differ from contemporary English.

If it *is* relevant, you should look for **patterns** in the spelling, and try to offer comments and explanations. Common spelling features include:

→ **Extra 'e' at the ends of words**   This usually reflects older pronunciation; also printers sometimes added extra letters to justify text (fill a line).
→ **Doubling of consonants** (as in *travell*)   Unnecessary consonants have fallen away over the centuries; the above point about printing is also sometimes an explanation for double consonants.
→ ***y* and *i/u* and *v* used in a reverse way to contemporary English** This occurred before the use of these letters became standardised into the contemporary pattern.

Look also for **inconsistencies** of spelling within a single text. This shows that spelling had not yet become standardised.

Lexis

Vocabulary is often **more formal** in older texts. In addition, look for:

→ **Archaisms**: words/expressions that have disappeared from the language, or are now used only rarely.
→ **Archaic meanings**: words/expressions where the meaning has changed (e.g. **narrowing** or **broadening** may have occurred).
→ **Archaic contractions** (e.g. *'tis*).
→ If you are comparing texts, words/expressions in the later text that are **unlikely to have existed at the time of the older text** (e.g. **neologisms**, modern colloquialisms, words referring to modern inventions etc.).
→ Vocabulary that reflects **social and cultural change** (e.g. the influence of political correctness in later texts).

Take note

You are unlikely to be asked to analyse a text from the Old English period, and texts from the Middle English period are only likely to appear on a question paper if they are set texts that you have studied as part of your course. Short unseen texts (i.e. ones you have not encountered before) from the other two periods are set more often, especially in the synoptic module (Unit 6).

Examiner's secrets

As there is an Old English period, you should not refer vaguely to texts being written in 'old English' when they are actually from the Middle or Early Modern English period. When referring to modern texts in your answer, the phrases 'contemporary English' and 'present-day English' are useful.

The jargon

Narrowing occurs when the meaning of a word narrows, becoming more specific (e.g. *meat* originally referred to food in general, not just animal flesh). **Broadening** is the opposite – the meaning of a word broadens (e.g. *dog* originally referred to a particular breed of dog, but now includes all breeds).

The jargon

A **neologism** is a new word or expression.

Checkpoint 1

Explain what is meant by **political correctness**.

Grammar

Sentences are often **longer** and **more complex** in older texts. In addition, look for:

→ **Archaic inflections** (e.g. *hath*, *did<u>st</u>*).
→ **Archaic pronouns** (e.g. *thee*, *thy*).
→ Differences in **word order**, and constructions that would be unlikely to occur in contemporary English.
→ **Archaic verb forms** (e.g. *art* for *are*).
→ Differences in the formation of: **the past tense/negatives/plurals/ interrogatives**.
→ **Punctuation** differences (e.g. more frequent use of colons).

Checkpoint 2

What are **interrogatives**?

Phonology

→ Older **pronunciation** may be reflected in the spelling of words.
→ Some older texts (e.g. the Authorised Version of the Bible) were intended to be **read aloud**, and the language used may reflect this.

Discourse structure/graphology

→ The **organisation** of the text may reflect the age of the text in some way (e.g. newspaper articles in the past tended to have longer paragraphs).
→ There may be old-fashioned **graphological features** (e.g. font styles).

Exam preparation (30 minutes)   answer: page 23

The text below is an extract from one of a series of letters written by Lady Brilliana Harley in the years 1625–1643. The letter is to her husband, Sir Robert Harley. In what ways does the language used in the letter differ from present-day English?

> Deare Sr – Your two leters, on from Hearifort and the other from Gloster, weare uery wellcome to me: and if you knwe howe gladly I reseaue your leters, I beleeue you would neeuer let any opertunity pase. I hope your cloche did you saruis betwne Gloster and my brother Brays, for with vs it was a very rainy day, but this day has bine very dry and warme, and so I hope it was with you; and to-morowe I hope you will be well at your journis end, wheare I wisch my self to bide you wellcome home. You see howe my thoughts goo with you: and as you haue many of mine, so let me haue some of yours. Beleeue me, I thinke I neuer miste you more then nowe I doo, or ells I haue forgoot what is past. I thanke God, Ned and Robin are well; and Ned askes every day wheare you are, and he says you will come to-morowe. My father is well, but goos not abrode, because of his fiseke*.

Examiner's secrets

The main aspects of language to look at here are spelling, lexis and grammar.

Take note

* *fiseke*: medical treatment ('physic').

21

Answers
Language terms and concepts

Word classes

Checkpoints

1 In the first sentence *paint* is a verb. In the second it is a noun.
2 An intensifier is a word that increases or decreases the intensity of another word or phrase. Examples include *really, very, hardly, scarcely.*

Exam preparation

Ten verbs in the extract: *was, made, shiver, Being, remove, jumped, running, knocked, tingled, howled.*

Lexis and semantics 1

Checkpoints

1 An extended metaphor is a metaphorical comparison that is developed and extended, for example over several lines of a poem.
2 Hyponyms of *poem* include *sonnet, ode, elegy, limerick* and so on.

Exam preparation

Used literally, the words listed would actually refer to parts of the body, as in *He used his foot to prevent me closing the door.* In the following sentences the words are used figuratively:
He agreed to foot the bill.
The house overlooked the mouth of the river.
You'll have to take it on the chin.
We see eye to eye on most things.
The president hadn't the stomach for another war.
His friends said he was under her thumb.
We must face facts.
I'm not going to shoulder the blame for this.
The dispute was coming to a head.
It cost me an arm and a leg.
Now we're getting to the heart of the matter.
The two teams are neck and neck in the championship race.

Lexis and semantics 2

Checkpoints

1 The play on words is based on the idea of spreading butter. Another linguistic feature of the headline is alliteration.
2 Bathos is the sense of comic anticlimax created when a literary work drops from an elevated or serious level to the absurd or ridiculous.

Exam preparation

The pairs are as follows (less formal word first):
chopper–helicopter; scarper–retreat; quiz–interrogate; drink–beverage; cop–police officer; chat–converse; brief–barrister; broke–impecunious; binmen–refuse collectors; job–occupation.

Grammar and syntax 1

Checkpoints

1 Auxiliary verbs are 'helping' verbs placed in front of main verbs, as in *I might see you tomorrow.* See page 4.
2 No. For example, the adverbial in the specimen sentence on page 10 could be moved to the beginning of the sentence: *Yesterday a visitor called the old house a ruin.*

Exam preparation

The noun phrases are: *She; He; his eyes; John; Mark; a key; Paula; The crowd; her; Leaves; the trees; Fiona; the money; her purse.* Examples of how some of these phrases could be extended by adding pre-modifiers or post-modifiers: *his tired eyes; a key attached to a red ribbon.*

Grammar and syntax 2

Checkpoints

1 Declarative – because it is a statement rather than a direct command.
2 The heavily syndetic listing emphasises the great abundance of food.

Exam preparation

Examples of the effects these kinds of sentences might be used to achieve: short, simple sentences – to create a sense of tension; long, complex sentence – to describe something happening slowly; declarative – to give information; interrogative – to suggest the narrator's doubts or uncertainties; imperative – to speak directly to the reader; exclamatory – to convey surprise or enthusiasm.

Phonology, discourse and graphology

Checkpoints

1 Onomatopoeia occurs when the sound of a word echoes its meaning (e.g. *splash*). Alliteration occurs when two or more words begin with the same sound (but not always the same letter).
2 Antonyms.

Exam preparation

Cohesive devices include: repetition (especially of *struggle, domination, ideal*); anaphoric references (*This, this struggle, It*); conjunctions (*then, But, and*).

Dialects and registers

Checkpoints

1 The Received Pronunciation (or RP) accent. This is the accent associated with educated, upper-class speakers of English.

2 The level of formality might well differ when speaking with friends rather than strangers. This might also be true when writing a letter rather than an essay, though this would depend on the type of letter and the recipient. Letters and essays also have different conventions of layout and structure.

Exam preparation

The register here is that of a newspaper sports report rather than a natural conversation. This is especially evident in the lexis, which includes a large amount of journalese (words and phrases that are especially common in newspapers). Examples include *shock FA Cup exit, Plucky Tranmere, a three-goal deficit, another Premiership scalp, the stuff of FA Cup legend, their lowly league placing, the in-form Reds*. None of these noun phrases is likely to occur in normal everyday speech. The contrived phonological effects – specifically, the use of alliteration – are also associated with newspapers rather than natural speech: *Terrific Tranmere, KO the Kop Kings*.

Language change

Checkpoints

1 Three important reasons are: the growth in education; movement of people around the country; the effects of the mass media.

2 Technological developments have brought in words such as *internet, online, texting, cyberspace* and so on. Borrowings from the USA include *chill out, pass the buck, sidetracked*. Changing ideas and attitudes have introduced words and phrases such as *ageism, grey power, pester power*.

Exam preparation

Word origins are shown in brackets: courtesy (French); exaggerate (Latin); citizen (French); amusement (French); anger (Old Norse); ill (Old Norse); romance (French); belittle (American); quotation (Latin); movie (American).

Analysing texts from the past

Checkpoints

1 The avoidance of language that might cause offence to particular minority groups.

2 Questions.

Exam preparation

This text is from the Early Modern English period and has several of the features associated with the language of that time.

There are numerous instances where the spelling of individual words differs from that found in contemporary English. Many words have an extra *e* ending: *deare, howe, warme, thinke* and so on. These endings are common in the English of the period. Also characteristic is the use of the letter *u* where now there would be *v*: *uery*. At the same time, there is a reverse pattern in the spelling of the time, with *v* instead of *u* at the beginning of words: *vs*. Use of *i* and *y* had not yet settled into the present English pattern, and this is reflected in the spelling of *journis*.

A feature of the punctuation of the period – reflected in this text – is that there was much more extensive use of the semi-colon than in contemporary English, used where we would have full stops or commas. Another feature of the time is that an apostrophe followed by an *s* is not used to show possession: this is evident in *your journis end*.

The vocabulary includes archaic words that have since passed out of use: *fiseke*. There are also expressions that are now obsolete or at least rarely heard: *did you saruis, goos not abrode, bide you wellcome home*.

In terms of grammar, many of the constructions used are similar to those found in contemporary English. Occasionally the word order is different: *more than nowe I do* instead of *more than I do now*. There are also constructions that would seem awkward and unnatural today: *or ells I haue forgoot what is past*. Verb endings are not always the same as in contemporary English: *miste* is used for *missed*.

Revision checklist
Language terms and concepts

By the end of this chapter you should be able to:

1	Understand and identify the main word classes (nouns, verbs, adjectives etc.).	Confident	Not confident. **Revise** pages 4–5
2	Recognise the different types of nouns, verbs, adjectives, pronouns and conjunctions.	Confident	Not confident. **Revise** pages 4–5
3	Explain the difference between denotation and connotation.	Confident	Not confident. **Revise** page 6
4	Explain the difference between figurative and literal language.	Confident	Not confident. **Revise** page 6
5	Distinguish between different levels of formality in a text.	Confident	Not confident. **Revise** page 8
6	Understand what is meant by ambiguity and irony.	Confident	Not confident. **Revise** pages 8–9
7	Explain the difference between a phrase and a clause.	Confident	Not confident. **Revise** pages 10–11
8	Identify whether sentences are simple, compound or complex.	Confident	Not confident. **Revise** page 12
9	Recognise subordinate clauses within a sentence.	Confident	Not confident. **Revise** page 12
10	Identify the four sentence moods (declarative, interrogative, imperative, exclamatory).	Confident	Not confident. **Revise** page 12
11	Recognise the main techniques used to achieve cohesion in a text.	Confident	Not confident. **Revise** pages 14–15
12	Understand what is meant by phonology and graphology.	Confident	Not confident. **Revise** pages 14–15
13	Explain the differences between dialect and accent.	Confident	Not confident. **Revise** page 16
14	Explain the main influences on register.	Confident	Not confident. **Revise** page 17
15	List the key periods in the history of English.	Confident	Not confident. **Revise** pages 18–19
16	Explain the main characteristics of English during each of these periods.	Confident	Not confident. **Revise** pages 18–19
17	Identify distinctive features of older texts, and recognise why they might be present.	Confident	Not confident. **Revise** pages 20–21

Spoken language

This chapter looks at two kinds of spoken language: spontaneous speech and prepared speech. The representation of speech in literature (dialogue in plays, for example) is dealt with separately, in the chapters on prose fiction (pages 82–83), drama (pages 104–107) and Shakespeare (pages 126–127).

Transcripts of spontaneous speech may look strange when you first encounter them, as often they are without conventional punctuation, and they may have special symbols to indicate such things as intonation and heavily stressed words. Because speech is normally listened to rather than read, these **prosodic features** are especially important, and when you are analysing a transcript of spoken language you should always try to imagine what it would *sound* like, and comment on this aspect of the text. Prepared speech (such as a speech made by a politician) may look more like a traditional written text, but it will probably include features (such as sentences which have a rhythmic effect) that are best appreciated when the speech is heard, and you should be careful to look for these.

Exam themes

→ Language features of spontaneous speech.

→ Language features of prepared speech.

→ Differences between spontaneous and prepared speech.

→ Speech genres (e.g. speeches, talks, sports commentaries etc.).

Topic checklist

○ AS ● A2	OCR	EDEXCEL	AQA A	AQA B	WJEC
Spoken language: an overview	○●	○●	○●	○●	○●
Features of spontaneous speech	○●	○●	○●	○●	○●
Phonological aspects of speech	○●	○●	○●	○●	○●
Elements of conversation	○●	○●	○●	○●	○●
Conversational interaction	○●	○●	○●	○●	○●
Conversation theory	○●	○●	○●	○●	○●
Prepared talk: speeches 1	○●	○●	○●	○●	○●
Prepared talk: speeches 2	○●	○●	○●	○●	○●
Other kinds of talk	○●	○●	○●	○●	○●
Specimen texts	○●	○●	○●	○●	○●

Spoken language: an overview

Spoken language comes in many different forms. This introductory section identifies some basic characteristics of speech, and also outlines some of the main influences on spoken language.

Speech and writing

Speech and writing are different **modes** of communication. Some of the main differences are summarised below:

→ Differences of **form** are most obvious if the speech is **spontaneous**. Unplanned speech is generally **much less structured** than most writing. While writing is organised into sentences and paragraphs, we do not usually speak in neatly formed sentences and our speech is likely to contain digressions and repetitions. Because we are making up what we say as we go along, hesitations, false starts and mistakes are inevitable.

→ Speech can be accompanied by **body language** and by **prosodic features** such as tone, pitch and stress.

→ Speech and writing tend to have different **purposes** or **functions**. For example, we especially favour speech for the purposes of social interaction. Writing is suited to the expression of complex ideas and is preferable when a permanent record is required.

Types of speech

→ Here the main distinction is between **spontaneous** and **prepared** speech. Conversation is the most common kind of spontaneous speech. Examples of prepared speech include public speeches, radio talks, advertising voice-overs and so on.

→ Some speech is **partly prepared** and **partly spontaneous**. Stand-up comedy is an example: performances by the same comedian will have similarities, but they are unlikely to be identical.

→ Another distinction is that between **face-to-face interaction** (such as a conversation in the street) and **non face-to-face interaction** (such as a telephone conversation).

→ **Literary representations** of speech include dialogue in novels, attempts to mimic the speaking voice in poetry, and scripted dialogue in plays and films.

Functions of speech

Here are some technical terms for the most common forms of speech. Note that a single **utterance** can have more than one function.

→ **Referential** utterances provide information (e.g. *The train station is two miles away*).

→ **Expressive** utterances express the speaker's feelings (*This burger is disgusting*).

→ **Phatic** utterances are more commonly known as 'small talk'. They mean very little but are important in maintaining social relationships. Examples of typical phatic utterances are *Hello*, *Nice to meet you*, remarks about the weather and so on.

Checkpoint 1

What is a **digression**?

Take note

Devices such as exclamation marks, underlining and so on are a graphic equivalent of prosodic features, and sentence structure or poetic metre can place emphasis on particular words. But the fundamental distinction – that speech is generally *heard* while writing is generally *read* – remains.

Take note

A further distinction is that between **monologue** (one person speaking) and **dialogue** (two or more people interacting).

Links

The chapters on poetry, prose fiction, drama and Shakespeare look at literary representations of speech in more detail. See also pages 44–45 in this chapter.

The jargon

An **utterance** is a single unit of speech – a remark, a question etc. It is roughly equivalent to a sentence in a written text.

→ **Directive** utterances occur when the speaker wants someone to do something (*Can you turn the television down?*).

→ **Transactional** exchanges are conversations in which the main emphasis is on getting something done. An example would be a conversation in a shop between a salesperson and a customer.

→ **Interactional** exchanges contrast with transactional exchanges in that the main emphasis is on the social relationship between the participants. Casual conversation between friends is an example.

Context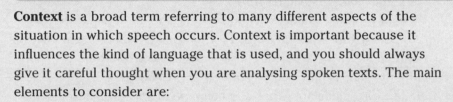

Context is a broad term referring to many different aspects of the situation in which speech occurs. Context is important because it influences the kind of language that is used, and you should always give it careful thought when you are analysing spoken texts. The main elements to consider are:

→ **Type of speech**   Different forms of spoken language have their own **conventions**. Jokes usually end with a punch line. If you are speaking to a doctor you might be asked at the beginning of the conversation to describe your symptoms.

→ **Speaker identity**   The kind of language a speaker uses can be influenced by such factors as the person's regional origin, occupation, gender and age.

→ **Audience**   Who is being addressed and what kind of relationship does the speaker have with them? Differences of **status** can have a significant impact: they might, for example mean that one speaker dominates another.

→ **Setting**   The **formality** of the setting is especially important. The language used at a casual social gathering would be different from that used at a job interview.

→ **Topic**   The subject being talked about will influence the lexis that is used. A conversation about photography, for example would probably contain a large amount of **field-specific lexis**: *shutter speed*, *zoom*, *focus* and so on.

→ **Purpose**   Think about what the speakers are trying to achieve and how this affects their language. If a parent is trying to get a child to do something, there will probably be a large number of directive utterances.

Take note

Conversations often begin with phatic exchanges.

Checkpoint 2

Directive utterances often involve the use of **commands**. What is the term for this kind of grammatical construction?

The jargon

Field-specific lexis is vocabulary associated with a particular topic or field.

Exam preparation (20 minutes)   answer: page 46

Make a list of the advantages that speech has as a means of communication compared with writing, and another list of the advantages that writing has. Do you think either mode is clearly superior to the other?

Features of spontaneous speech

The features listed in this section can often be found in transcripts of spontaneous speech. Having a check-list of features to look for is useful when you are analysing transcripts.

Lexis

→ Vocabulary is likely to be **less formal** than in written texts. Ways this may be evident include:
  → Use of **colloquial** words and expressions (e.g. *mate* instead of 'friend', *chuck* instead of 'throw').
  → Use of **regional dialect** vocabulary (e.g. *sarnie* for 'sandwich').
  → Use of **elision**: shortened word forms such as *can't* for 'cannot' and *I'll* for 'I will' (these are also known as **contractions**).
→ **Phatic** utterances may occur (*Take care, How do you do?* etc.).
→ **Deictic** expressions are especially common in speech. These have a 'pointing' function and refer in some way to the immediate context of an utterance. Often they relate to time (*now, then, yesterday, next week*) or place (*here, over there, these, those*).

Grammar

The main point about the grammar of spontaneous speech is that much of it is likely to be **non-standard** – that is, it will not follow the rules and conventions of standard written English. One obvious example of this is that spontaneous speech is not arranged into neatly separated sentences. The structure is much looser, and it can be difficult to determine where one grammatical construction ends and another begins. This is why transcripts of genuine spontaneous speech are not usually punctuated with full stops and commas. It is important when analysing transcripts such as this not to refer to 'sentences' – there aren't any! Instead you should refer to **utterances** or **constructions**.

Other grammatical features found in spontaneous speech include:

→ **Non-standard forms** such as *We was late* or *I don't know nothing about it*. If these occur in the text try to explain how the construction is non-standard. In the first example a plural subject (*We*) is followed by a singular verb (*was* – Standard English would use the plural verb *were*).

→ **Ellipsis** This is when grammatical elements are missing from a construction – words that would be included if the construction appeared as a conventional sentence in a written text are omitted. Take the following exchange:

  X: seen Mark lately
  Y: saw him yesterday

Both these utterances are ellipitical. If they were changed into complete grammatical constructions, they would become:
Have you seen Mark lately? – I saw him yesterday.

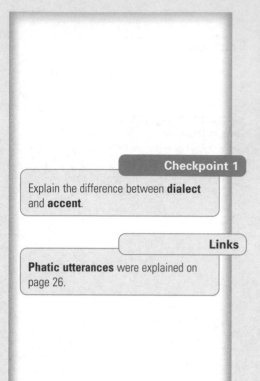

Checkpoint 1

Explain the difference between **dialect** and **accent**.

Links

Phatic utterances were explained on page 26.

Links

There are some transcripts of spontaneous speech on pages 44–45.

→ **Disjointed constructions** These are constructions that would appear clumsy if they were in a written text:

he's good at Modern Languages (.) French and that

In a written text this would be something like *He is good at Modern Languages, including French.*

→ **Interrupted constructions** (or **false starts**) Changes from one grammatical construction to another (before the initial construction has been completed) occur when speakers change their minds about what they want to say: *I want to will you marry me.*

Non-fluency features ●●●

This is a broad term referring to a range of features that might interrupt the flow of a person's speech. They occur naturally when a person is speaking spontaneously. They include:

→ **Fillers** These are words and expressions that have little meaning but are often inserted into everyday speech. Examples include *you know*, *like*, *sort of*, *I mean*. Some speakers use them out of habit and they also give a speaker more time to think.

→ **Filled pauses** (also known as **voiced pauses**) These are voiced hesitations, such as *um* and *er*.

→ **Unvoiced pauses** are silent pauses usually indicated in transcripts by the symbol (.). Often they are natural pauses for breath (the equivalent of full stops and commas in written texts), but they can also indicate hesitation.

→ **Unintentional repetition**, either of single words or of several words at a time: *where where was it.* (Note that if the repetition is deliberate it is not a non-fluency feature.)

→ **False starts** (see **Interrupted constructions** above).

Discourse structure ●●●

In the same way that individual utterances are not made up of neat grammatical sentences, longer stretches of speech are not organised into paragraphs. Transcripts of spoken English can appear disorganised and repetitive. There may be **digressions** – deviations from the main theme or topic – and ideas or information may not be presented in a logical sequence. However, transcripts of spontaneous speech do usually have *some* discernible structure. Spoken narratives, for example, usually have a broadly chronological sequence, and conversations often develop along predictable lines (see pages 32–33).

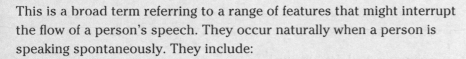

Watch out!

Fillers are virtually meaningless. The expressions listed here are *not* fillers when they clearly mean something. For example, *you know* is not a filler in the utterance *You know why I've asked to see you.*

Examiner's secrets

Try to use the relevant technical terms when referring to non-fluency features, rather than simply saying something like 'the speaker stumbles over her words'.

Checkpoint 2

What do you understand by the term **discourse**?

Exam preparation (30 minutes) answer: page 46

Text A on page 44 is a transcript of a woman speaking to a friend about a holiday she has recently had in Turkey. In what ways is the speaker's use of language typical of spontaneous spoken English?

Phonological aspects of speech

When we say something, a great deal of meaning is conveyed by the *way* that we say it. Phonological aspects of speech such as intonation, pitch and volume are collectively known as **prosodic features**.

Intonation

This can significantly alter meaning. *Well done!* can be made to sound like sarcasm or genuine praise. Variations of tone enliven our speech, making different shades of meaning or emotion more distinct and helping to retain a listener's attention. Contrastingly, a flat monotone will not engage the listener and will lessen the listener's ability to comprehend fully what is being said. In plays or novels there may be **stage directions** or **authorial description** to indicate a speaker's tone of voice, as in this example from Charles Dickens's *Great Expectations*:

> I whimpered, 'I don't know.'

Pitch

Pitch is most noticeable when it is unusually high or low. Researchers who have studied the voices produced by people in different emotional states have found that someone who is depressed usually speaks slowly and with a low and falling pitch. A raised pitch can indicate excitement, enthusiasm or anxiety.

Pace

Slow, measured speech can convey calmness and reassurance, while interest or enthusiasm is often reflected in more rapid delivery. Fast, muddled speech may be the result of anxiety or panic.

Liaison

When two words are run together in speech so that a new sound is produced, this is known as **liaison**. For example, *Where are you?* might be pronounced *Where rare you?*, the 'r' sound in 'where' carrying over into the next word.

Juncture

The gap between words that make it possible for us to distinguish between them is known as **juncture**. In spontaneous speech this is usually a silence lasting a fraction of a second.

Pauses

Pauses in a conversation may reflect awkwardness between the participants and can have a menacing effect, but often they are relaxed and free of tension. Hesitation occurs naturally in speech but may also be an indication of uncertainty, stress or fatigue. An **unvoiced pause** is a silent pause; a **filled** or **voiced pause** is a sound such as *er* or *um*. When dramatists indicate pauses in dialogue, they are usually aiming for very specific effects, and you should consider what these might be.

Check the net

The **International Phonetic Alphabet** (**IPA**) is a way of indicating how words are **pronounced**. You can see the alphabet at the website of the International Phonetic Association: www.arts.gla.ac.uk/IPA/ipachart.html

Volume

Loudness can reflect attitudes and emotional states. For example, if *Close the door, please* is said quietly it is likely to be a request; shouted loudly it will sound like an angry demand. Volume level may be linked to status: superiors are more likely to raise their voices to subordinates than the other way round.

Stress

Stress draws our attention to particular words and may change the meaning of an utterance: note the different implications of *He gave the money to me* and *He gave the money to me*.

Accent

Accent – the pronunciation of words – is an important expression of regional and social identity, and influences the impressions that others form of a speaker. Researchers have investigated the associations, positive and negative, that particular accents have. The **RP** accent, for instance, is socially prestigious and is associated with authority and competence, but it is regarded by many as sounding less warm and friendly than most rural accents. Writers sometimes use non-standard spelling to indicate that a character is speaking with a regional accent.

Oral signals

Oral signals are expressive sounds such as laughs, sighs, gasps and so on. In transcripts they may be represented by 'words' such as *mmm* and *ah*.

Transcription conventions

Some of the symbols commonly used in transcripts are listed below. Note that if you are given a transcript to analyse in an exam, there will usually be a key explaining the symbols that are used

→ A **micropause** of half a second or less is indicated by (.). Longer pauses are shown as a figure in seconds, as in (2).
→ **Stress** is marked by <u>underlining</u> or by *italics*.
→ Loud speech is shown by CAPITAL LETTERS.
→ **Overlapping speech** and **interruptions** are indicated by [ ] or //.

Checkpoint 1

List some effects that a pause in dramatic dialogue might have.

Checkpoint 2

How could stressing other words in this utterance produce yet more variations in meaning?

The jargon

RP (Received Pronunciation) is the accent associated with upper-class speakers of English.

Watch out!

Be careful not to confuse **oral signals** and **filled pauses** (see page 29). If *mm* is simply a hesitation, it is a filled pause. But if it means something (e.g. *I understand*) it is an oral signal.

Links

The **International Phonetic Alphabet** (**IPA**) can be used in transcripts to indicate how words are pronounced. See opposite page.

Exam preparation   answer: page 46

Transcribe approximately 60 seconds of dialogue from a television soap or comedy programme. Make sure your transcript indicates prosodic features. Then write an analysis of the extract, commenting in particular on phonological aspects of the language used.

Elements of conversation

This section is mainly concerned with the **structure** of conversation. Although conversations are usually spontaneous, much of what is said nevertheless follows predictable patterns.

Opening and closing a conversation

Most conversations begin with a conventional **opening sequence** and end with a conventional **closing sequence**. Standard ways of opening a conversation include: exchange of greetings; self-identification (*Hello, I'm Jennifer Reid*); politeness formulas (*Excuse me*). There may be further **phatic utterances** before the conversation gets properly underway. Phatic expressions such as *Nice talking to you* are also common as conversations near their end. Other conventional closing sequences include remarks that conclude or sum up the conversation in some way (*So that's agreed?*), and discussing arrangements to meet again. The last words spoken are usually an exchange of farewells.

Turn-taking

One of the most important features of conversations is that we take turns at speaking. Research has shown that we are very accurate judges of the precise moment when it is appropriate for us to contribute to a conversation. If we weren't, conversation would be chaotic: full of interruptions, simultaneous (or **overlapping**) speech and awkward silences. Conversations work so efficiently because despite its informality and spontaneity, conversation has its own rules and conventions, which speakers follow even though for the most part they are not consciously aware of them. We are also sensitive to a range of verbal and non-verbal **cues**, which signal that a speaker is reaching the end of an utterance, or that a listener wishes to speak. Sometimes there are direct invitations for us to speak, most obviously when we are asked a question or when our name is mentioned (*Sarah can tell you more about that than I can*). Another cue for us to speak is when the other speaker reaches the end of a grammatical construction (the equivalent of a full stop at the end of a sentence). When speakers approach the end of an utterance their voice also usually begins to fall, and they look directly at the person they are addressing – non-verbal signals that we unconsciously understand and respond to.

Adjacency pairs

Adjacency pairs are important building blocks of conversation. An adjacency pair is a two-part exchange that follows a predictable pattern. Common forms of adjacency pairs include:

→ Question – Answer (*What's the time? – Three o'clock.*)
→ Greeting – Greeting (*Hello. – Hello.*)
→ Summons – Answer (*Dad! – Yes?*)
→ Statement – Agreement (*It's time to leave. – You're right.*)

Checkpoint 1

Explain what is meant by **phatic utterances**.

Links

The pattern of turn-taking in a conversation is an important indication of the **relationship** between the participants. See pages 34–35.

Examiner's secrets

Try to remember these different kinds of adjacency pairs. A common mistake made by students is only to identify question–answer exchanges as adjacency pairs.

→ Apology – Acceptance (*Sorry.* – *That's OK.*)

→ Invitation – Acceptance or refusal (*D'you want a drink?* – *No thanks.*)

Adjacency pairs make an important contribution to the structure of a conversation, and a typical conversation will contain a large number of them.

Topics ●●●

The **topic** of a conversation (what is being talked about) also helps to give it coherence and structure. Generally, utterances will be relevant to the current topic or will attempt to initiate new topics. An utterance that establishes a topic at the beginning of a conversation is known as a **topic marker**: *So how did the driving test go?*

Changes of topic are known as **topic shifts**. If a conversation returns to an earlier topic, this is known as a **topic loop**. Initiating topics, and controlling changes of topic, is called **agenda-setting** (see page 35).

Repairs ●●●

A **repair** resolves a problem that has arisen in a conversation. An example is a speaker correcting himself (*I paid twenty no fifteen pounds for it*). Alternatively, the repair may be carried out by another speaker (*I paid twenty pounds for it* – *No, fifteen*).

Feedback ●●●

An important element in a conversation is the **feedback** that those being addressed give to the speaker to show that they are listening. Feedback (also known as **back-channel behaviour**) can take various forms:

→ **Verbal responses** such as *Yeah*, *Really?* etc.

→ **Oral signals** such as *mm*, *uh huh*, laughs, sighs etc.

→ **Non-verbal responses** such as nods and smiles.

Failure to give such feedback can be very disconcerting for the speaker. Note also that feedback can be negative as well as positive (e.g. looking away can indicate boredom or impatience).

Take note

The second half of an adjacency pair does not always occur immediately – the speaker's response may be delayed. There may be an **insertion sequence**, which means that one adjacency pair is embedded within another:

A: Can you buy a bottle of lemonade as well?

B: Are you sure you've given me enough money?

A: Yes.

B: OK.

Here the first and last utterances form one adjacency pair, and the middle two utterances form another. An interruption to an adjacency pair which is longer, lasting for several utterances, is termed a **side sequence**.

Take note

As well as adjacency pairs, **three-part exchanges** can also occur, with the second speaker's response generating a further utterance from the first speaker. Teacher–pupil interaction often has this pattern:

Teacher: Who wrote *1984*?

Pupil: George Orwell.

Teacher: That's right.

Checkpoint 2

In a transcript, would *mm* always be an oral signal?

Exam preparation (30 minutes) answer: page 46

Text B on page 44 is from a radio phone-in programme. Comment on the interaction between the two speakers. In what ways is the language they use typical of spontaneous speech?

Conversational interaction

This section is essentially concerned with the **relationship** that speakers have with each other in a conversation.

Face-to face?

In considering the **context** of a conversation, whether or not the exchange is **face-to-face** can be important. In conversations that are not face-to-face (such as telephone calls), body language (nods, facial expressions and so on) cannot be used to communicate. This means speech, including prosodic features such as intonation and stress, is more important. Correspondingly, the absence of speech – pauses and silences – is also more significant, and can make the participants very uncomfortable. Face-to-face and non face-to-face interactions also tend to have different **discourse conventions**. For example, the opening sequence of a telephone conversation often involves self-identification (*Hi, it's Susie here*).

Speech acts

Speech act theory suggests that when we say things we are in effect performing actions. The nature of the action will reflect the function that the utterance has. We might, for example, be making a prediction or a promise, or giving someone a warning or an order. Note that the purpose of an utterance (known technically as the **illocutionary force**) can very much depend on its context and on paralinguistic features such as stress and intonation. If one person tells another, *We'll discuss this tomorrow*, it could be a promise ('I promise I won't forget about it'), an order ('Don't try to discuss this with me now') or a warning ('I'm not going to let this drop'). Usually speech acts are understood correctly, but there is obviously the potential for misinterpretation.

Take note

Analysing the kinds of speech acts performed by speakers (in real-life transcripts or in a literary text such as a play) can reveal much about attitudes and relationships. A speaker who habitually gives orders, for instance, may be someone who is dominant and controlling.

Status and power

If you are studying a transcript or a piece of dialogue, the balance of **power** between the speakers can be an interesting and important dimension to consider. Sometimes the **context** of the conversation will clearly indicate that one speaker has more authority or **status** than another. This status might, for example, derive from the speaker's occupation, age, specialist knowledge, or relationship with the other speaker(s). In this case, you should look for how the status is reflected in the speaker's language and conversational behaviour. (Be careful not to *assume* the higher status speaker is in control – you might find the other speaker refuses to accept a subordinate role and instead tries to dominate.) In other cases differences of status might not be apparent from the context of the conversation, but analysis of the interaction nevertheless reveals that one speaker exercises more control over the conversation than another.

Some of the ways that conversational dominance might be expressed are listed here.

Take note

Speakers whose status depends on their occupation will usually only have that status when they are in their occupational role. For example, a doctor will only have superior status in an occupational context such as a doctor–patient interview. Even then, it is becoming increasingly common for patients to challenge and question what doctors tell them.

Modes of address

The most common modes of address available to speakers include first name (*Hannah*), title (*Doctor*) and title followed by last name (*Doctor Jones*, *Mrs Hughes*).

Asymmetrical or **non-reciprocal** address forms, which occur when people address each other in different ways, usually reflect a difference in status. School students are likely to use respectful forms in addressing their teachers: the formal title *Sir* or *Miss*, or title followed by last name (*Mr Webster*). Teachers will address students by their first names or, in more traditional schools, by their last name only. Students who leave school and go on to college where they are encouraged to address their teachers by their first names often feel uncomfortable at first about doing this.

Agenda-setting

Deciding what should be talked about, and for how long, can be an indicator of status. If you are analysing a conversation, consider whether one of the speakers controls the interaction by initiating and changing topics.

Making requests

Where clear difference of status exists, **imperatives** (commands) may be used by superiors to subordinates (e.g. a parent to a child: *Come here now!*). Where there is equality of status, or a subordinate is addressing a superior, requests tend to be less direct (*Would you mind opening the window?*).

Other indications of status

Other ways that status might be asserted or revealed in a conversation include:

→ **Asking questions** (especially in certain contexts – e.g. a police officer interrogating a suspect).
→ **Interrupting** other speakers.
→ **Saying more** than other speakers.
→ **Ignoring** other speakers.
→ Using **complex** or **specialist vocabulary** to demonstrate superior knowledge.
→ Expressing dominance through **body language** and **prosodic features** such as intonation, stress and volume.

Checkpoint 1

In Shakespeare's plays, what are the differences between *thou* and *you* as modes of address?

Checkpoint 2

Can you think of any contexts or situations where asking questions might indicate inferior status?

Exam preparation (20 minutes)   answers: page 47–48

Text C on page 45 is from the play *Glengarry Glen Ross* by David Mamet. Examine how Mamet uses dialogue to reveal the two characters and the relationship between them.

Conversation theory

Here we look at some theories and research findings related to conversation. In the exam you will not be directly tested on your knowledge of theory, but occasional reference to relevant theory can strengthen answers to analysis questions.

The co-operative principle

H.P. Grice (1975) saw co-operation between the participants as the fundamental principle underlying conversation. He argued that conversations proceed on the assumption that those taking part have common goals and agreed ways of achieving these goals. He called this assumption the **co-operative principle**, and developed his theory by identifying four specific **maxims** (rules or principles), which he said participants in a conversation usually follow:

1 **Quantity**   In making a contribution to a conversation, you should say neither more nor less than is required.
2 **Relevance**   What you say should be relevant to the ongoing context of the conversation.
3 **Manner**   You should avoid ambiguity and obscurity and be orderly in your utterances.
4 **Quality**   You should also be truthful and not say anything that you suspect to be false.

When these principles are not abided by, the maxims are said to be **flouted**. Flouting of the maxims can lead to conversational difficulties and breakdown. Other participants may show their dissatisfaction by insisting that speakers answer the question or 'get to the point', and speakers themselves may apologise if they fear they are flouting the maxims (e.g. *I'm sorry if I'm not explaining this very clearly*).

Face

Erving Goffman (1955) used the term **face** for the image of ourselves that we present to others in a conversation. The face we present can vary: for example, we may present ourselves as a good friend in one context and as a knowledgeable student or teacher in another. Usually others accept the face that we offer, or at least behave as if they do. If something is said or done that challenges or rejects another's face, this is termed a **face-threatening act**. An example would be bluntly telling somebody *You don't know what you're talking about*. If, in contrast, we are respectful and deferential, we are being attentive to the other person's **face needs**.

Politeness

Having regard for another person's face is an important aspect of **politeness**, a broad term for the sensitivity that we show to others in conversation. Examples of politeness include:

Checkpoint 1

If I ask someone the way to a railway station and am simply told *It's not far*, what maxim is being flouted?

Checkpoint 2

Criticisms of the way people speak can often be explained in terms of Grice's maxims. For example, if someone is described as a 'windbag', what maxim is that person being accused of flouting?

Watch out!

Do not feel you need to apply Grice's maxims to every spoken text. Only use them when they are clearly relevant and help to reveal important aspects of the text.

Take note

Also relevant to conversation is **accommodation theory**, developed by Howard Giles and others in the 1970s. This suggests we adjust our speech to 'accommodate' the person we are addressing. Most commonly, **convergence** occurs. This is when the speech styles of individual speakers move closer together.

→ Using appropriate forms of address.
→ Speaking to others in a way that is appropriate to the social relationship you have with them.
→ Speaking with a degree of formality appropriate to the occasion.
→ Understanding the conventions of language associated with particular situations (e.g. accepting or refusing an invitation, beginning and ending a conversation).
→ Understanding the conventions of turn taking.

Robin Lakoff (1973) argued that much conversational interaction is governed by what she called the **politeness principle**. **Brown and Levinson** (1987) speak of face needs being met by positive and negative politeness. **Positive politeness** is demonstrated when we show people that they are liked and admired. **Negative politeness** is shown when we avoid intruding on others' lives, taking care not to impose our presence on them or pry into their personal affairs.

Gender ●●●

An important aspect of the study of conversation is the question of **gender difference** in conversational behaviour. Researchers have found that women tend to be more supportive in their conversational behaviour than men. In essence, women's approach to conversation tends to be **co-operative**, whereas men's approach tends to be **competitive**.

Specifically, women tend to:

→ Ask more questions (showing interest in what other speakers think, and encouraging them to participate).
→ Give more supportive feedback when listening (e.g. through oral signals such as *mm* and through expressions of agreement and understanding such as *I know*, *Yes* etc.).
→ Pay more compliments.
→ Initiate more topics of conversation.
→ Make more effort to bring others into the conversation.
→ Use *you* and *we* more often (i.e. they address others more and involve them more in what is being said).
→ Develop the ideas of previous speakers more than men do.

In contrast, men are more likely to:

→ Interrupt.
→ Express disagreement.
→ Ignore the other person's utterances.
→ Show reluctance to pursue topics initiated by others.

Watch out!

Researchers have identified trends and tendencies, but many individual men and women do not conform to the expected pattern. It is important not to assume that all men and women are the same!

Take note

Researchers have also investigated what men and women talk about. Women's conversation often relates to personal experiences, relationships and family issues. Male conversation tends to focus more on information, facts, objects and activities. Again, it is important not to over-generalise: these findings do not apply to all men or all women, nor to all conversations.

Take note

Another research finding is that women's speech tends to be closer to Standard English than men's.

Take note

Some specifications require a coursework assignment that investigates spoken language. Transcripts that enable you to comment on gender can be useful for this.

Exam preparation   answer: page 47

Record a few short snippets of conversation (no more than about 60 seconds each), involving male and female friends. Do the conversations support the view that there are gender differences in conversational behaviour?

Prepared talk: speeches 1

Public speeches are one of the main forms of spoken language studied at AS and A2. This first section on speeches looks at some important grammatical features associated with speeches.

Grammatical features

Parallelism

Parallelism involves the use of phrases, clauses or sentences with a similar grammatical structure. Earl Spencer began his speech at the funeral of his sister, Diana Princess of Wales, with the following sentence:

> I stand before you today the representative of a family in grief, in a country in mourning, before a world in shock.

Here the parallel phrases are *a family in grief*, *a country in mourning* and *a world in shock*. Parallelism helps to create a strong, emphatic rhythm, and it can be used to stress key ideas. In this example, the extent of the grief caused by Diana's death is emphasised (note the progression from *family* to *country* to *world*).

Repetition

This can be of single words or of complete phrases or sentences. As with parallelism, the effect is often to emphasise important words or ideas and to create a powerful rhythm. Repetition can give a speech **cohesion**, as in the famous Martin Luther King speech where he repeated the words *I have a dream*. A simpler example of repetition is Tony Blair's declaration that the priorities of his government were *Education, education, education*.

Contrast and antithesis

A balanced rhythm is created by the use of words and phrases that contrast in some way. Antithesis is an especially powerful kind of contrast, as the words involved have directly opposite meanings. This quotation is from Abraham Lincoln's address at the Gettysburg military cemetery in 1863:

> The brave men living and dead, who struggled here, have consecrated it far above our power to add or detract. The world will little note, nor long remember what we say here, but it can never forget what they did here.

Note the series of contrasts here: *living–dead*; *add–detract*; *little–long*; *remember–forget*; *what we say here–what they did here*.

Tripling

Three-part lists (also known as **sets of three**) have a memorable rhythm and often feature in speeches. The earlier quotation from Earl Spencer is an example. In a wartime speech Winston Churchill referred to *blood, toil, tears and sweat*. This is a four-part list, but over the years it has

The jargon

The techniques used by speakers to make their speeches powerful and persuasive are known as **rhetorical features**.

The jargon

The term **cohesion** refers to the techniques used to connect different parts of a text with each other.

Take note

Parallelism is also present here: *little note – long remember, remember what we say here – forget what they did here.*

become a well-known expression, modified to the more easily remembered set of three: *blood*, *sweat and tears*.

Listing

Lists have a cumulative effect, and are often used to reinforce an idea or argument. In a speech in October 2001, delivered a few weeks after the September 11th terrorist attack on the World Trade Centre in New York, President Bush used listing to emphasise the strength and solidarity of the American response:

> Our nation is grateful to so many Americans who are rallying to our cause and preparing for the struggle ahead: FBI agents, intelligence officers, emergency response workers, public health authorities, state and local officials, our diplomats abroad, law enforcement teams who safeguard our security at home, and soldiers, sailors, marines and airmen who defend us so far away.

Sentence length

Sentences in speeches are often notable for being short, direct and powerful. Alternatively, long sentences which build to a climax may be present (they are especially common towards the ends of speeches). Abraham Lincoln's Gettysburg address ended with the following climactic sentence:

> It is rather for us to be here dedicated to the great task remaining before us – that from these honoured dead we take increased devotion to that cause for which they gave the last full measure of devotion – that we here highly resolve that these dead shall not have died in vain – that this nation, under God, shall have a new birth of freedom – and that government of the people, by the people, for the people, shall not perish from the earth.

Use of first and second person

The use of first person plural pronouns (*we*, *our*) promotes a feeling of unity and solidarity between speaker and audience. Second person pronouns (*you*, *your*) involve the audience by addressing them directly.

Interrogatives

Asking questions is another way of involving the audience, though usually of course they are not expected to answer them. A question may be answered by the speaker: *And what has the government done about it? Nothing!* Alternatively, it may be a **rhetorical question** – that is, a question that does not require an answer (usually because the answer is obvious). Asking a question requires a change in intonation, so questions make the delivery of a speech more varied and dynamic.

Checkpoint 1

What is the difference between **syndetic** and **asyndetic listing**?

Checkpoint 2

What other **rhetorical features** can you identify in this extract?

Example

In Martin Luther King's *I have a dream* speech, the repeated use of first person plural pronouns shows that King identifies with his audience, and also stresses that they are united in a common cause:
> In the process of gaining our rightful place we must not be guilty of wrongful deeds. Let us not seek to satisfy our thirst for freedom by drinking from the cup of bitterness and hatred. We must forever conduct our struggle on the high plane of dignity and discipline.

Exam preparation   answer: page 47

See page 41 for a practice question relevant to this and the following section.

Prepared talk: speeches 2

We now consider the lexical and phonological aspects of speeches. There is also a practice question on a Tony Blair speech.

Lexical features

Simple vocabulary

Simple, possibly **monosyllabic** vocabulary may be used in order to be clear, direct and forceful. However, speeches can also employ **elaborate**, **elevated vocabulary** to add solemnity and weight to a speech, or to make it sound dramatic and uplifting.

Emotive vocabulary

Vocabulary intended to stir the emotions of the audience is common in speeches. In a speech early in the Second World War, Churchill used emotive language to stress the iniquity of Nazi Germany:

> Side by side, the British and French peoples have advanced to rescue not only Europe but mankind from the foulest and most soul-destroying tyranny which has ever darkened and stained the pages of history.

Hyperbole

This is the use of exaggeration. Again it is often used for emotive effect, or for dramatic impact. In a powerful speech during the General Election of 1987, the Labour Party leader Neil Kinnock spoke of the battle during the 20th century to eradicate privilege and secure equality of opportunity for ordinary people ('Glenys' is a reference to his wife):

> Why am I the first Kinnock in a thousand generations to be able to get to university? Why is Glenys the first woman in her family in a thousand generations to be able to get to university?

Taken literally, this implies that universities have existed for *a thousand generations* – which, of course, they haven't.

Figurative language

Metaphors and **similes** can make a speech more vivid and memorable. Martin Luther King's *I have a dream* speech makes extensive use of figurative language. He says that the abolition of slavery in the USA was *a joyous daybreak to end the long night of captivity*. However, one hundred years later black Americans still inhabited *a lonely island of poverty in the middle of a vast ocean of material prosperity*.

Phonology

If you are analysing a speech, never forget that it is intended to be *heard*. This means **sound** and **rhythm** are especially important. Consider the rhythm of specific parts of the speech (e.g. stress on

Checkpoint 1

Explain the difference between **monosyllabic** and **polysyllabic** vocabulary.

Checkpoint 2

Which words and phrases in this extract are especially emotive?

particular words) and of the speech as a whole. As was noted, several of the grammatical features listed in the previous section (pages 38–39) have a rhythmic effect. Look also for phonological devices such as **alliteration**, **assonance** and **rhyme**.

Links

For more on phonological devices such as alliteration and assonance, see page 65.

Checkpoint 3

Before beginning your answer to this question, answer the following as fully as possible: who are the audience for this speech?

Exam preparation (45 minutes)   answer: page 47

The text below is the beginning of a speech given by Prime Minister Tony Blair at the Labour Party Conference in 2001. The speech was delivered a few weeks after the September 11th terrorist attacks on New York. Comment on the language of the speech, focusing in particular on Blair's use of rhetorical techniques associated with public speeches.

Conference, in retrospect the millennium marked a moment in time, but it was the events of the 11 September that marked a turning point in history. When we confront the dangers of the future and assess the choices facing human kind. It was a tragedy, an act of evil and from this nation goes our deepest sympathy and prayers for the victims and our profound solidarity with the American people. We were with you at the first, we will stay with you to the last . . .

Just two weeks ago in New York after the church service I met some of the families of the British victims, and it was in many ways a very British occasion, tea and biscuits, raining outside and around the edge of the room strangers making small talk, trying to be normal people, in a very abnormal situation. And as you crossed the room you felt the longing and the sadness. Hands that were clutching photos of sons and daughters, wives and husbands, imploring you to believe that when they said there was still an outside chance of their loved ones being found alive it could be true, when in truth you knew that all hope was gone.

Then a middle aged mother looks you in the eyes and tells you that her only son has died and asks you why, and I tell you, you do not feel like the most powerful man in the country at times like that. Because there is no answer. There is no justification for the pain of those people. Her son did nothing wrong, the woman seven months pregnant whose child will never know its father did nothing wrong. And they don't want revenge. They want something better in memory of their loved ones. And I believe that their memorial can and should be greater than simply the punishment of the guilty. It is that out of the shadow of this evil should emerge lasting good. Destruction of the machinery of terrorism wherever it is found, hope amongst all nations of a new beginning where we seek to resolve differences in a calm and ordered way. Greater understanding between nations and between faiths, and above all, justice and prosperity for the poor and dispossessed so that people everywhere can see the chance of a better future through the hard work and creative power of the free citizen, not the violence and savagery of the fanatic. (This is the Labour Party's transcript of the speech).

Other kinds of talk

During your AS and A2 course it is likely you will be asked to analyse many different kinds of spoken language. This section offers some guiding principles, and also looks more closely at the nature of broadcast speech.

Talk in literature

Some examining boards have a specific requirement that you study the spoken word as it is presented in **literature**. This usually means examining the presentation of speech in plays, novels and short stories. You might be asked to analyse a single extract, or to compare an extract with a transcript of a different kind of spoken language (such as spontaneous speech). With all the specifications it is also possible that you will encounter a literary extract involving speech in the synoptic module (Unit 6). For more advice on analysing speech in literature, see the relevant sections of the chapters on Prose Fiction, Drama and Shakespeare (pages 82–83, 104–107, 126–127).

Importance of context

Apart from literary extracts, you are likely during your AS or A2 course to come across transcripts of speech from a range of situations. These could include job interviews, telephone conversations, stand-up comedy routines or exchanges between doctors and patients, teachers and pupils, sales assistants and customers and so on. As far as the exam is concerned, you really need to be prepared to analyse *any* kind of spoken language. This is not as daunting as it sounds, as there are certain guiding principles that are relevant to the analysis of any spoken text.

You should think about the **context** of the transcript. What type of speech situation are you dealing with? It might, for instance, be one of the situations referred to above. Develop your thoughts about context by asking the following questions:

➜ What are the **conventions** of this kind of speech situation, and are any of these apparent in the transcript? (For example, there are standard ways of beginning and ending a telephone conversation.)

➜ Is the speech **scripted** or **spontaneous**? This will have an important influence on language – for example, spontaneous speech is more likely to have grammatically incomplete constructions, non-fluency features, interruptions and overlaps; scripted speech is more likely to be in standard grammatical sentences. Note that in some situations the speech may be **partly scripted** and **partly spontaneous** (this is often the case with stand-up comedy).

➜ What is the **status** of the speakers and the nature of the **relationship** between them? How is this reflected in the language the speakers use? If one speaker has a higher status than the other (as in a job interview), there may be evidence of **conversational dominance**.

➜ What are the speakers **trying to achieve**, and how is this evident in their language?

Take note

As well as being prepared to analyse different kinds of spoken language, you should also watch for **writing that resembles speech**. Written texts sometimes seek to imitate speech, and this may be apparent in the presence of such language features as colloquial vocabulary, contractions and non-standard grammar. In addition, patterns of intonation associated with speech may be suggested by the use of italics (to show emphasis) and exclamation marks.

→ Are there any other ways in which the language used **reflects the context**? For example, there may be **field-specific lexis** (e.g. transcripts of a court hearing may contain legal terms and expressions).

Broadcast talk ●●●

Transcripts of **broadcast speech** are often set for study. Again the range is enormous: weather forecasts, cookery programmes, radio phone-ins, news programmes, sports commentaries, chat shows etc. The questions listed above can usually be profitably applied to any of these. The role of the viewing or listening **audience** is also important. How do speakers address, or interact with, the audience? Do members of the audience participate (as in radio phone-ins)? If so, think about the relationship between host and audience, and how their language differs.

The **football commentary** is a good example of a speech genre with a set of characteristic language features. These include:

→ Often there are **two speakers**: the main commentator, who describes the action on the pitch, and an expert summariser (often an ex-player), whose role is to provide analysis and comment. The main commentator will appear to be in overall charge of proceedings, but his or her manner towards the summariser is likely to be both respectful and good-humoured.
→ What is said will be mostly **spontaneous**, but if (as is likely) the speakers are experienced broadcasters there may be relatively few non-fluency features. Parts of the commentary (such as what is said before the match starts) may sound more prepared.
→ There will be **field-specific lexis** relating to football (*offside*, *throw-in*, *tackle* etc.).
→ **Grammatically incomplete constructions** will occur (e.g. *Gerard through to Owen* instead of *Gerard passes the ball through to Owen*).
→ Much of the commentary will be in the **present tense**, describing events as they happen.
→ **Prosodic features** such as intonation, stress, pace and volume will be important. Exciting phases of the game are likely to be reflected in the commentator speaking at a faster pace and more loudly.
→ **Radio** and **television** commentaries have important differences. In particular, a radio commentator needs to describe what is happening in more detail.

Checkpoint 1

Explain the term **field-specific lexis**.

Checkpoint 2

What is another term for a grammatically incomplete construction?

Exam preparation (20 minutes) answer: page 47

Text D on page 45 is an extract from a television commentary on an England football match. Comment on the speakers' use of language, considering how far it might be said to be typical of the genre.

Specimen texts

The texts below are for use with the practice exam questions for this chapter.

Take note

Key for these texts:
(.) a micropause
(2.0) a longer pause, in seconds
// overlapping speech
CAPITAL LETTERS louder speech
accel faster pace

Take note

The question for this text is on page 29.

Text A

We'd read the brochure and the hotel sounded brilliant (.) course they always exaggerate and everything but anyhow (.) we thought it'd be pretty good (.) I mean should be for that money (.) when we got there you wouldn't believe the room it was it was OK but the view from the balcony we were right opposite a flaming building site (.) here look we took a photograph look at this (*shows friend a photograph*) you know you see on telly them holidays from hell well it was like that (.) we complained and got another room the next day (.) the rep didn't want to (.) no couldn't care less (.) we did it all through reception (.) anyway we complained and got a different room (.) it was right above the bar you know the terrace no no privacy at all (.) you went out on the balcony and all these eyes looked up (*laughs*) then at night the music came on (.) real loud (.) constant you know thud thud thud (.) so anyway we had to go through it all again (.) you know complaining and all that (.) then we got one on a higher higher floor and it was OK (.) but that view look at it like a bomb site (.) just imagine we'd just arrived there from the airport dead tired opened the curtains and saw that (.) I mean (.) we'll try and get some money back cos the first few days were just a waste of time

Take note

The question for this text is on page 33.
A BBC radio phone-in presenter, Brian Alexander (**BA**), is interviewing Tracey Edwards (**TE**) about leadership.

Text B

BA: Tracey Edwards the er the former erm yachtswoman is on the line as well (.) hello Tracey

TE: good morning

BA: now you read er you read (*laughs*) you you run leadership um courses I think in some shape or form

TE: yup

BA: so what what what is a leader as far as you're concerned

TE: a leader is someone that erm people will follow (.) er that's that's common sense (.) erm it's really someone (.) for me it's someone who can see through all the obstacles and all the sort of (.) surrounding erm problems and can always have an eye on on the end goal erm and (.) convey that message to the people around them so that the people can concentrate on their jobs and (.) what they're doing so that they can reach the end goal (.) and it's someone that takes those // people with them

BA: mm mm // (.) so someone like you

TE: erm hopefully (*laughs*)

BA: you have to have it though don't you

TE: yes I do but (.) er it's down to also the age-old erm question (.) are born er are leaders born or are they (.) do you do you learn how to be a leader (.) and I think it's a mixture of both I think if

you don't want to be a leader (.) and if you don't have that erm
need to to to sort of lead from the front then I think you probably
won't be a leader (.) but if you do have that erm that sort of
motivation and that belief in yourself then I think you can learn (.)
erm the the characteristics that go with good leadership

Text C

Lingk: It's not me, it's my wife.
Roma: (*pause*) What is?
Lingk: I told you.
Roma: Tell me again.
Lingk: What's going on here?
Roma: Tell me again. Your wife.
Lingk: I told you.
Roma: You tell me again.
Lingk: She wants her money back.
Roma: We're going to speak to her.
Lingk: No. She told me 'right now'.
Roma: We'll speak to her, Jim.
Lingk: She won't listen. (*pause*) She told me if not, I have to call the State's Attorney.
Roma: No, no. That's just something she 'said'. We don't have to do that.
Lingk: She told me I *have* to.
Roma: No, Jim.

Take note

The question for this text is on page 35.
Richard Roma, an American real estate
salesman, has earlier persuaded James
Lingk to invest a large amount of money
in a property deal. Lingk has now changed
his mind and wants to withdraw from the
transaction.

Text D

JM: this has not been a (.) smooth performance in any department at
the moment by England (3.0) no real conviction about their game
yet but here's Heskey (2.0) (*accel*) NOW ROONEY'S FOLLOWING
UP HERE (.) AND THERE'S CONVICTION NOW (.) WAYNE ROONEY
HAS BECOME THE YOUNGEST GOALSCORER IN ENGLAND'S
INTERNATIONAL HISTORY (.) he's got to be careful how he
celebrates in view of the supporters who shouldn't really be here
in the FA's opinion (.) but 53 minutes gone and Rooney at 17 has
scored his first goal for England (.) and he's just produced it when
England looked to be REALLY in trouble (*a replay of the goal is
shown*) the ball up to Emile Heskey the header down Rooney
strikes and it's beyond the goalkeeper's left side

TB: (*another replay*) terrific ball from Beckham (.) the substitute
Heskey does his job (.) a little knockdown (.) look where the 13 is
brought on to do a manmarking job on Rooney (.) Rooney's lost
him a couple of yards (*another replay*) still a lot of work to do for
the youngster it's just on the edge of the penalty area (.) drills it
down low (.) the minute it left his foot it was going to beat the
keeper

Take note

The question for this text is on page 43.
In this BBC television commentary, John
Motson (**JM**) is the main commentator.
The other speaker, Trevor Brooking (**TB**),
is a former England player. The match is
Macedonia v. England in September 2003.

Answers
Spoken language

Spoken language: an overview

Checkpoints

1 A digression is a temporary departure from the main topic or theme of a spoken utterance or written text. The speaker goes 'off the point', but then comes back to it.
2 A command is known as an imperative.

Exam preparation

Advantages of speech include: it can be accompanied by body language and prosodic features, to increase clarity and show emphasis; feedback is often instantaneous (e.g. in a conversation), so adjustments (e.g. additional explanations) can be made. Advantages of writing include: it can be carefully planned and organised, unlike most spontaneous speech; punctuation and structural devices such as paragraphs assist comprehension; it can be edited/corrected before it is read; it can be kept, read again and referred back to if desired.

The superiority of one over the other depends entirely on context. Speech is more suited to some situations, writing to others.

Features of spontaneous speech

Checkpoints

1 The term *accent* refers to the pronunciation of words. *Dialect* is a broader term, referring to the way language is used by a particular group of speakers (usually from a specific geographical region). This can include accent, but it also refers to vocabulary and grammar.
2 The term *discourse* is used for an extended stretch of spoken or written language. This usually means more than a sentence long.

Exam preparation

Much of the lexis is informal, incorporating colloquial words and expressions (*pretty good*, *dead tired*, *flaming* etc.), abbreviations (*cos*) and numerous contractions. Another feature is the presence of deixis (vocabulary that refers to the immediate situation). This is more common in spoken than written English. Examples here occur when the speaker points to a photograph: *look at this*, *here look*.

The grammatical constructions present include examples of the disjointed constructions often found in spontaneous speech: *the view from the balcony we were right opposite a flaming building site*. Ellipsis is also evident: *I mean should be for that money*. Non-standard grammar includes *them holidays from hell* and *real loud*.

Non-fluency features include: unvoiced pauses; repetition (*it was it was OK*); false starts (*the rep didn't want to – no couldn't care less*); fillers (*you know*).

In terms of discourse structure, the transcript generally follows an orderly chronological sequence. Towards the end there is a topic loop as the speaker returns to the photograph mentioned earlier.

Phonological aspects of speech

Checkpoints

1 The effect will depend on the context. Possible effects include: tension; reflecting the emotional mood of a character – e.g. uncertainty, distress; reflecting in some way the relationship between characters – e.g. awkwardness, intimacy; giving what is said before or after the pause additional emphasis.
2 Stressing *He* would emphasise that the money wasn't given by someone else. Stressing *money* would emphasise that he gave the money and not something else.

Exam preparation

Depending on your exam board specification, you might find that analysing your own transcripts can form part of a coursework assignment.

Elements of conversation

Checkpoints

1 Phatic utterances are 'small talk' – utterances that have no real meaning but which are an important part of social relationships. See page 26.
2 No. It might be a filled pause. An oral signal has to mean something.

Exam preparation

BA as the programme presenter controls the conversation. He introduces the other speaker, initiates the main topic (*what is a leader*) and asks a series of questions (the conversation contains several adjacency pairs). TE speaks more, but this is because she is asked for her views as an expert on the topic. BA encourages TE to develop her contributions and gives feedback (the oral signal *mm*). Features typical of spontaneous speech include informal lexis (*on the line*, *have an eye on* – note that the more formal lexis tends to be field-specific: *leadership*, *motivation*, *end goal*); ellipsis (*so someone like you*); frequent false starts; fillers (*sort of*); filled and unvoiced pauses; unintentional repetition (*that's that's common sense*).

Conversational interaction

Checkpoints

1 As explained on page 124, *thou* was only used as a singular pronoun. It was also more intimate and less formal than *you*, and used towards those of lower rank.
2 The speaker might for example be asking questions of someone in authority, seeking permission to do something or asking for guidance or instruction.

Exam preparation

Lingk's first utterance suggests that he is weak. He shifts the responsibility for his objections to his wife. Later utterances suggest he is dominated by her (e.g. *She told me I have to*). Lingk is also dominated by Roma, who controls the conversation. He makes Lingk repeat what he has told him, using an imperative (*Tell me again*). His refusal to retreat from his position is shown by his repetition of *No* towards the end of the extract. At the same time, he tries to appear friendly to Lingk by addressing him as *Jim*. He cleverly uses the first person plural *we* to imply solidarity between them, and to suggest they are united against Lingk's wife.

Conversation theory

Checkpoints

1 The maxim of quantity is being flouted. The speaker needs to give a more detailed reply.
2 The maxim of quantity. The person says more than is required.

Exam preparation

It is also interesting to compare same-sex and mixed-sex conversations involving the same speakers, examining how far the conversational behaviour of individual speakers remains consistent.

Prepared talk: speeches 1

Checkpoints

1 Syndetic listing occurs when conjunctions (such as *and*) are used to join the items in a list. Asyndetic listing occurs when a list has no conjunctions.
2 Other rhetorical features include: parallelism (*that ... that ... that ... that*); repetition (*devotion, dead, people*); tripling (*of the people, by the people, for the people*); use of first person (*we, us*).

Prepared talk: speeches 2

Checkpoints

1 Monosyllabic words have one syllable. Polysyllabic words have three or more.
2 Emotive vocabulary includes *foulest, soul-destroying tyranny, darkened, stained*.
3 As the speech was delivered at the Labour Party Conference, the immediate audience (those present in the hall) would be Labour Party members. However, the speech would be reported in the media (and broadcast on television and radio), so Blair would also be aware of a much broader domestic audience. At one point he also speaks directly to the American people (*We were with you at the first*).

Exam preparation

Grammatical features of the speech include: parallelism (*our deepest sympathy ... and our profound solidarity*; *sons and daughters, wives and husbands*); contrast, often combined with parallelism (*the hard work and creative power of the free citizen, not the violence and savagery of the fanatic*); antithesis (*trying to be normal people, in a very abnormal situation*); short, emphatic sentences (*Because there is no answer.*); use of first person plural pronouns *we* and *our*, to suggest Blair is speaking on behalf of his the audience and the nation; use of second person (*you*) when he describes his experience in New York, encouraging audience to imagine themselves in Blair's position; use of first person singular in *I tell you ...*, which implies Blair is confiding in the audience, revealing his feelings.

Lexical features include: emotive vocabulary (*evil, savagery, longing* etc.); simple, concrete vocabulary (*tea and biscuits*), which contrasts with the large number of abstract nouns (*understanding, justice*); metaphor (*out of the shadow of this evil ...*).

Other kinds of talk

Checkpoints

1 Field-specific lexis is vocabulary associated with a particular field or topic.
2 Ellipsis.

Exam preparation

JM is the main commentator. He describes the action as it takes place, and also supplies some background information (*Wayne Rooney has become the youngest goalscorer in England's international history*). TB is the expert summariser and is more analytical (*look where the 13 is brought on to do a manmarking job on Rooney*). The lexis includes numerous examples of field-specific lexis (*header, substitute* etc.). Grammatical features include ellipsis (*terrific ball from Beckham*) and non-standard constructions (*Rooney's lost him a couple of yards*). The most noticeable phonological feature is JM's increased pace and volume as the goal is scored.

Revision checklist
Spoken language

By the end of this chapter you should be able to:

1	Explain the main differences between speech and writing.	Confident	Not confident. **Revise** page 26
2	Distinguish between different types of speech.	Confident	Not confident. **Revise** page 26
3	Explain the main functions of speech.	Confident	Not confident. **Revise** pages 26–27
4	Understand the main contextual influences on speech.	Confident	Not confident. **Revise** page 27
5	Recognise the main features of spontaneous speech.	Confident	Not confident. **Revise** pages 28–29
6	Understand what is meant by the term non-fluency features.	Confident	Not confident. **Revise** page 29
7	Identify prosodic features of speech, such as pitch and intonation.	Confident	Not confident. **Revise** pages 30–31
8	Understand the symbols and conventions associated with the transcription of speech.	Confident	Not confident. **Revise** page 31
9	Identify the main elements in the structure of conversations, such as turn taking and adjacency pairs.	Confident	Not confident. **Revise** pages 32–33
10	Understand what is meant by speech act theory.	Confident	Not confident. **Revise** page 34
11	Explain how conversational behaviour might reflect differences of status or power.	Confident	Not confident. **Revise** page 34
12	List and explain Grice's maxims.	Confident	Not confident. **Revise** page 36
13	Understand the concepts of face and politeness.	Confident	Not confident. **Revise** pages 36–37
14	Outline research findings related to gender differences in conversational behaviour.	Confident	Not confident. **Revise** page 37
15	Identify the main grammatical, lexical and phonological features of public speeches.	Confident	Not confident. **Revise** pages 38–41
16	Approach with confidence the analysis of a variety of types of spoken language.	Confident	Not confident. **Revise** pages 42–43

Literature has three broad genres: poetry, prose fiction and drama. Within the genre of poetry, there are many different poetic **forms**, such as the sonnet and the ballad. As well as studying different types of poem, you will also encounter on your course poems from different historical periods. The first great English poet was Geoffrey Chaucer (who lived in the 14th century), and you may find that you are studying as a set text one of his *Canterbury Tales*. Poets tend to use language in an especially intense, concentrated way, and individual words, lines and images are often ambiguous, with different layers of meaning. When you are writing an analysis of a poem you need to show you are aware that what you are analysing is a poem rather than another kind of literary text, and the poet's use of rhyme, rhythm and metre is also relevant here.

Exam themes

→ Different poetic forms.

→ Poetry from different periods.

→ Literary and linguistic features of poetry.

Topic checklist

○ AS ● A2	OCR	EDEXCEL	AQA A	AQA B	WJEC
Historical overview	○●	●	○●	○●	○●
Chaucer	○●	●	○●	○●	○●
Poetic form and structure	○●	●	○●	○●	○●
Poetic imagery	○●	●	○●	○●	○●
Lexis in poetry	○●	●	○●	○●	○●
Grammar in poetry	○●	●	○●	○●	○●
Rhythm and metre	○●	●	○●	○●	○●
Sound in poetry	○●	●	○●	○●	○●
Analysing poetry	○●	●	○●	○●	○●
Specimen texts	○●	●	○●	○●	○●

Historical overview

This section offers a brief overview of some of the principal writers and movements in the history of English poetry.

Medieval English poetry

The leading English poet of the Middle Ages was **Geoffrey Chaucer**, who was born around 1340 and died in 1400. He is discussed in the next section of this chapter (pages 52–53). Longer works by medieval writers other than Chaucer are not usually set for AS/A2 study, though shorter poems may feature in examining board anthologies. The language of the period, known as **Middle English**, was very different from today's English and is described more fully on page 18.

Metaphysical poetry

Metaphysical poetry is a term used to refer to the works of a group of 17th-century poets, including **John Donne**, **Andrew Marvell** and **George Herbert**. The Metaphysicals are associated with an intellectual approach to emotional topics, and with the use of strikingly unusual **images**. Donne's love poetry, for example, displays his considerable learning and is full of references to scientific and geographical discoveries. His poems often take the form of complex, carefully developed arguments, incorporating clever **paradoxes** and **puns**. He is also noted for his ingenious **conceits**: surprising comparisons between things that are apparently dissimilar. In *Batter my heart* (*Holy Sonnet XIV*), he compares himself to a besieged town, and in *A Valediction: forbidding mourning* the souls of two lovers are compared to a pair of geometric compasses:

> If they be two, they are two so
> As stiff twin compasses are two,
> Thy soul the fixed foot, makes no show
> To move, but doth, if th'other do.

18th-century poetry

The 18th century includes the **Augustan** period in English Literature, which is generally identified as lasting from 1700 to 1745. The most important English poet from this time is **Alexander Pope**. In 18th-century poetry there is less emphasis on love and religion (the major themes addressed by 17th-century poets) and a greater preoccupation with society, manners and morals. There was also a belief in order, reason and control, and this was reflected in the widespread use of the **heroic couplet**: pairs of rhyming **iambic pentameter** lines, a verse form noted for its rhythmic balance and precision.

Romantic poetry

The **Romantic** period runs roughly from 1789 (the year of the French Revolution) to the middle of the 19th century. Notable Romantic poets include **William Blake**, **William Wordsworth**, **Samuel Taylor Coleridge**, **John Keats**, **Percy Bysshe Shelley** and **Lord Byron**. The Romantic

---

Take note

Other important medieval poets include **William Langland** (who wrote *Piers Plowman*), **Sir Thomas Malory** and **John Skelton**.

Checkpoint 1

Define the terms **paradox** and **pun**.

Checkpoint 2

What does this image tell us about the relationship between the lovers?

Take note

During the Augustan period, there was a strong interest in the classical writers of the ancient world, whose works were admired and imitated (the original Augustan age was under the Roman Emperor Augustus, from 27BC to AD14).

The jargon

Iambic pentameter is a metre comprising five pairs of syllables, with the stress falling on the second syllable in each pair.

movement can be seen as a reaction against the 18th-century commitment to order and reason. The Romantic poets stress the importance of human emotions, and celebrate and explore the individual consciousness (they had a particular interest in the power of the imagination). There is an enthusiasm for nature, especially those parts of the landscape that had not been shaped and ordered by human intervention; mountains are a recurring symbol of beauty and mystery in Romantic verse. There is also a nostalgia for simple rural society, for an environment in which people lived and worked in harmony with nature, and a new interest in the attitudes and experiences of ordinary country people. The regard for unspoilt, natural man was accompanied by an exploration of the insights of childhood, an interest that is most evident in the poetry of Wordsworth and Blake. In Wordsworth's *Immortality Ode*, the child is addressed as *Thou best Philosopher* and *Mighty Prophet*.

Later poetry   ○○○

Poetry since 1900 has been immensely varied, but it is possible to identify some broad patterns and movements. The poets of the **First World War**, such as **Wilfred Owen**, brought a new kind of realism to English poetry, with shocking images of violence and suffering. **Modernist poetry**, which is associated with the first half of the 20th century, can be seen in part as a response to the horrors of global conflict, and to the uncertainties of a world experiencing continual industrial and technological change. Modernist poets such as **T.S. Eliot**, **W.B. Yeats** and **Ezra Pound** deliberately rejected old poetic forms and conventions, producing complex, experimental poetry which reflected a sense of disintegration and confusion. They developed **free verse**, which broke the conventions of traditional metre, with its patterns of regularly stressed syllables and standard line lengths. The modernist approach has continued to be influential, and much late-20th-century poetry is in this tradition. In contrast, there have also been more conventional, anti-experimental poets – notably **Thomas Hardy**, who began writing in the 19th century but lived until 1928, and **Philip Larkin**, who became established as a major poet in the 1950s. The later decades of the century also saw the emergence of a number of important women poets, coinciding with the growing influence of **feminism**. Examples include **Sylvia Plath**, **Carol Ann Duffy** and **Fleur Adcock**.

Take note

English language poetry has also become increasingly **multicultural**. The poetry of **Grace Nichols**, for example, reflects on her experiences as a black woman living in Britain, and on the slavery of her West Indian ancestors.

Exam preparation (30 minutes)

Select a poem from the poetry text you are studying and consider how the poem reflects the time that it was written. (Alternatively, use a poem from the *Specimen texts* section, pages 68–69.) Consider such aspects as: language; form and structure; subject matter; attitudes and values; social and historical references.

Chaucer

Take note

Chaucer was born around 1340 (his exact date of birth is unknown) and died in 1400. His father was a prosperous wine merchant, so Chaucer was familiar with the middle-class world of business from an early age. Later he moved in aristocratic circles, holding several positions in the royal court. His equivalent today would be a high-ranking civil servant: his posts included controller of customs in the port of London, and he also frequently travelled abroad on diplomatic missions.

Examiner's secrets

Don't forget:
→ In the exam you will have to refer to the original text, so you need to get used to quoting and analysing Chaucer's language.
→ Don't get so immersed in trying to understand the language that you lose sight of the bigger picture – the **characters** and **themes**. When you engage with the text on this level you should find that it is very accessible. Many of Chaucer's storylines are humorous and entertaining, and his tales have survived through the centuries because his characters have retained an instantly recognisable humanity.

Checkpoint 1

Name three groups of foreign invaders who influenced the development of English before the arrival of the French in 1066.

If you are studying a Chaucer text and have not encountered Chaucer's poetry before, the text will inevitably appear strange when you first look at it. It is more than 600 years since Chaucer wrote *The Canterbury Tales*, and written English has changed a great deal in that time. However, the language hurdle is really not too difficult to overcome, and it is worth the effort – Chaucer's poetry has tremendous energy, wit and descriptive power.

Chaucer's language

The key to coming to terms with Chaucer's language is perseverance. If you try reading a page of Chaucer, you should find that you can pick up the general gist of much of it, though there will probably be some passages that are incomprehensible. You should make full use of the notes and glossary that are included in all good editions of Chaucer texts, and work carefully through the poem, a section at a time.

Here are some important aspects of Chaucer's language:

Historical context

Chaucer's life coincided with an important period in the history of the English language. Following the Norman conquest in 1066, French became the language of the ruling class and, in terms of prestige, English was a poor third to French and Latin (the language of the church). For centuries English, while continuing in use as a spoken language, was rarely written down. But during Chaucer's time English was slowly re-establishing itself. In 1362 Parliament was opened in English for the first time, and in 1399 (the year before Chaucer died) the first English-speaking king for three centuries, Henry IV, came to the throne. The English language of Chaucer's day (known as **Middle English**) had however been transformed by the influence of French: an estimated 10,000 words of French origin were added to our vocabulary over a 300-year period. These new words were often elegant and refined, in contrast to the older Anglo-Saxon vocabulary, which was more earthy and direct.

Lexis

The lexis of Chaucer's poems reflects the contrast between French and Anglo-Saxon: he often uses French-derived vocabulary to achieve a grander, more elevated tone, and Anglo-Saxon vocabulary when he is describing ordinary people or situations, or being deliberately crude and blunt. Many words used by Chaucer are recognisable to a modern reader, but some caution is needed, as in some cases the meaning of the word has changed over time. For example, the meaning of *sentence* when used by Chaucer is 'meaning' or 'opinion'.

Grammar

Word order is sometimes different from today's English. Syntax is often **inverted** (meaning the order of the grammatical elements is the reverse of what we would expect). The description of Alison in *The Miller's Tale* begins *Fair was this yonge wyf*, not 'This yonge wyf was fair' (incidentally, note how Chaucer's construction has the advantage of stressing *Fair*). Another grammatical feature of Middle English is that several **inflections** (word endings that serve a grammatical function) were in use that later disappeared from the language. These include *-th* or *-eth* at the ends of verbs (*maketh*, *toucheth*) and *-en* as a verb ending (*slepen*) or to indicate a noun is plural (*eyen* for 'eyes').

Phonology

Sound is especially important in Chaucer's poems because he was working within an **oral** literary tradition. Poetry was generally intended to be read aloud to groups of listeners. As you are reading your text, try to imagine how it would sound when spoken, and look for effects achieved by the sounds of words. If you can, listen to a tape of the text being read in Middle English. Alternatively, many editions of Chaucer's poems include some guidance on pronunciation.

The Canterbury Tales ●●●

The Canterbury Tales consists of stories told by a group of pilgrims who are on their way from London to Canterbury. In the opening poem, *The General Prologue*, the narrator (who identifies himself as one of the pilgrims) gives a description of his companions and explains the proposal for a story-telling competition. Each pilgrim is to tell four stories, two on the outward journey and two as they return. As there are over 30 pilgrims, a complete *Canterbury Tales* would have comprised over 120 tales. In fact Chaucer never completed the work, and there are only 24 tales, spread over an assortment of manuscripts, some containing sequences of several tales, some only one tale.

Chaucer seems to have chosen the situation of a pilgrimage because it enabled him to present a marvellous panorama of medieval life. His pilgrims cover a range of ages, occupations and classes, and their personalities and moral natures are equally varied. This diversity is also reflected in the stories they tell. In most of the poems there is a close relationship between the tale and its teller, and if you are studying one of the tales you will probably find that the **role of the narrator** is a key topic. The portrait of the relevant pilgrim in *The General Prologue* is a good place to start. You then need to look closely at how the tale reflects the pilgrim's attitudes, values and personality.

Checkpoint 2

Give two examples of inflections that still exist in contemporary English.

Take note

With some tales it is also useful to consider how the poem relates to other tales. For example, *The Miller's Tale* immediately follows *The Knight's Tale*, and while there are interesting parallels between the two stories, the contrasts are even more striking.

Exam preparation (45 minutes)

Write an essay examining the character and role of the narrator in the tale that you are studying. Refer closely to Chaucer's use of language in your answer.

Poetic form and structure

Examiner's secrets

Remember your primary focus must always be on the **meaning** of the poem. How does the poet **use** the form of the poem to convey thoughts, feelings and ideas?

Links

Metre and **rhyme** are important aspects of poetic form. See pages 62–65.

Links

For more on the **iambic pentameter**, see page 62.

Checkpoint 1

Name three Romantic poets.

This section is concerned with the overall shape and organisation of poems. The terms **form** and **structure** are often used interchangeably, but form is really a narrower term referring to the kinds of poetry poets use to organise their thoughts and ideas – sonnets, couplets, blank verse and so on. Structure refers to the overall arrangement of a poem. This can include the poem's form, but it also includes such elements as the sequence of ideas (for example, how the poem begins and ends).

Stanzas

A **stanza** is a section of a poem consisting of several lines of verse. Many poems are divided into stanzas of equal length (e.g. three or four lines). Four-line stanzas, known as **quatrains**, are especially common, and are often combined with a regular **metre** and **rhyme scheme**. If a poem is organised into stanzas, you should think about why this is and about the relationship between the stanzas. How does the poem develop as it moves from stanza to stanza? Are there important contrasts between individual stanzas?

Lyric poetry

The majority of poems can be classified as **lyric poetry**. A lyric poem expresses an individual's thoughts and feelings. Lyrics are usually quite short, and the most common subject is love. **Sonnets**, **odes** and **elegies** (see below) are all examples of lyric poetry. Apart from the lyric, the other dominant type of poetry is **narrative poetry** (see opposite page).

Sonnets

A **sonnet** is a poem of 14 lines, with a rhythm usually based on the **iambic pentameter**. The two most common kinds of sonnet are the **Petrarchan** and the **Shakespearean**:

→ The **Petrarchan** sonnet uses a rhyme scheme that divides the poem into two sections, an **octave** (the first eight lines) and a **sestet** (the last six lines). The rhyme scheme is usually *abbaabba*, *cdecde* (or *cdcdcd*).

→ The **Shakespearean** sonnet has three **quatrains** (units of four lines each) and ends with a **couplet** (a pair of rhyming lines). The usual rhyme scheme is *abab*, *cdcd*, *efef*, *gg*.

The sonnet is an Italian form that entered English poetry in the 16th century. The earliest English sonnets were love poems. Love has continued to be the topic most strongly associated with sonnets, but poets have used the form for a great variety of subjects; religious sonnets are also common, and the Romantic poets wrote many sonnets about nature.

If you are analysing a sonnet, you should look closely at the relationship between the different sections of the poem, as the divisions often mark shifts in meaning or attitude. In Petrarchan sonnets, for instance, the octave sometimes outlines a situation or problem, while the sestet offers a response to it. In Shakespearean sonnets, the final couplet may express a concluding thought or introduce a new idea.

Odes

An **ode** is an elaborate lyric poem, often extending over several stanzas, usually addressed to a person, object or idea. Odes are also usually serious poems that praise the person or thing addressed, and meditate upon its qualities. Famous odes include Shelley's *Ode to the West Wind*, Keats's *Ode to Autumn* and Marvell's *Horatian Ode upon Cromwell's Return from Ireland*.

Elegies

An **elegy** is a poem that mourns someone's death, such as Tennyson's *In Memoriam*, which was written in memory of A.H. Hallam, a friend of the poet. The term is also sometimes applied more generally to solemn, contemplative poems. Thomas Gray's famous *Elegy Written in a Country Churchyard* is a reflective poem about death.

Narrative poetry

Narrative poetry is poetry that tells a story. Before novels became popular in the 18th century, stories were usually told in verse, and even after the advent of the novel many poets continued to write narrative verse. The two main forms of narrative poetry are the **epic** and the **ballad**:

→ **Epics** are long poems, often about mythical heroes, and often with grand, impressive settings and elements of the supernatural.
→ **Ballads** tell stories in simple, everyday language. The emphasis is on action and dialogue, with description usually kept to a minimum. Many ballads use the traditional **ballad metre**, which comprises rhyming **quatrains** (four-line stanzas) of alternate four-stress and three-stress lines. Also common is the use of a **refrain** – the regular repetition of words or lines, usually at the end of a stanza.

Links

The *Specimen texts* section on pages 68–69 includes three examples of sonnets.

Examiner's secrets

As well as identifying the form of a poem, consider other elements of its structure. How does it begin, develop and end? Does the structural pattern of the poem change or break down at any point?

Checkpoint 2

An example of an **epic** poem is *Paradise Lost*, a long 17th-century religious poem about the fall of man. Who wrote it?

Exam preparation (30 minutes)   answer: page 70

Text A on page 68 is a sonnet by Shakespeare, *My mistress' eyes are nothing like the sun*. Explore the poet's attitude towards the woman described in this poem, referring closely to his use of language and of the sonnet form.

Poetic imagery

The term **imagery** is sometimes used very broadly to refer to any aspect of a piece of writing that appeals to the reader's senses – a visual description, for example, or a description of a sound or a taste. More narrowly, the term also refers specifically to the use in literature of **comparisons**, especially **similes**, **metaphors** and **personification**. Imagery can occur in any kind of text, but is especially common in poetry.

Figurative and literal language

Literal language means what it says. **Figurative** language is language that is not literally true. If the sentence *He kicked the bucket* refers to someone who lost their temper and kicked over a pail of water, it is literal. If it is a colloquial remark meaning someone died, it is figurative.

In the texts you are studying you will probably encounter a large amount of figurative language. Poets in particular use comparisons to make their writing more vivid, suggestive or precise. When you come across an image, you should ask yourself these questions:

→ What are the two things that are being compared? Here the terms **tenor** and **vehicle** are useful – see **metaphors** below.
→ How are they similar? Often there is more than one similarity.
→ What is conveyed or achieved by the comparison? For example, the comparison may highlight a particular characteristic of the thing that is being described.
→ What is the significance of the comparison in relation to the text as a whole? There may be links with other images in the text, or the comparison may relate in some way to an important theme.

Similes

A **simile** is a comparison that uses the words *like* or *as*. This example is from Wordsworth's *Composed upon Westminster Bridge* (see page 67).

> This City now doth, like a garment, wear
> The beauty of the morning

The simile *like a garment* compares London's early morning splendour to a beautiful piece of clothing. It suggests how the buildings are bathed in sunlight, and also implies that the beauty is transitory, that London is not always as beautiful as this (clothing is not worn all the time).

Checkpoint 1

List five other figurative expressions in everyday use.

Take note

A word or expression that is not meant to be taken literally is also known as a **figure of speech**.

Examiner's secrets

Never simply write, 'There is a metaphor in the third stanza'. Always explain what is being compared, and what the effect or significance of the comparison is.

Metaphors

Whereas a simile acknowledges that the things being compared are separate (by using *like* or *as*), a **metaphor** goes one stage further and describes something as if it actually were something else – what is said is not literally true. In the following extract from the poem *Last Lesson of the Afternoon*, D.H. Lawrence (who briefly worked as a teacher) uses the metaphor of a hunt to describe the situation in a classroom as the school day draws to a close:

> When will the bell ring, and end this weariness?
> How long have they tugged the leash, and strained apart,
> My pack of unruly hounds! I cannot start
> Them again on a quarry of knowledge they hate to hunt,
> I can haul them and urge them no more.

Much of the language here is metaphorical. For example, the pupils are not really a pack of hounds, and they have not been tugging on a leash. The image is effective because the comparison with a hunt works in several different ways. The pupils are like a pack of hunting hounds in that they are noisy and restless. The teacher resembles a huntsman who has the hounds on a leash but is struggling to control them, just as the teacher is struggling to control the class. The pupils are meant to be searching for knowledge, in the same way that hounds are meant to pursue a *quarry* (which might, for example, be a fox). However, the pupils are not interested in the search for knowledge, so that they are like hounds being urged to pursue a quarry *they hate to hunt.*

A metaphor such as this which is introduced and then **developed**, either over several lines (as here) or over a complete text, is called an **extended metaphor**. Two other relevant terms are **tenor** and **vehicle**: the tenor is the subject of the metaphor (in this case, the situation in the classroom), the vehicle is what it is compared with (here, a hunt).

Personification

Personification occurs when something that is not human or alive is described as if it were. The earlier quotation from *Composed upon Westminster Bridge* is an example of personification, because London is compared to someone wearing a garment. There is more personification elsewhere in the poem:

> Dear God! the very houses seem asleep,
> And all that mighty heart is lying still!

Checkpoint 2

Comment on the effectiveness of the verbs in this extract.

The jargon

There are also terms for the ways that images appeal to our senses:
→ a **visual** image appeals to our sense of sight;
→ an **auditory** (or aural) image appeals to our sense of hearing;
→ a **tactile** image appeals to our sense of touch;
→ an **olfactory** image appeals to our sense of smell;
→ a **gustatory** image appeals to our sense of taste.

Watch out!

The term **tenor** can also mean 'register'.

Exam preparation (30 minutes)   answer: page 70

Text B on page 68 is *Holy Sonnet XIV*, written by the Metaphysical poet John Donne (see page 50). Examine Donne's use of imagery in this poem.

Lexis in poetry

The jargon

The term **poetic diction** is sometimes used for the vocabulary employed by poets. **Lexical choice** is a term used for a writer's choice of vocabulary.

Watch out!

Be careful before making sweeping statements about how 'formal' or 'informal' a text is. Sometimes there are different levels of formality within the same text.

"I like working in both Standard English and Creole. I tend to want to fuse the two tongues because I come from a background where the two worlds were constantly interacting… Some Creole expressions are very vivid and concise and have no equivalent in English."

Grace Nichols

Checkpoint 1

What points could be made about **phonology** and **grammar** in the extract from *Caribbean Woman Prayer*?

Lexis is of course important in any kind of text, but as poems usually contain relatively few words, the words that are there have to work that much harder. As a result, poets choose their words with particular care and are very conscious of their suggestive power.

Levels of formality

As with other kinds of text, an initial point to consider when examining the lexis of a poem is how **formal** it is. Formal vocabulary tends to be associated with more serious subjects and also with older texts. If there is evidence of **informality**, you should look for examples to quote, and should also consider *why* the poet has chosen to use informal lexis. For example, it may help to suggest a speaking voice, give us a sense of the character of the narrator, or be appropriate in some way to the attitudes expressed in the poem or to the poem's subject matter. Although informality is more common in modern poetry, it can occur in older poems, as the opening of *The Good Morrow* by the 17th-century poet John Donne illustrates:

> I wonder by my troth, what thou, and I
> Did till we lov'd?

Here the direct, largely monosyllabic vocabulary, the colloquial-sounding expression *by my troth*, and the rhythmic stress on *Did* combine to create the impression of natural speech.

The informal lexis may include **non-standard vocabulary**, especially if the poem seeks to recreate a regional or national **dialect**. Some of Grace Nichols's poems, for example, combine **Creole** and **Standard English** in order to reflect the narrator's Afro-Caribbean background. This extract is from *Caribbean Woman Prayer*:

> An talking bout politics Lord
> I hope you give de politicians dem
> de courage to do what they have to do
> an to mek dem see dat tings must grow
> from within
> an not from without

Connotation

The **connotations** of a word are its associations – the emotions, sensations and attitudes that it evokes. Very broadly, words can have **positive** or **negative** connotations, but you should also try to be more precise about the particular connotations of specific words. Consider, for example, the beginning of William Blake's *London*:

> I wander thro' each charter'd street
> Near where the charter'd Thames does flow,
> And mark in every face I meet
> Marks of weakness, marks of woe.

The connotations of several of the words in this stanza can be commented upon. Most obviously, *weakness* and *woe* both have connotations of suffering (though *weakness* may also suggest powerlessness). *Charter'd* is a more complex word. Literally, it means having official approval and recognition, usually from the ruling monarch or the government. In Blake's poem as a whole a theme of oppression emerges, and his use of *charter'd* suggests how much of life is controlled and regulated – even the River Thames, which ought to *flow* freely. The **repetition** of *charter'd* reinforces the point: there is no escape from the power of authority. *Marks* is **ambiguous** (i.e. it has more than one meaning). As an **abstract** word, it suggests that the expressions on people's faces are an indication of their misery. As a **concrete** word, it is more powerful, implying that people's suffering is physically etched on their faces. Again, **repetition** is important: as well as *marks* occurring twice, there is also *mark*, which here means 'notice'. The pattern of repetition in the poem suggests that the despair Blake observes is all around him, and creates linguistically a feeling of imprisonment – a sense of being trapped in a cycle of words.

Archaisms and neologisms ●●●

An **archaism** is a word or expression that is no longer in general use. Obviously the presence of archaic diction will usually indicate an older text, though poets occasionally use archaisms deliberately, for example if a poem is set in the past and the poet wants to create an authentic mood and atmosphere.

A **neologism** is a newly **coined** word or expression. A poet might use up-to-date language to give the poetry an added sense of contemporary relevance, or because neologisms have a freshness and vitality sometimes lacking in older vocabulary. Poets also sometimes create words and expressions of their own. In *Dulce et Decorum Est* Wilfred Owen describes a group of First World War soldiers:

> Many had lost their boots,
> But limped on, blood-shod.

The **coinage** here is the **compound** *blood-shod*. 'Shod' means 'wearing on the feet', and is usually applied to shoes. Owen means the soldiers who have lost their boots have feet caked with blood. He has created an original expression by combining two words in an unexpected way, and by changing a single vowel in the existing word 'bloodshed'.

Take note

This analysis illustrates some important aspects of lexis that can be noted when you are analysing a poem. Look for:
→ words with similar **connotations**;
→ words with **contrasting** meanings or connotations (in this example, *charter'd* and *flow* contrast);
→ **repetition** of particular words;
→ **ambiguity**;
→ whether words are **abstract** or **concrete**, and the effects this has.

Example

The use of *mark* to mean 'notice' in the Blake extract above is an example of an **archaism**.

Checkpoint 2

What is a **compound**?

Exam preparation

See page 61 for a practice question relevant to this and the following section.

Grammar in poetry

Watch out!

When analysing texts, refer to 'non-standard' grammar rather than to 'wrong' or 'incorrect' grammar.

Checkpoint 1

Explain the difference between **dynamic** and **stative** verbs.

Links

The terms for different types of sentence are explained on page 12.

There is more deviation from the usual rules of grammar in poetry than in prose. This is partly because a flexible attitude to elements of grammar such as word order is sometimes needed to meet the demands of poetic form (e.g. rhyme and metre). At the same time, modern poetry tends to be less respectful of traditional poetic conventions (see page 51), and part of this freer approach is a greater willingness to break normal grammatical rules. This section looks at some areas of grammar to focus on if you are analysing a poem.

Word classes

Does a particular type of **word class** tend to recur, either in the poem as a whole or in a particular part of it? If so, does this have any effect? For example, a large number of **dynamic verbs** might create an impression of action and excitement.

Types of sentence

What **kinds of sentence** are used – **declarative**, **imperative**, **exclamatory**, **interrogative**? In *Composed upon Westminster Bridge* (see page 67), exclamatory sentences stress how moved Wordsworth is by the scene before him:

> Dear God! the very houses seem asleep;
> And all that mighty heart is lying still!

Sentence length

Consider the effects of **unusually long** or **short sentences**. Philip Larkin's *MCMXIV* describes Britain at the outbreak of the First World War. The entire poem, which is 32 lines long, consists of a single sentence. Because the poem never moves forward to another sentence, the effect is to reinforce the impression that Larkin has tried to freeze a moment in time, evoking a world that was about to change irrevocably (the last line of the poem is *Never such innocence again*).

Word order

Look for unusual **word order**, which may cause particular words to be **foregrounded** (brought to the reader's attention). In *The Best of School*, D.H. Lawrence (the author of *Last Lesson of the Afternoon*, referred to on page 57) describes teaching children who are absorbed in their studies:

> and I,
> As I sit on the shores of the class, alone,
> Watch the boys in their summer blouses
> As they write, their round heads busily bowed

Note how the word order and the punctuation stress the word *alone* by isolating it (Lawrence does not write 'As I sit alone'). The positioning of the word at the end of the line reinforces this. The effect is to emphasise the teacher's separation from the pupils.

Look also for **patterns** in the grammatical constructions used, such as **parallelism** (the repetition of similar grammatical structures). In the second stanza of Blake's *London* (see page 58), parallelism strengthens the impression that Blake is surrounded by misery and oppression:

> In every cry of every Man,
> In every Infant's cry of fear,
> In every voice, in every ban,
> The mind-forg'd manacles I hear.

The parallelism here is created by the series of **noun phrases** beginning *every* . . .

Take note

The word *ban* in this extract means 'curse' (though the word may have a double meaning).

Checkpoint 2

What do you think Blake means by *mind-forg'd manacles*?

Non-standard grammar ●●●

As explained in the introduction to this section, **non-standard grammar** occurs more commonly in poetry than prose. Nevertheless, when you encounter it, it is still important to consider why it is a feature of a particular poem. For example, as with non-standard vocabulary (see page 58), non-standard grammar may be part of an attempt to evoke a narrator's social or regional background.

Use of first person ●●●

If the poem is written in the **first person** (using words such as *I* and *me*), be careful not to assume that the poet is necessarily the narrator. What kind of feelings, attitudes and tone does the narrator have, and how does the language of the poem reflect this? What view of the narrator does the poet have, and what view is the reader intended to have?

Tense ●●●

Tense may be significant, especially if it changes (e.g. switching from past to present, or vice versa). The present tense tends to be associated with a feeling of immediacy.

Exam preparation (30 minutes)   answer: pages 70–71

William Blake's *London* has been referred to in this section and the preceding one (pages 58–59). The poem in full appears on page 69 (**Text C**). Write an analysis of the poem, focusing in particular on Blake's use of lexis and grammar.

Rhythm and metre

Rhythm is a general term for the pace, speed or 'movement' of a poem. An important component of rhythm is **metre**, which is a more technical term for the regular patterns of stressed and unstressed syllables used by poets – the 'beat' that a poem has.

Metre ●●●

The **metre** of a line or lines of poetry is the distribution within the verse of stressed and unstressed syllables. Especially in older poetry, this distribution will usually conform (with occasional variations) to a standard pattern. Depending on the metre, this pattern will be made up of groups of two or three syllables. Each of these groups is called a **foot**. There are five main patterns or metres:

Iambic

Here an unstressed syllable is followed by a stressed one:

> The *cur*few *tolls* the *knell* of *par*ting *day*

This line has five pairs of syllables, or five feet. This particular form of the iambic metre is known as the **iambic pentameter**, the most common metre in English poetry. Unrhymed poetry based on the iambic pentameter is known as **blank verse**.

Trochaic

This is the second most common metre, and is the reverse of the iambic metre. Again there are pairs of syllables, but here the pattern is stressed-unstressed:

> *Sim*ple *Si*mon *met* a *pie*man

As this example illustrates, the strong 'marching' rhythm makes this a common metre in nursery rhymes.

Dactylic

Each foot has three syllables, one stressed followed by two unstressed:

> *Half* a league, *half* a league,
> *Half* a league *on*ward

In this example the last foot is trochaic: '*on*ward'.

Anapaestic

Again the feet have three syllables, this time two unstressed followed by a stressed:

> Through *all* the wide *bor*der his *steed* was the *best*

The first foot here – 'Through *all*' – is iambic.

Spondaic

Two successive stressed syllables; this metre is usually only found in part of a line:

Watch out!

As some of the examples on this page illustrate, individual lines will often contain slight variations on the metre the poet is using. These prevent the metre sounding rigid and predictable.

Checkpoint 1

The example of dactylic metre is from Tennyson's *The Charge of the Light Brigade*. Is the metre appropriate to a description of cavalry charging into battle?

Rocks, *caves*, *lakes*, *fens*, *bogs*, *dens* and *shades* of *death*

Here there are three spondaic feet, then the poem returns to its usual iambic metre for the last two feet.

Rhythm: other terms

Enjambement
This occurs when the sense of one line continues into the next, and the end of the first line has no punctuation mark. This example is from Wordsworth's *Composed upon Westminster Bridge*:

Ships, towers, domes, theatres, and temples lie
Open unto the fields, and to the sky

End-stopped line
This is when the end of a line coincides with a grammatical pause, which is usually indicated by a punctuation mark.

Caesura
This is a pause, usually in the middle of a line, and usually shown by a punctuation mark:

To be, or not to be: that is the question

Here the caesura is indicated by a colon.

Analysing rhythm

Metre can be difficult and you need not worry too much if you cannot identify the metre being used in a poem. It is certainly not worth wasting precious time in an exam trying to work out the metre if it is not clear to you quite quickly. It should still be perfectly possible to comment intelligently on the rhythm of the poem. Try to imagine how the poem would sound when read aloud, and think about the effects of heavily stressed words, of enjambement and of the pauses suggested by the punctuation. Does the rhythm seem to be fast or slow? Look for changes in the rhythm and, above all, try to identify places in the poem where the rhythm corresponds in some way to the **meaning**. In Coleridge's *The Ancient Mariner*, for example, the rhythm quickens when it is describing a ship travelling at high speed:

The fair breeze blew, the white foam flew

Later, when the ship is becalmed, the rhythm slows:

Day after day, day after day,
We stuck, nor breath nor motion

Checkpoint 2

This example of spondaic metre describes a difficult journey. Why is the spondaic metre appropriate here?

Checkpoint 3

Comment on the effect of the **enjambement** in this example.

Examiner's secrets

If you are able to identify the metre, remember to comment on how and why it is used.

Checkpoint 4

Identify and comment on some of the other **phonological** features present in these two examples.

Exam preparation

See page 65 for a practice question relevant to this and the following section.

Sound in poetry

This section looks at some of the phonological techniques commonly associated with poetry. Remember that devices such as alliteration and sibilance should never be mentioned for their own sake; you should always try to explain the effects that the poet's use of sound has.

Rhyme ●●●

The most common form of **rhyme** occurs when the last one or two syllables of two or more lines of poetry have a matching sound. A pair of rhyming lines is called a **couplet**, though rhyming lines are not always next to each other. Rhymes are easy to spot, and you won't get much credit for simply saying they're there. Instead, you should think about what **effect** the rhymes have. This effect will very much depend upon the individual poem. Sometimes rhymes help to give a poem a lively, jaunty rhythm, a sense of narrative pace or a feeling of order and harmony. The **words** that are rhymed may be significant – rhyming brings them together, and you should consider whether linking them in this way has any effect. In *Essential Beauty*, Philip Larkin rhymes words with very different connotations in order to emphasise the contrast between the images of perfection that appear on advertising hoardings and the drab reality of the streets they occupy:

> High above the gutter
> A silver knife sinks into golden butter

Internal rhyme is when words rhyme *within* the line:

> The ship was cheered, the harbour cleared

Half-rhymes occur when the rhyme is not quite complete; usually the consonants in the rhyming words match but the vowels do not. Many 20th-century poets, such as Wilfred Owen (whose poems are mostly about the First World War), use half-rhymes. In the poem *Miners*, thinking about miners digging for coal reminds Owen of soldiers digging to make trenches in France:

> I thought of some who worked dark pits
>   Of war, and died
> Digging the rock where Death reputes
>   Peace lies indeed.

Half-rhymes can have a jarring, discordant effect. The half-rhymes here (*pits – reputes, died – indeed*) – as in other Owen poems – are unsettling, and confirm that Owen wants to disturb the reader rather than to reassure us.

The arrangement of rhymes within a poem as a whole is called the **rhyme scheme**. Certain types of poem, such as the **sonnet** (see page 54) have standard rhyme schemes. The rhyme scheme is part of the overall **structure** of a poem. Think about the effect the rhyme scheme has.

Checkpoint 1

Comment on the use of **pre-modifiers** in this extract.

Checkpoint 2

Does this extract have any other significant **phonological** features?

For example, it may help to divide the poem into different stages or sections. Any change in the pattern of rhyming lines may correspond to a significant change or development in the meaning of the poem.

Onomatopoeia

Onomatopoeia occurs when words imitate the sounds they describe: when we say the words out loud, we can actually hear the sound. *Wind*, a poem by Ted Hughes describing a violent storm, begins with these lines:

> This house has been far out at sea all night,
> The woods *crashing* through darkness, the *booming* hills

Alliteration

This is when two or more words begin with the same sound. You should only refer to alliteration if you can also explain the effect that you think it has. In *Ageing Schoolmaster* by Vernon Scannell, the narrator recalls his schooldays:

> And think of when I rolled, a gormless boy,
> And rollicked round the playground of my hours

Sibilance, assonance and dissonance

Sibilance, which is from a Latin word meaning 'hissing', is the repetition of *s*, soft *c*, *sh* and *z* sounds.

Assonance is the rhyming of vowel sounds within two or more words. This quotation from Philip Larkin's *The Trees* illustrates both assonance and sibilance:

> Yet still the unresting castles thresh
> In fullgrown thickness every May.
> Last year is dead, they seem to say,
> Begin afresh, afresh, afresh.

Dissonance contrasts with assonance as it occurs when sounds are so different that they clash with each other. In Ted Hughes's *Wind* (see above), the effect the strong wind has on birds is described:

> The wind flung a magpie away and a black-
> Back gull bent like an iron bar slowly

Checkpoint 3

Comment on the use of **imagery** in the first line of this extract.

Watch out!

Words sometimes begin with the same letter but not the same sound: *the whole world*. This is *not* alliteration.

Take note

Note how the repeated *r* sounds in *rolled*, *rollicked* and *round* help to convey a sense of energetic activity.

Take note

The **sibilance** creates an effect of rustling trees, and combines with **assonance** (*unresting* – *thresh* – *every* – *afresh*) and other kinds of **repetition** to evoke an impression of natural growth and movement.

Take note

Here the difficult sequence of sounds in *black-/Back gull bent like* prevents the verse flowing smoothly, reflecting the gull's hard struggle against the wind.

Exam preparation (30 minutes)   answer: page 71

Text D on page 69 is *God's Grandeur* by Gerard Manley Hopkins. Write an analysis of the poem, focusing in particular on Hopkins's use of rhythm, metre and sound.

Analysing poetry

This section offers some tips on analysing poems. They are especially relevant if you are studying a poem for the first time or tackling a previously unseen poem in an exam.

Stage one

Begin by asking yourself these questions about the poem:

→ What is it about?
→ What is it *really* about?

In answering the first question, you only need to address the simple, surface meaning of the poem. Who is narrating the poem? What are they describing? If the poem tells some kind of story, what happens? In answering the second question, you need to think more deeply about the poet's intention. What attitude does he or she have towards the subject matter of the poem? How is the reader intended to react? How would you describe the theme (or themes) of the poem? Does the poem have some kind of moral or 'message'?

Stage two

Develop your response to the poem by looking in more detail at what different parts of the poem mean, and by looking at the poem's **style**. Identify important literary and linguistic features, and consider how these contribute to the overall effect and to the meaning the poem has. Key aspects to consider include:

Form and structure

How has the poem been organised? Does it conform to an identifiable poetic form (e.g. the sonnet)? How does it begin, develop and end? Do particular sections of the poem contrast with each other?

Poetic voice

What tone does the poem have – bitter, playful, ironic, regretful? If the poem is in the first person, has the poet created a **persona** (a narrator who is clearly distinct from the author)? If so, what view does the poet have of this character, and what view is the reader intended to have (sympathetic? disapproving?).

Lexis

What general points can be made about the lexis of the poem? Is it formal or informal? Simple or complex? What kind of mood or atmosphere does the lexis create? Are there any other **patterns** in the lexis, such as groups of words with similar connotations? Are there individual words and phrases that are especially powerful or significant? Are there words that contrast with each other?

Imagery

Does the poem make use of metaphors, similes or personification? How do the comparisons work and what effects do they have? Are there any links between the images used?

Grammar

What types of sentence are used (interrogative, declarative, imperative, exclamatory)? How about sentence length – are any sentences unusually long or short? Are there parts of the poem where word order is especially unusual or significant? Is any of the grammar non-standard? What tenses are used in the poem (past, present, future)? Are there changes of tense that are significant?

Phonology

Does the poem have a regular rhythm or metre? Are there places where the rhythm changes? If so, why? Is there any use of devices such as alliteration, assonance and onomatopoeia?

Stage three ●●●

Finally, how successful do you consider the poem to be? Which aspects of the language are especially effective? Does the poem 'work' for you?

Checkpoint 1

Give brief definitions of the four types of sentence mentioned here.

Checkpoint 2

What is the opposite of **assonance**?

Exam preparation (30 minutes)   answer: page 71

Earlier in this chapter references have been made to Wordsworth's poem *Composed upon Westminster Bridge* (see pages 56, 57 and 60). The poem appears in full below. Write an analysis of the poem, examining closely the attitudes expressed in it and the poet's use of language. How does Wordsworth's vision of London compare with Blake's vision in the poem *London* (**Text C** on page 69)?

> Earth has not anything to show more fair:
> Dull would he be of soul who could pass by
> A sight so touching in its majesty:
> This City now doth, like a garment, wear
> The beauty of the morning; silent, bare,
> Ships, towers, domes, theatres, and temples lie
> Open unto the fields, and to the sky;
> All bright and glittering in the smokeless air.
> Never did sun more beautifully steep
> In his first splendour, valley, rock, or hill;
> Ne'er saw I, never felt, a calm so deep!
> The river glideth at his own sweet will:
> Dear God! the very houses seem asleep;
> And all that mighty heart is lying still!

Examiner's secrets

You will get credit for including a genuine, well argued personal response to the poem.

Specimen texts

The poetry texts below are for use with the practice exam questions for this chapter.

Take note

The question for this text is on page 55.
→ *dun*: a dull greyish-brown colour;
→ *damask'd*: decorated with a varying colour (a damask rose is pink or light red in colour).

Text A

My mistress' eyes are nothing like the sun;
Coral is far more red than her lips' red:
If snow be white, why then her breasts are dun;
If hairs be wires, black wires grow on her head.
I have seen roses damask'd, red and white,
But no such roses see I in her cheeks;
And in some perfumes is there more delight
Than in the breath that from my mistress reeks.
I love to hear her speak, yet well I know
That music hath a far more pleasing sound:
I grant I never saw a goddess go –
My mistress, when she walks, treads on the ground:
    And yet, by heaven, I think my love as rare
    As any she belied with false compare.

William Shakespeare (1564–1616)

Take note

The question for this text is on page 57.
→ *usurpt*: taken illegally by force;
→ *faine*: gladly, with pleasure.

Text B

Batter my heart, three person'd God; for, you
As yet but knocke, breathe, shine, and seeke to mend;
That I may rise, and stand, o'erthrow mee, and bend
Your force, to breake, blowe, burn and make me new.
I, like an usurpt towne, to another due,
Labour to admit you, but Oh, to no end,
Reason your viceroy in mee, mee should defend,
But is captiv'd, and proves weake or untrue.
Yet dearely I love you, and would be loved faine,
But am betroth'd unto your enemie:
Divorce mee, untie, or breake that knot againe,
Take mee to you, imprison mee, for I
Except you enthrall mee, never shall be free,
Nor ever chaste, except you ravish mee.

John Donne (1572–1631)

Text C

I wander thro' each charter'd street
Near where the charter'd Thames does flow,
And mark in every face I meet
Marks of weakness, marks of woe.

In every cry of every Man,
In every Infant's cry of fear,
In every voice, in every ban,
The mind-forg'd manacles I hear.

How the Chimney-sweeper's cry
Every black'ning Church appalls,
And the hapless Soldier's sigh
Runs in blood down Palace walls.

But most thro' midnight streets I hear
How the youthful Harlot's curse
Blasts the new born Infant's tear,
And blights with plagues the Marriage hearse.

William Blake (1757–1827)

Take note

The question for this text is on page 61.
→ *mark* (l.3): notice;
→ *ban*: a curse or oath.

Text D

The world is charged with the grandeur of God.
    It will flame out, like shining from shook foil;
    It gathers to a greatness, like the ooze of oil
Crushed. Why do men then now not reck his rod?
Generations have trod, have trod, have trod;
    And all is seared with trade; bleared, smeared with toil;
    And wears man's smudge and shares man's smell: the soil
Is bare now, nor can foot feel, being shod.

And for all this, nature is never spent;
    There lives the dearest freshness deep down things;
And though the last lights off the black West went
    Oh, morning, at the brown brink eastward, springs –
Because the Holy Ghost over the bent
    World broods with warm breast and with ah! bright wings.

Gerard Manley Hopkins (1844–1889)

Take note

The question for this text is on page 65.
→ *reck*: pay heed or attention to;
→ *rod*: a staff or stick that is a symbol of authority;
→ *shod*: wearing shoes.

Answers
Poetry

Historical overview

Checkpoints

1 A paradox is a statement that appears to contradict itself but is nevertheless true. A pun is a play on words, usually involving the use of a word with a double meaning.
2 The image emphasises that the lovers are inseparable; even when they are physically apart their souls are still joined. It may also imply that the woman is more faithful and steadfast (*Thy soul the fixed foot*).

Chaucer

Checkpoints

1 The Romans invaded in the first century BC, though Latin left little mark on the language at this time. More influential were the Angles, Saxons and Jutes, who invaded England from northern Germany and southern Denmark in the fifth century. Viking invaders began arriving towards the end of the eighth century.
2 Two examples are *-s*, used at the end of a word to indicate it is plural, and *-ed*, used to indicate past tense.

Poetic form and structure

Checkpoints

1 The best known Romantic poets include Wordsworth, Blake, Keats, Shelley, Byron and Coleridge.
2 John Milton.

Exam preparation

The poem consists of a series of comparisons, all of which are rejected as *not* applicable to the woman described. These comparisons are generally conventional romantic images of Shakespeare's time (cheeks like roses, walking like a goddess etc.). Shakespeare's rejection of these images can be interpreted in a variety of ways: 1. The woman is not conventionally attractive, but he still loves her. 2. He loves her for her inner qualities, implying this is more important than physical beauty. 3. He is mocking the traditional love poetry of his time, emphasising that the romantic clichés included in the poem are unrealistic.

It is important to note the element of humour in the poem, and also how the sonnet form is used in the final couplet, where the poet reveals that despite all that has been said earlier he thinks the woman is *rare* or special.

Poetic imagery

Checkpoints

1 Examples of figurative expressions in everyday use: *under a cloud, miss the boat, round the bend, bend over backwards, a fair crack of the whip*.
2 The dynamic verbs *tugged* and *strained* convey the restless energy of the pupils, and how the teacher struggles to control them. His exhausting efforts to

stimulate their interest in learning are evident in the verbs *haul* and *urge*. The use of several dynamic verbs effectively helps to create the atmosphere of a noisy, unruly class.

Exam preparation

In this poem Donne calls upon God to take possession of his soul and wrest him away from the devil. In the first four lines of the poem Donne compares himself to a piece of metal that has to be hammered into a new shape. Two extended metaphors appear in the remainder of the poem. The first is the idea of a besieged town, introduced in line 5. Donne means he is under the control of the devil but wants God to take him back. His powers of reason should be like the *viceroy* in a town, representing the authority of the ruler (God). But the viceroy is *captiv'd* and *weake*. Other words that relate to this image are *defend, enemie* and *imprison*. The other image is of a love relationship (in which Donne is the woman). He is *betroth'd* to the devil but calls on God to *divorce* and *ravish* him.

Lexis in poetry

Checkpoints

1 Non-standard spelling suggests the narrator's accent: *an, bout, mek* etc. Non-standard grammar similarly suggests her speaking voice and also her dialect: *I hope you give de politicians dem/de courage to do what they have to do*.
2 A word formed by joining two other words together.

Grammar in poetry

Checkpoints

1 Dynamic verbs refer to actions. Stative verbs refer to states or processes.
2 This is an unusual image, which combines abstract and concrete words. It suggests that people are repressed and restricted by society's – and their own – attitudes and values. The *manacles* that limit their freedom are forged in the *mind*.

Exam preparation

The first stanza is analysed on page 59, and there is some comment on the second stanza on page 61. A feature of the lexis in this second stanza (and in much of the poem) is its directness and simplicity. However, on a semantic level (i.e. in terms of meaning) some of the lexis is more complex. For example, *ban* means an oath or curse, but it also has connotations of today's usual meaning, and therefore strengthens the idea of repression. For a comment on *mind-forg'd manacles*, see answer to Checkpoint 2 above. In the rest of the poem Blake focuses on more specific social ills, and on the institutions that must bear some responsibility for them. The *Chimney-sweeper's cry* symbolises poverty and child labour, the *black'ning Church* pollution but also how the established church is shamed by the existence of social injustice. The *hapless Soldier* seems to represent those who are sent out to die in wars, while the state that sends them has a stony indifference to their fate (the soldier's blood runs down *Palace walls*). The last stanza is about prostitution. Young women are driven into it by poverty, and the pregnancies that result are a curse rather than a blessing. The last line suggests the diseases spread by prostitution. As in the first two stanzas, Blake uses striking visual and auditory imagery to convey his ideas. The use of language is very concentrated, with powerful and evocative pre-modifiers (e.g. *black'ning Church*). In the final stanza, noun phrases combine words with contrasting associations in order to show the corrupting effect of prostitution (*youthful Harlot*, *the Marriage hearse*). Parallelism is a feature (*the Chimney-sweeper's cry . . . the hapless Soldier's sigh*) and word order foregrounds certain words (e.g. *But* and *Blasts* are both positioned at the beginning of a line).

Rhythm and metre

Checkpoints

1 Yes – the metre suggests galloping horses.
2 The spondaic metre slows the line down with a series of heavy stresses. This helps to suggest a long, arduous journey.
3 The enjambement reflects the 'openness' of the scene. The buildings merge seamlessly with the fields and the sky.
4 In the first quotation, alliteration helps to quicken the pace of the line. In the second, the repetition of sounds reinforces the idea of a lack of movement.

Sound in poetry

Checkpoints

1 The pre-modifiers *silver* and *golden* both have connotations of luxury. These contrast strongly with the connotations of *gutter*.
2 The alliteration of the hard *d-* sound suggests the difficult physical work of the miners and the soldiers.
3 The house is compared to a ship at sea. This creates a sense of isolation and instability, and suggests how the house has been lashed by wind and rain.

Exam preparation

Hopkins was a very original poet. The aspects of style he is noted for include powerful phonological features and strong, energetic rhythm. Both are evident in this poem, which celebrates natural beauty as an expression of God. Even though nature has been partially spoilt by man, its essential glory remains. The opening of the poem has a tremendous energy, which reflects the idea that the world is *charged* with God's grandeur. This is partly created by the use of alliteration (*flame/foil*, *shining/shook*, *gathers/greatness*). Onomatopoeia is another feature, used for example to suggest an intense, concentrated beauty: *like the ooze of oil/Crushed*. In the second half of the octet, repetition of sound evokes the dreariness of men's daily lives, and the deadening effect this has on the world: *have trod, have trod, have trod/And all is seared with trade; bleared, smeared with toil*. In the last four lines of the poem the emergence of daylight, and the hope it represents, is mirrored in the use of enjambement over successive lines.

Analysing poetry

Checkpoints

1 An interrogative sentence ends with a question mark, an exclamatory sentence with an exclamation mark. A declarative sentence makes a statement. An imperative sentence gives a command.
2 Dissonance.

Exam preparation

The opening line of this sonnet immediately evokes a scene of breathtaking beauty. Words with connotations of magnificence are used to describe the city: *majesty*, *splendour*, *mighty*. Exclamatory sentences stress the poet's sense of awe. The man-made elements of the scene blend appealingly with the natural beauty of the surrounding countryside, suggested by the enjambement of lines 6–7. It is the serenity of the scene that Wordsworth responds most strongly to, especially at the close of the poem. However, the imagery of the last two lines suggests the transience of this calmness. If the houses are *asleep* they must soon awake, and if the city is not dead the *mighty heart* must resume beating. The earlier image of the beauty of the morning being worn like a *garment* similarly indicates that it is transitory.

Revision checklist
Poetry

1	Outline the main phases in the development of English poetry.	Confident	Not confident. **Revise** pages 50–51
2	List the main poets associated with these periods.	Confident	Not confident. **Revise** pages 50–51
3	Identify the key features of Chaucer's language.	Confident	Not confident. **Revise** pages 52–53
4	Explain the concept behind *The Canterbury Tales*.	Confident	Not confident. **Revise** page 53
5	Identify the main forms of poetry, including lyric poetry, sonnets, odes, elegies and narrative poetry.	Confident	Not confident. **Revise** pages 54–55
6	Understand how to analyse poetic imagery.	Confident	Not confident. **Revise** pages 56–57
7	Recognise how levels of formality can differ in poetry.	Confident	Not confident. **Revise** page 58
8	Understand the importance of connotation.	Confident	Not confident. **Revise** pages 58–59
9	Explain the difference between archaisms and neologisms.	Confident	Not confident. **Revise** page 59
10	Comment on significant grammatical features in poems.	Confident	Not confident. **Revise** pages 60–61
11	Explain the five main types of metre in English poetry.	Confident	Not confident. **Revise** pages 62–63
12	Understand the terms enjambement, end-stopped line and caesura.	Confident	Not confident. **Revise** page 63
13	Identify different types of rhyme, such as internal rhyme and half-rhyme.	Confident	Not confident. **Revise** page 64
14	Understand the terms onomatopoeia, alliteration, sibilance, assonance and dissonance.	Confident	Not confident. **Revise** page 65
15	Approach with confidence the analysis of a poem.	Confident	Not confident. **Revise** pages 66–67

This chapter looks at the features of novels and short stories. You are likely to be studying a prose fiction set text, but also need to be prepared in the exam to analyse extracts from prose fiction texts you have not read before. With some specifications the way **dialogue** is presented in fiction is especially important, and you need to consider the stylistic features of fictional dialogue and how it differs from real-life conversation. **Plot**, **narrative viewpoint**, **characters** and **themes** are other important aspects. As with all kinds of texts, you will also be expected to analyse closely the ways writers of prose fiction use language.

Exam themes

→ Literary and linguistic features of prose fiction texts.

→ Dialogue in novels and short stories.

→ Characters and themes.

→ Prose fiction texts of different periods.

Topic checklist

○ AS ● A2	OCR	EDEXCEL	AQA A	AQA B	WJEC
Historical overview	○●	○●	○●	○●	○●
Plot and setting	○●	○●	○●	○●	○●
Narrative viewpoint	○●	○●	○●	○●	○●
Characters and themes	○●	○●	○●	○●	○●
Dialogue in prose fiction	○●	○●	○●	○●	○●
Lexis and imagery	○●	○●	○●	○●	○●
Grammar and phonology	○●	○●	○●	○●	○●
Analysing prose fiction extracts	○●	○●	○●	○●	○●
Specimen texts	○●	○●	○●	○●	○●

Historical overview

Before the 18th century, drama and poetry were the dominant forms of literature. The tremendous growth in the popularity of the novel since then (especially in the 19th and 20th centuries) has meant that it has become the leading modern literary form. This section identifies some important developments and some major authors in the history of prose fiction.

18th century

Although there are earlier forms of writing that can be seen as antecedents of the novel, the first true English novels appeared in the early 18th century, notably **Daniel Defoe**'s *Robinson Crusoe* and *Moll Flanders*. The other major 18th-century novelists, who came after Defoe, were **Samuel Richardson**, **Henry Fielding** and **Laurence Sterne**.

19th century

The 19th century, especially the middle decades, is regarded as the great age of the novel. The major novels of the period are generally characterised by a combination of **psychological complexity** and **social realism**. They explore the morality and emotional life of individual characters, while also addressing broader contemporary issues such as the effects of the Industrial Revolution and of social class divisions. Important authors include:

→ **Jane Austen**   Austen's novels typically focus on the dilemmas of upper-class young women, torn between the expectations of society and the promptings of their own moral conscience. Her books remain popular today, celebrated for their social comedy and astute, ironic observation. Austen's novels include *Pride and Prejudice*, *Emma* and *Mansfield Park*.

→ **Charles Dickens**   Dickens was enormously popular in his own lifetime, in Britain and the USA. His novels are notable for their memorable characters and exposure of the injustices and corruption of 19th-century society. Dickens's many works include *Great Expectations*, *Hard Times*, *David Copperfield* and *Bleak House*.

→ **Emily Brontë**   *Wuthering Heights* was Emily Brontë's only novel, and was only recognised as a masterpiece after her death. Emily was one of the Brontë sisters. **Anne** wrote *The Tenant of Wildfell Hall* and *Agnes Grey*. **Charlotte's** major novels were *Jane Eyre* and *Villette*.

→ **Thomas Hardy**   Hardy's novels appeared later in the century. They show an interest in rural life (they are usually set in Hardy's native West Country), and a sympathy for characters who rebel against social conventions. The lives of his central characters often follow a tragic pattern, their downfall demonstrating the power of fate. *Tess of the D'Urbevilles*, *Far From the Madding Crowd* and *The Mayor of Casterbridge* are among Hardy's novels.

Take note

Samuel Richardson wrote **epistolary** novels, where the story is told through letters written by the major characters. Fielding's works (such as *Joseph Andrews* and *Tom Jones*) are comic, and closer in form to the modern novel. In particular, he made use of an **intrusive omniscient narrator**, a device discussed on page 79.

Checkpoint 1

Other important 19th-century novelists include: **George Eliot**, **Anthony Trollope**, **W.M. Thackeray**, **Elizabeth Gaskell** and **Henry James**. Can you name any of their books?

Checkpoint 2

Can you name any of **Charles Dickens's** other works?

Take note

Wuthering Heights tells of the doomed, passionate relationship between Catherine Earnshaw and the mysterious Heathcliff. Catherine decides, disastrously, to marry for social advantage. The novel explores Catherine's motives and the consequences of her action, and vividly evokes the wild Yorkshire moors that are the story's setting.

20th century ●●●

The tendency for the novel to focus on the individual consciousness increased in the 20th century. Many modern novels have heroes who are **alienated**, unable to connect with the world around them. 19th-century novels were **realist** in their approach, in that they generally sought to make the reader believe in a fictional world. This tradition has continued to the present day, but during the 20th century there were also many novelists who were more **experimental** in their approach. Instead of trying to hide the fact that they were writing fiction, they drew attention to the novel as a constructed work of art, and to their own role as author, by playing with different narrative voices, mixing genres and incorporating unexpected time-shifts.

Important 20th-century writers include:

→ **Joseph Conrad**   Conrad came to Britain as a Polish sailor, and many of his novels and short stories are based on his experiences at sea. His works are carefully structured and technically sophisticated, often involving the use of a fictional character, Marlow, as narrator. His novels and stories include *Heart of Darkness*, *Nostromo* and *The Secret Agent*.

→ **E.M. Forster**   Forster's works often concern the barriers people have to overcome in forming relationships. *A Passage To India* portrays India under British rule, exploring relationships between people of different races. In *A Room With A View* the central characters have to overcome social convention and prejudice to find love.

→ **James Joyce**   Joyce was an experimental writer who is especially associated with the **stream of consciousness** technique, which seeks to capture as accurately as possible an individual's flow of thoughts. *Ulysses*, a novel about a day in the life of its central character, is in this tradition. Joyce also wrote the autobiographical novel *A Portrait of the Artist as a Young Man* and *Dubliners*, a collection of short stories.

→ **D.H. Lawrence**   Lawrence's novels focus on relationships between men and women, and on the pursuit of individual fulfilment. He grew up in a mining community, and industrialisation often provides a threatening backdrop to his novels. His works include *The Rainbow* and *Women In Love*.

→ **Graham Greene**   Greene's heroes are often morally flawed, wrestling with feelings of guilt and desire. Catholicism is an important element in many of his novels, which include *The Power and the Glory*, *The Heart of the Matter* and *Brighton Rock*.

Exam preparation

Find out when the prose fiction text you are studying was first published. (You may already know this; if not, you should be able to find the date at the beginning of the book.) What other prose fiction was published around this time? How is the text typical (or untypical) of the period? How was it received when it was first published?

Take note

One type of experimentation, **magic realism**, was especially influential in the 1970s and 1980s. Magic realism blends realistic representations of life with the improbable and fantastic, often drawing on fairy tale and myth. Authors associated with this approach include **Salman Rushdie** and **Angela Carter**.

Take note

Other significant 20th-century English novelists include: **Virginia Woolf**, **George Orwell**, **Evelyn Waugh**, **Kingsley Amis**, **William Golding**, **Martin Amis**. There have also been important American and Canadian novelists, such as **Margaret Atwood**, **F. Scott Fitzgerald**, **J.D. Salinger**, **Joseph Heller** and **Saul Bellow**. Noted African and Caribbean writers include **V.S. Naipaul** and **Chinua Achebe**.

Take note

Useful sources for the Exam preparation exercise might include:
→ The introduction, notes etc. in your edition of the text.
→ Biographies of the author.
→ English Literature reference books.

Plot and setting

This section looks at the importance in novels and short stories of the main storyline (or **plot**) and of the writer's use of locations and **settings**. Remember that in an exam answer you should never fall into the trap of simply 'telling the story' (examiners sometimes call this **narrative paraphrase**). You should only refer to details of the plot in order to support points about characters, themes, intended effects on the reader and so on.

Plot and structure

The term **plot** refers to the events of a novel and how these are *organised* by the novelist. The pattern or plan that the author imposes on the action of the novel reflects the author's underlying purposes – for example, a sequence of events may be devised that encourages us to be sympathetic towards a character.

The structure of a novel can also be influenced by the novel's form or **genre**. **Epistolary** novels (popular in the 18th century) tell the story through letters written by the main characters. Other novels may take the form of a diary, or have **multiple narrators**, so that events are described from different characters' perspectives. Usually narratives are **linear**, which means events are presented in a chronological sequence, but this is not always the case. For example, there may be **flashbacks**.

When you are considering plot, think about how the overall organisation of the novel, and particular events or sequences of events, illustrate important themes in the novel, or help to convey aspects of the novel's characters. Think also about the kinds of effects the development of the plot has on the reader – for example, parts of the plot may generate a feeling of **suspense**, or the story may have an exciting **climax**.

Setting and themes

The **settings** or locations in a novel, and the ways they are described, can have a range of purposes. Often they reflect the **themes** of the novel in some way. A setting may have a **symbolic** purpose, which means it is used to **represent** something – usually, a set of ideas, attitudes or values. In *Wuthering Heights*, the two main settings are Wuthering Heights itself (a farmhouse on the Yorkshire moors) and another house nearby, Thrushcross Grange. The houses represent contrasting values and approaches to life. Wuthering Heights, a working farm, is associated with the forces of nature and with intense, unrestrained emotion. Thrushcross Grange, a luxurious family residence, is associated with social refinement and control of the emotions. The location of the houses reflects this contrast: Wuthering Heights is set in wild and unprotected moorland ('wuthering' means exposed to violent winds), whereas Thrushcross Grange is set in a sheltered park.

Take note

Examples of novel genres include science fiction, detective novels, gothic novels and historical novels.

Example

Time's Arrow is an experimental novel by Martin Amis which tells the story of a man's life backwards in time, beginning with his death and ending with his childhood.

Take note

As this example illustrates, **contrasts** between settings in a novel can be important.

The jargon

Pathetic fallacy occurs when natural elements (such as landscape or the weather) are used to reflect human moods and emotions. When Heathcliff runs away from Wuthering Heights, fracturing his relationship with Catherine, a violent storm splits a tree in two.

Setting and character

Settings can also be used to reflect aspects of the novel's **characters**. In the case of *Wuthering Heights*, the characters who live at Wuthering Heights tend to be strong and passionate, while those at Thrushcross Grange are delicate and sensitive. In *A Painful Case*, a short story in James Joyce's *Dubliners*, the central character (Mr Duffy) is a morose, emotionally repressed man who avoids human company. His character is reflected in his bleak surroundings and sparsely furnished room:

> He lived in an old sombre house and from his windows he could look into the disused distillery or upwards along the shallow river on which Dublin is built. The lofty walls of his uncarpeted room were free from pictures. He had himself bought every article of furniture in the room: a black iron bedstead, an iron washstand, four cane chairs, a clothes-rack, a coal-scuttle, a fender and irons and a square table on which lay a double desk.

Checkpoint 1

Write a short analysis of this extract, considering how Joyce uses language (especially lexis) to evoke the atmosphere of Mr Duffy's home.

Setting and atmosphere

The **mood** or **atmosphere** evoked by an author's description of a setting can also be important. *The Fall of the House of Usher* is a 19th-century horror story, written by Edgar Allan Poe. The opening sentence, which describes the narrator's journey to the House of Usher, immediately creates an ominous, unsettling atmosphere:

> During the whole of a dull, dark and soundless day in the autumn of the year, when the clouds hung oppressively low in the heavens, I had been passing alone, on horseback, through a singularly dreary tract of country; and at length found myself, as the shades of evening drew on, within view of the melancholy House of Usher.

Checkpoint 2

How does the author's use of **pre-modifiers** contribute to the effectiveness of this extract?

Short stories

As explained on page 73, most of the material in this chapter is relevant to **short stories** as well as novels. The Poe and Joyce extracts above illustrate this. In the case of **plot**, that of a short story is obviously usually less complex than that of a novel. In fact, short stories often focus on a single revealing incident in the life of a single character. When analysing a story such as this, look for how the central incident is used to explore the character, and how the character changes or develops in the story.

Examiner's secrets

If you are studying a collection of short stories, look for similarities and contrasts between the stories. Make a list of the main themes running through the stories, and of the distinctive ways in which the writer uses language.

Exam preparation

See page 85 for a practice question relevant to this section and the section on *Lexis and imagery*.

Narrative viewpoint

Watch out!

If you are studying a text that doesn't have a first-person narrator, that doesn't mean you should skip this section! Narrative viewpoint is an important aspect of all prose fiction texts.

At a simple level, looking at **narrative viewpoint** involves answering the question, 'Who is telling the story?' For example, the narrator might be one of the characters. Alternatively, the narrator might be invisible, someone outside the story who describes what happened. At a deeper level, examining narrative viewpoint means establishing the narrator's attitudes and values. Even when the narrator is invisible, the way a story is told almost inevitably implies a view of the characters and events described. In analysing a text you need to decide what this view is, and how far it appears to be shared by the author.

First-person narration

There are two main types of narration: **first-person narration** and **third-person narration**.

A first-person narrator refers to *I* and *me*. The narrator is usually the novel's central character, but can also be a secondary character who is a witness to the events described (Nelly Dean, one of the main narrators in *Wuthering Heights*, is an example of this). An advantage of first-person narration is that it enables the author to present a character's thoughts and emotions very directly. Often the narrator is viewing events **retrospectively**, recognising with the wisdom of hindsight their own foolishness or naivety. In Charles Dickens's *Great Expectations* the narrator, Pip, is a mature adult, recalling the illusions and misjudgements of his childhood and youth.

Because we view events from the narrator's perspective, and because their private thoughts are shared with us, there is a tendency for the reader to identify with the narrator. In some cases, this may be what the author intended, but remember the narrator is a character the author has created, and may well have been given flaws and weaknesses. Try to identify these, and consider how far the narrator's view of events can be relied upon (see *Unreliable narrators* below).

The jargon

If a novel has **multiple narrators**, this means several different characters tell the story (the novel will often alternate between them). This device often gives the reader **different perspectives** on the same events.

Narrative voice

The character of a narrator is created partly through the opinions and attitudes they express, and partly through the **language** the narrator uses. The **narrative voice** might, for example, reflect the narrator's personality, age or regional background. The narrator of Kazuo Ishiguro's *The Remains of the Day*, a novel set in 1956, is Stevens, the butler to an English aristocrat. The opening of the novel immediately conveys the narrator's stiffness and formality:

> It seems increasingly likely that I really will undertake the expedition that has been preoccupying my imagination now for some days. An expedition, I should say, which I will undertake alone, in the comfort of Mr Farraday's Ford; an expedition which, as I foresee it, will take me through much of the finest countryside of England to the West Country, and may keep me away from Darlington Hall for as much as five or six days.

Checkpoint 1

Explain how the language of this extract gives the reader a sense of Stevens's character.

Unreliable narrators

An **unreliable narrator** is a narrator whose judgement is flawed. Lockwood, one of the two main narrators in *Wuthering Heights*, is an example. In the novel's opening chapters he comically makes several mistaken assumptions about the people he meets. The device of an unreliable narrator is a way of drawing the reader into the novel, as it forces us to question the narrator's views and form our own judgements.

Third-person narration

A **third-person narrator** is not involved in the world of the story and refers to characters using third-person pronouns such as *he*, *she* and *they*. This is the most common form of narration. The narrator is usually **omniscient**, which means 'all-knowing'. In other words, everything in the novel's fictional world is known to them, and they can switch freely from character to character, and from location to location.

An omniscient narrator can be **intrusive** or **unintrusive**. Intrusive narrators intervene in the novel to comment directly on characters and events, often making explicit moral judgements. 19th-century authors such as George Eliot and Jane Austen are associated with this approach. Unintrusive narrators are invisible. They describe the events of the story but do not comment on them, although a view may well be **implicit** in the language that is used.

Address to reader

Some authors use their narrators (whether first- or third-person) to **speak directly to the reader**. In a novel such as *Jane Eyre* this occurs only rarely (the famous example is *Reader, I married him*), but in other novels it happens more regularly, and the interaction between reader and narrator is an important element in the novel's overall effect. In Julian Barnes's *Love, etc* multiple narrators compete for the reader's trust and attention. Here Gillian is the narrator:

> What you have to understand is that Stuart wants you to like him, needs you to like him, whereas Oliver has a certain difficulty imagining that you won't ... And me? Well, I'd prefer you to like me rather than the reverse, but that's normal isn't it? Depending on who *you* are, of course.

Checkpoint 2

Explain what *implicit* means as used here. What word is the opposite of *implicit*?

Take note

First- or third-person narrators may use the **second person** (*you*) to address their readers. The Julian Barnes extract is an example of this.

Checkpoint 3

In what ways does the language here resemble that of speech?

Exam preparation

See page 87 for a practice question relevant to this section and the section on *Grammar and phonology*.

Characters and themes

In this section we consider how writers present **characters** and how you might approach analysing them. There is also a brief discussion of **themes**, though all the other elements discussed in this chapter (plot, dialogue and so on) usually contribute to the development of a novel's themes.

Ways of presenting characters

Listed below are some of the main techniques used by novelists in the presentation of character.

Appearance

Physical **appearance** (including clothing) is often used to express important aspects of a character. In *Wuthering Heights* Lockwood is shown a portrait of Edgar Linton:

> I discerned a soft-featured face, exceedingly resembling the young lady at the Heights, but more pensive and amiable in expression. It formed a sweet picture. The long light hair curled slightly on the temples; the eyes were large and serious; the figure almost too graceful.

The portrait suggests Edgar's strengths – his gentleness and sensitivity – but also hints at an underlying weakness of character (*the figure almost too graceful*).

Imagery and symbolism

A character may be strongly associated with particular **images** or **symbols**. In *Wuthering Heights* Heathcliff is associated with natural imagery, reflecting his primitive strength and savagery. Two characters compare him to *whinstone* (hard rock). Nelly Dean says that the contrast between Heathcliff and Edgar Linton *resembled what you see in exchanging a bleak, hilly, coal country for a beautiful fertile valley*. Even the name *Heathcliff* has connotations of wild, rugged nature.

Speech and thought

Characters are also revealed through what they say and think. As well as *what* characters say, you should consider *how* they say it: a character's **idiolect**, or use of language, is often significant. In many novels we also gain an insight into characters' minds, and are told about their attitudes and feelings. For more on both these aspects of characterisation, see the following section on dialogue (pages 82–83).

Action

How a character **acts** is important. This includes both physical actions (Heathcliff, for example, often acts violently towards other characters) and patterns of behaviour (Heathcliff's carefully plotted revenge against the Linton family shows his malevolence and ruthlessness). Characters

Checkpoint 1

Comment on the writer's **lexical choice** (choice of vocabulary) in this extract.

The jargon

Idiolect refers to a particular individual's use of language.

may have revealing physical habits. In *Great Expectations* the lawyer Jaggers frequently gnaws the side of his finger, suggesting the intimidating toughness of his character.

Analysing characters ●●●

Here are some of the ways you can approach the analysis of a character:

→ Consider how the character is **presented** in the novel (see above).

→ Think about the author's **attitude** to the character, and the attitude readers are intended to have.

→ Look at how the character **develops** in the course of the novel. Do their attitudes change? Have they learned anything by the end of the novel?

→ Think about the character's **importance** to the novel as a whole. How central are they? Consider the character's importance in terms of:

   → The **plot** How important are they to the storyline? How do they influence the events that occur in the novel?

   → The **themes** Does the character represent or illustrate any of the main ideas in the novel?

   → **Relationships with other characters** Do they have important relationships with any of the other characters? Are these relationships used to reveal anything about the other characters? Does the character **contrast** with any of the other characters?

Themes ●●●

The **themes** of a novel are the main ideas running through it. Usually the themes are **implicit** – that is, they are implied rather than explicitly stated. All of the elements in a novel – plot, setting, imagery, characters, dialogue, narration – can contribute to the development of a theme, and you should always look for how particular episodes might be relevant to one or more of the book's themes. A theme in *Great Expectations* is the hollowness of material values and the folly of judging others according to their wealth and social position. This theme emerges over the duration of the novel as we see how Pip comes to value the simple goodness of Joe, the village blacksmith who helped to raise him, and makes the ironic discovery that he owes his fortune to the generosity of an ex-convict. During the course of the novel the theme is reinforced by numerous other characters and incidents.

Watch out!

Remember not to write about fictional characters as if they are real people. Imagining the characters created by an author is of course part of the enjoyment of reading novels, but you should only refer to what is disclosed about them in the pages of the book. Don't speculate about additional biographical details, such as relationships you imagine they might have had before the story started. Instead, show that you are aware the character has been created by the author to serve specific purposes and functions within the novel.

Checkpoint 2

If one character is said to be the **antithesis** of another, what does this mean?

Exam preparation (15 minutes) answer: page 92

Text C on page 90 is a description of Mr Duffy, the central character in *A Painful Case*, a short story in James Joyce's *Dubliners*. Examine Joyce's presentation of the character, referring closely to his use of language.

Links

On page 77 there is an extract from earlier in the story, describing the room Mr Duffy lives in.

Dialogue in prose fiction

Links

Much of the material in the sections on *Dialogue in plays* (pages 104–107) and *Conversational interaction* (pages 34–35) is also relevant to this topic.

Watch out!

Although fictional dialogue differs from genuine speech, many novelists do of course strive to make their dialogue appear realistic, writing what is known as **naturalistic dialogue**. In most cases, this is still more coherent than real speech.

Checkpoint 1

Do you know another term for **indirect speech**?

Your prose fiction set text is likely to contain passages of **dialogue**, but you may also come across unseen dialogue extracts in other exam papers (as always, it is advisable to check your specification). Questions might ask you to consider how far the extract resembles genuine speech, or how the writer uses dialogue to reveal character.

Fictional dialogue and real speech

The main difference between fictional dialogue and genuine spontaneous speech is that fictional dialogue is usually more orderly and more organised. Characters are more likely to speak in grammatical sentences, and the non-fluency features we associate with spontaneous speech (hesitations, false starts and so on) are not usually present. In terms of conversational interaction, there are fewer interruptions, and overlapping speech is difficult to present on the printed page. The other important difference is that dialogue often has an **accompanying commentary** from the author, giving the reader more information about how characters speak and how what they say should be interpreted.

Functions of dialogue

Dialogue can be used in a novel to:

→ **Reveal character** or **develop relationships** between characters. An author will often give a character a distinctive **idiolect**, an individual way of speaking that reflects the character's personality and attitudes.
→ Illustrate and develop a **theme**.
→ Move the **plot** forward.
→ Gain a specific **response from the reader** (e.g. the dialogue may be humorous and intended to entertain).

Forms of dialogue

There are four main ways of presenting dialogue:

→ **Direct speech** Here the actual words spoken are quoted, accompanied by an explanatory clause such as *He said*:

  He asked, 'How are you?'

→ **Indirect speech** The exact words spoken are not quoted; instead, the narrator reports what was said. Verbs usually change to the past tense and pronouns change to the third person:

  He asked her how she was.

→ **Free direct speech** This is a form of direct speech in which accompanying explanation and comment from the narrator are omitted – the words that are spoken stand alone:

  'How are you?'
  'I'm fine.'

→ **Free indirect speech**   As with indirect speech, the words spoken are not quoted. However, the narrator is missing so there is also a resemblance to direct speech:

> He told her he was pleased to see her. How was she?

The first sentence here is indirect speech, the second free indirect speech.

In considering the **effects** of these forms of dialogue, here are some points to consider:

→ Because they present the actual words the characters are meant to have spoken, direct and free direct speech can make the dialogue seem more immediate and real. The author can give each character a distinctive voice or idiolect.
→ Free direct speech, which eliminates the narrator, can be used to quicken the pace of dialogue, or to focus attention more closely on what is being said.
→ Direct speech and indirect speech can both be accompanied by narrative comment, describing for example a character's tone of voice or body language.
→ Indirect speech tends to distance the reader from characters more, though this is less true of free indirect speech.
→ Authors will frequently switch between different forms of presentation, so their dialogue has variety.

Presentation of thought ●●●

The same forms of presentation can be used for describing a character's thoughts. For example, the second sentence in the following is direct thought:

> He looked across to where she was standing. How are you? he wondered.

Free direct thought and free indirect thought take the reader especially close to the inner workings of a character's mind. In the short stories in *Dubliners*, James Joyce often uses a free indirect style to capture the inner life of his characters, as in this example from *The Dead*:

> He was trembling now with annoyance. Why did she seem so abstracted? He did not know how he could begin. Was she annoyed, too, about something? If she would only turn to him or come to him of her own accord!

Take note

Here is a summary of points to look for when analysing dialogue:
→ What form of **presentation** is used?
→ How **naturalistic** is the dialogue?
→ What kind of **language** does each speaker use? How is language used to reflect **character**?
→ Are there **contrasts** in the kinds of language used by each speaker?
→ What does the dialogue reveal about the characters' **attitudes and values**?
→ How do the characters **interact**? What kind of **relationship** do they have?
→ How does the **accompanying narrative** (comments, description etc. by the author) influence the reader's response to the dialogue?
→ What **purposes** and **functions** does the dialogue have in relation to the novel or short story as a whole?

Checkpoint 2

Present this thought as: free direct thought; indirect thought; free indirect thought.

The jargon

Stream of consciousness writing is writing that seeks to express as directly as possible the flow of a person's thoughts. Free direct thought and free indirect thought are both associated with this kind of writing.

Exam preparation (15 minutes) answer: page 92

Text D on page 91 is an extract from *Bridget Jones's Diary* by Helen Fielding. Referring closely to the use of language, consider how Fielding uses dialogue to reveal character and create humour.

Lexis and imagery

As is the case with all kinds of literary texts, the writer's use of **lexis** and **imagery** is a key aspect of language to consider.

Formality ●●●

The **level of formality** can be a significant aspect of a writer's lexical choice. Sometimes formal vocabulary can be an indication of an older text, or of serious subject matter. It can also be used to reflect **character**. In the first chapter of *Wuthering Heights*, Lockwood meets Heathcliff, the owner of the house where he will be staying. This is how he introduces himself:

> 'Mr Lockwood, your new tenant, sir. I do myself the honour of calling as soon as possible after my arrival, to express the hope that I have not inconvenienced you by my perseverance in soliciting the occupation of Thrushcross Grange: I heard yesterday you had had some thoughts –'

Lockwood is being very polite, but his formality and **circumlocutory** (roundabout) way of speaking seem excessive. The formal words and phrases he uses include *do myself the honour*, *express the hope*, *perseverance*, *soliciting*, *occupation*. The effect is to make Lockwood appear a pompous and rather ridiculous figure, an effect reinforced by the contrast with Heathcliff, whose reply is much more direct:

> 'Thrushcross Grange is my own, sir,' he interrupted, wincing. 'I should not allow anyone to inconvenience me, if I could hinder it – walk in!'

Note how Heathcliff's vocabulary is much **simpler**: most of the words are **monosyllabic**, whereas much of Lockwood's vocabulary is **polysyllabic**. As this example shows, lexis can be used in **dialogue** to give individual characters distinctive ways of speaking – that is, it can help to create a character's **idiolect**. It can also be used to highlight **contrasts** between characters.

Informality ●●●

Lexis can also be notably **informal**, as in the extract below, which is the opening sentence of J.D. Salinger's *The Catcher in the Rye*. The narrator, Holden Caulfield, is an American teenager:

> If you really want to hear about it, the first thing you'll probably want to know is where I was born, and what my lousy childhood was like, and how my parents were occupied and all before they had me, and all that David Copperfield kind of crap, but I don't feel like going into it.

Take note

Note how the length and complexity of Lockwood's second sentence reflects his long-windedness.

Checkpoint 1

Explain the terms **monosyllabic** and **polysyllabic**.

Checkpoint 2

Comment on the grammatical features of this extract.

The informality here is evident in the use of **simple, direct vocabulary** (again much of it is **monosyllabic**), **colloquial expressions** (*the first thing, lousy childhood, going into it*) and **non-standard lexis** (*all that David Copperfield kind of crap, and all*). The vocabulary helps to create an authentic **narrative voice**, and the narrator immediately strikes up a lively, informal relationship with the reader. This extract also illustrates some other points about lexis in prose fiction:

→ Although the extract is not dialogue, the narrative style clearly resembles **speech**. This approach is especially common in modern novels that have first-person narrators.

→ Lexis can reflect a character's **regional** or **national identity**. *And all* is an American expression, and is one of the many examples of **American English** in the novel.

→ Lexis can indicate the **historical period** of a text. Phrases such as *my lousy childhood* and *all that David Copperfield kind of crap* are clear signs that this is a relatively modern text (the novel was published in 1951).

Checkpoint 3

What term is used for a variety of English associated with a particular geographical region?

Connotations ●●●

As in all kinds of literary text, the **connotations** (or associations) of the vocabulary used in a work of prose fiction are very important. Look for **positive** or **negative** connotations, and also for the more specific associations that particular words can have. Try to find **patterns** in the writer's use of vocabulary, such as the repeated use of words with similar or contrasting associations. *Counterparts* in Joyce's *Dubliners* is a short story about an embittered, frustrated clerk in a solicitor's office. Words with connotations of anger and aggression run through the story: *furious, rage, savage, revengeful, annoyed, enraged*.

Imagery ●●●

The term **imagery** is sometimes applied to any aspect of a text that appeals to the reader's senses. For example, prose fiction often includes passages of **visual description**, perhaps describing a novel's **setting** (see page 76) or a character's **appearance** (see page 80). More specifically, imagery means the use of **comparison**. Look for examples of **metaphor**, **simile** and **personification**, and for the effects that they have. A **symbol** is something used to represent something else, such as an abstract idea or concept.

Examples

In another *Dubliners* story, *A Mother*, Joyce uses a humorous **simile** to describe a woman's relationship with her husband: *She respected her husband in the same way as she respected the General Post Office, as something large, secure and fixed.*

William Golding's *The Spire* is a novel about the building of a medieval cathedral. The cathedral spire is a complex **symbol**, used to represent a variety of ideas, including religious faith and sexual desire. This is apparent in the **imagery** used to describe the spire: it is seen as both a *diagram of prayer* and a phallus.

Exam preparation (20 minutes)   answer: pages 92–93

Text A on page 90 is an extract from *Hard Times* by Charles Dickens. The extract describes Coketown, the industrial town that is the novel's setting. Referring closely to such aspects of language as lexis, imagery and sentence structure, consider how Dickens presents the town.

Grammar and phonology

This section offers advice on **grammatical features** that might be found in prose fiction texts, and also includes a brief discussion of **phonology**.

Word classes

When you are analysing a text, you should look for patterns in the types of words that are used, thinking about the effects that these have and how these relate to the meaning of the text. For example, are **concrete** or **abstract nouns** frequently used? Concrete nouns tend to create a sense of physical reality, while abstract nouns are associated more with the presentation of an argument, or with descriptions of feelings and ideas. If **adjectives** are present, the **connotations** that they have may be significant. Are the **verbs** that are used **dynamic** or **stative**? **Active** or **passive**? Dynamic verbs are often used to evoke an impression of action, movement or excitement. Passive verbs might be used to suggest a feeling of powerlessness or helplessness. In the following extract from *Great Expectations*, describing Magwitch (an escaped convict), passive verbs encourage sympathy in the reader by presenting the character as a victim:

> A man who had been soaked in water, and smothered in mud, and lamed by stones, and cut by flints, and stung by nettles, and torn by briars.

Sentences

Sentence types

The types of sentences that are used (**declarative**, **imperative**, **interrogative**, **exclamatory**) reflect the tone or purpose of a text, and can also suggest changes in mood or atmosphere. In this extract from *Eveline*, a story in Joyce's *Dubliners*, Eveline is contemplating leaving the home she shares with her father and running away with Frank. The exclamatory and interrogative sentences create a sense of urgency and help to suggest the character's desperation and anxiety:

> She stood up in a sudden impulse of terror. Escape! She must escape! Frank would save her. He would give her life, perhaps love, too. But she wanted to live. Why should she be unhappy? She had a right to happiness. Frank would take her in his arms, fold her in his arms. He would save her.

Sentence length

Sentences that are noticeably **long** or **short** can have a variety of effects. Think about the meaning of the text, and consider why it is appropriate to have short or long sentences. In the above extract from *Dubliners*, short sentences suggest the rapid succession of thoughts passing through Eveline's mind, and reinforce the impression of emotional turmoil.

Links

The terms used here are explained earlier in the book:
- → **concrete** and **abstract nouns**: page 4
- → **connotations**: page 6
- → **dynamic** and **stative verbs**: page 4
- → **active** and **passive verbs**: page 4

Checkpoint 1

Comment on the grammatical structure of this extract.

Sentence structure

Whether sentences in a text are **simple**, **compound** or **complex** might be important. A large number of simple and compound sentences might indicate a deliberate attempt to avoid complexity (the text might, for example, be aimed at children). Simple sentences are also usually short, and can have similar effects to those described above (most of the sentences in the *Dubliners* extract are simple sentences). Other aspects of sentence structure include **word order** and **parallelism**. Word order may have the effect of **foregrounding** (highlighting) important words or phrases. Along with **punctuation**, it can also affect the **rhythm** of sentences. The following sentence by D.H. Lawrence describes the movement of a train:

> The small locomotive engine, number 4, came clanking, stumbling down from Selston with seven full wagons.

The broken rhythm of the sentence reflects the train's slow, clumsy motion (try reading the sentence aloud, pausing after each comma).

Non-standard grammar

Non-standard grammar occurs when the conventional grammatical rules of Standard English are broken. It might be used in **dialogue** to make the characters' speech more **realistic**, or to suggest the **idiolects** of individual characters. It can also create a distinctive **narrative voice**, and be part of a narrative style that resembles speech, so that the narrator appears to be speaking conversationally to the reader.

Phonology

Phonological techniques such as **onomatopoeia** and **alliteration** are used more frequently in poetry, but they can be found in prose. In this example, Thomas Hardy uses **sibilance** and onomatopoeia to create the sounds heard in a wood:

> To dwellers in a wood, almost every species of tree has its voice as well as its feature. At the passing of the breeze, the fir trees sob and moan no less distinctly than they rock; the holly whistles as it battles with itself; the ash hisses amid its quiverings; the beech rustles while its flat boughs rise and fall.

Checkpoint 2

Explain the differences between **simple**, **compound** and **complex sentences**.

Links

Parallelism is explained on page 13.

Take note

The rhythm of this sentence would have been different if only one **verb** had been used instead of two (omitting *clanking* or *stumbling*), and if *number 4* had been earlier. The sentence then would have read: *The small number 4 locomotive engine came clanking down from Selston with seven full wagons.* Note how the rhythm of the sentence is no longer as effective.

Take note

Other important aspects of grammar include **person** and **tense**. Many novels and short stories have **first-person narrators** (see page 78). The **second person** (*you*) may be used to address the reader directly. The **present tense** is associated with a feeling of immediacy (it is as if events are happening *now*). **Changes in tense** usually correspond to changes in time (e.g. from past to present) and can also mark significant changes in perspective.

Take note

Phonological effects are also likely in **dialogue**, and when the narrative style resembles speech.

The jargon

Sibilance is the repeated use of *s*, *z* and *sh* sounds.

Exam preparation (30 minutes)   answer: page 93

Text B on page 90 is the opening of *The Adventures of Huckleberry Finn*, a novel by Mark Twain. Consider how Twain uses language to create a narrative voice, referring closely to lexis, grammar and spoken language features.

Analysing prose fiction extracts

The types of exam questions set on **prose fiction extracts** vary according to the specification, and within each specification different kinds of questions are also set for different units or modules. If the extract is from a set text, you might have to compare it with an extract from another set text, or analyse the extract in a way that shows how it relates to the novel as a whole. If the extract is unseen (i.e. you have never seen it before), you will probably have to compare it to other extracts, which may again be unseen or from texts you have studied.

Getting started ●●●

Whether the extract is unseen or from a set text, a good way to start is to read the extract once or twice and develop an **overview** of it. What are the **purposes** of the extract? For example, is the writer portraying **characters**, or describing a **place** or a piece of **action**? What is the **narrative viewpoint** (see below)? What kinds of **feelings** and **attitudes** does the writer seem to be encouraging in the reader? Are characters portrayed sympathetically or unsympathetically? If a setting is described, are the impressions you form of it generally positive or negative?

If the extract is from a set text, your knowledge of the rest of the book will help you answer these questions. You will also need to think about the **context** of the extract. **Where** in the set text does it occur? How is what happens here important? What aspects of the **characters** are illustrated? Are any of the novel's **themes** evident? Do any elements in the extract **echo**, or **contrast** with, other parts of the book?

In your answer you should explore these aspects of the extract more deeply, looking closely at how the writer's purposes and intentions are reflected in the **language** used. Listed below are some detailed aspects of style and technique that you might consider.

Narrative viewpoint ●●●

→ Is the narration **first-person** or **third-person**?
→ What kind of **narrative voice** is created (especially important with first-person narration)?
→ What kind of relationship exists between **narrator and reader**? Is the reader addressed directly?

Dialogue ●●●

→ How is the dialogue presented (**direct/indirect/free direct/free indirect**)?
→ How close is the dialogue to **natural speech**?
→ How does the speech of **individual characters** differ?
→ How do characters **interact**? What does the dialogue reveal about **relationships** between characters?

Watch out!

Check your specification and look at past exam papers so you know the kind of question to expect.

Watch out!

Always read the question carefully. It might ask you to focus on specific aspects of the text.

Checkpoint 1

Explain the difference between **first-person** and **third-person narration**.

→ How does the author's (or narrator's) **accompanying commentary** influence the way we interpret the dialogue?

→ Are characters' **thoughts** presented – if so, how?

Lexis

→ How **formal** or **informal** is the lexis used?

→ Is any of the vocabulary **non-standard**?

→ What are the **connotations** of individual words? Are there groups of words with similar connotations?

→ Is any use made of **imagery**, including **simile**, **metaphor** and **personification**?

→ How are the impressions we form of the **characters** influenced by the lexis used (either in their own speech, or in descriptions of them)?

→ Does the lexis reflect the **period** the text was written, or the time it is set?

Examiner's secrets

Remember that if you identify a language feature, you should always quote one or more **examples**, and **comment** on the effect or significance of the feature.

Grammar

→ What types of words (**verbs**, **adjectives** etc.) are used, and to what effect?

→ What types of sentences are used (**declarative**, **imperative**, **interrogative**, **exclamatory**)?

→ Are any sentences unusually **long** or **short**?

→ Is any of the grammar **non-standard**?

→ Is **word order** important in any of the sentences?

→ Are techniques such as **parallelism** and **repetition** used in structuring any of the sentences?

→ Does the structure of any of the sentences have a **rhythmic** effect?

→ Are any effects achieved by the use of **first**, **second** and **third person**?

→ Is **tense** significant?

→ Does the grammar reflect **historical period** in any way?

Checkpoint 2

Explain what is meant by **non-standard grammar**.

Phonology

→ Are any phonological devices (**onomatopoeia**, **alliteration** etc.) used?

Discourse structure

→ How is the extract **organised**, and how does it **develop**?

→ Are there any particular comments you can make about how the extract **begins** and how it **ends**?

→ Is **paragraphing** significant? Do changes in paragraph correspond to changes in perspective (point of view) or tone?

Exam preparation

See the next section (pages 90–91) for some prose fiction extracts that can be used for exam practice.

Specimen texts

The texts below are for use with the practice exam questions for this chapter.

Text A

It was a town of red brick, or of brick that would have been red if the smoke and ashes had allowed it; but as matters stood it was a town of unnatural red and black like the painted face of a savage. It was a town of machinery and tall chimneys, out of which interminable serpents of smoke trailed themselves for ever and ever, and never got uncoiled. It had a black canal in it, and a river that ran purple with ill-smelling dye, and vast piles of building full of windows where there was a rattling and a trembling all day long, and where the piston of the steam-engine worked monotonously up and down like the head of an elephant in a state of melancholy madness. It contained several large streets all very like one another, and many small streets still more like one another, inhabited by people equally like one another, who all went in and out at the same hours, with the same sound upon the same pavements, to do the same work, and to whom every day was the same as yesterday and tomorrow, and every year the counterpart of the last and the next.

Take note

The question for this text is on page 85.

Text B

You don't know about me without you have read a book by the name of The Adventures of Tom Sawyer; but that ain't no matter. That book was made by Mr Mark Twain, and he told the truth, mainly. There was things which he stretched, but mainly he told the truth. That is nothing. I never seen anybody but lied one time or another, without it was Aunt Polly, or the widow, or maybe Mary. Aunt Polly – Tom's Aunt Polly, she is – and Mary, and the Widow Douglas is all told about in that book, which is mostly a true book, with some stretchers, as I said before.

Now the way that the book winds up is this: Tom and me found the money that the robbers hid in the cave, and it made us rich. We got six thousand dollars apiece – all gold. It was an awful sight of money when it was piled up. Well, Judge Thatcher he took it and put it out at interest, and it fetched us a dollar a day apiece all the year round – more than a body could tell what to do with. The Widow Douglas she took me for her son, and allowed she would sivilize me; but it was rough living in the house all the time, considering how dismal regular and decent the widow was in all her ways; and so when I couldn't stand it no longer I lit out. I got into my old rags and my sugar-hogshead again, and was free and satisfied. But Tom Sawyer he hunted me up and said he was going to start a band of robbers, and I might join if I would go back to the widow and be respectable. So I went back.

Take note

The question for this text is on page 87. Mark Twain (1835–1910) was an American novelist. *The Adventures of Huckleberry Finn* was a sequel to *The Adventures of Tom Sawyer*, referred to in this extract.

Text C

Mr Duffy abhorred anything which betokened physical or mental disorder. A medieval doctor would have called him saturnine. His face, which carried the entire tale of his years, was of the brown tint of Dublin streets. On his long and rather large head grew dry black hair, and a tawny moustache did not quite cover an unamiable mouth. His cheekbones also gave his face a harsh character; but there was no harshness in the eyes which, looking at the world from under their tawny eyebrows, gave the impression of a man ever alert to greet a redeeming instinct in others but often disappointed. He lived at a little distance from his body, regarding his own acts with doubtful side-glances. He had an odd autobiographical habit which led him to compose in his mind from time to time a short sentence about himself containing a subject in the third person and a predicate in the past tense. He never gave alms to beggars, and walked firmly, carrying a stout hazel.

Text D

11.45 p.m. Ugh. First day of New Year has been day of horror. Cannot quite believe I am once again starting the year in a single bed in my parents' house. It is too humiliating at my age. I wonder if they'll smell it if I have a fag out of the window. Having skulked at home all day, hoping hangover would clear, I eventually gave up and set off for the Turkey Curry Buffet far too late. When I got to the Alconburys' and rang their entire-tune-of-town-hall-clock-style doorbell I was still in a strange world of my own – nauseous, vile-headed, acidic. I was also suffering from road-rage residue after inadvertently getting on to the M6 instead of the M1 and having to drive halfway to Birmingham before I could find anywhere to turn round. I was so furious I kept jamming my foot down to the floor on the accelerator pedal to give vent to my feelings, which is very dangerous. I watched resignedly as Una Alconbury's form – intriguingly deformed through the ripply glass door – bore down on me in a fuchsia two-piece.

'Bridget! We'd almost given you up for lost! Happy New Year! Just about to start without you.'

She seemed to manage to kiss me, get my coat off, hang it over the banister, wipe her lipstick off my cheek and make me feel incredibly guilty all in one movement, while I leaned against the ornament shelf for support.

'Sorry. I got lost.'

'Lost? Durr! What are we going to do with you? Come on in!'

She led me through the frosted-glass doors into the lounge, shouting, 'She got lost, everyone!'

'Bridget! Happy New Year!' said Geoffrey Alconbury, clad in a yellow diamond-patterned sweater. He did a jokey Bruce Forsyth step then gave me the sort of hug which Boots would send straight to the police station.

'Hahumph,' he said, going red in the face and pulling his trousers up by the waistband. 'Which junction did you come off at?'

'Junction nineteen, but there was a diversion . . .'

'Junction nineteen! Una, she came off at Junction nineteen! You've added an hour to your journey before you even started. Come on, let's get you a drink. How's your love-life, anyway?'

Oh *God*. Why can't married people understand that this is no longer a polite question to ask?

Take note

The question for this text is on page 81.
→ *saturnine*: gloomy in character (from the supposed astrological influence of the planet Saturn);
→ *predicate*: the part of a sentence that makes a statement about the subject, usually containing a verb.

Take note

The question for this text is on page 83. *Bridget Jones's Diary* was published in 1996. In this extract Bridget, a single woman in her thirties, describes a New Year's Day party hosted by Una and Geoffrey Alconbury, friends of her parents.

Answers
Prose fiction

Historical overview

Checkpoints

1 Books by the authors include: George Eliot –
   Middlemarch, *The Mill on the Floss*; Anthony
   Trollope – *Barchester Towers*, *Can You Forgive Her?*;
   W.M. Thackeray – *Vanity Fair*; Elizabeth Gaskell – *Cranford*,
   Wives and Daughters; Henry James – *Washington Square*,
   Portrait of a Lady.
2 Other novels by Charles Dickens include *Oliver Twist*,
   Nicholas Nickleby, *Martin Chuzzlewit*, *Dombey and Son*,
   Little Dorrit.

Plot and setting

Checkpoints

1 The house in which Mr Duffy lives is described as
   sombre, and the nearby distillery is *disused*, suggesting
   decay and neglect. The room is cold and functional, with
   nothing that suggests comfort. It is *uncarpeted* and the
   walls have no pictures. The final sentence uses syndetic
   listing to show that the room is only furnished with
   essentials. The repetition of *iron*, and the *square* table,
   give the room a hardness and severity that matches
   Mr Duffy's character.
2 The pre-modifiers help to create a sense of gloom and
   foreboding: *dull*, *dark*, *soundless*, *singularly dreary*,
   melancholy.

Narrative viewpoint

Checkpoints

1 The lexis is very formal, with several polysyllabic words:
   undertake, *expedition*, *preoccupying*. The careful,
   repetitive grammatical structure of the second sentence
   suggests a narrative voice that is measured and precise.
2 *Implicit* means implied rather than openly stated. The
   opposite of *implicit* is *explicit*.
3 The register is quite informal: the frequent contractions,
   the use of *Well*. The use of interrogative sentences
   suggests interaction with another person. Ellipsis (. . .)
   suggests a pause in speech, while the italicised *you*
   makes us imagine the narrator stressing the word.

Characters and themes

Checkpoints

1 Much of the lexis suggests delicacy: *soft-featured*, *sweet*,
   long light hair, *curled slightly*, *graceful*.
2 This would mean the characters are direct opposites of
   one another.

Exam preparation

Mr Duffy is described as *saturnine*, which means gloomy and
deliberate. This is confirmed by the rest of the description,
including that of his physical appearance, where modifiers
suggest a hard, uncharitable nature: *dry black hair*, *an
unamiable mouth*, cheekbones that give his face a *harsh*
character. He is self-contained and keeps himself at a
distance from others, never giving money to beggars. He is
even detached from himself, examining his own behaviour
and commenting on it in his mind. He has a pessimistic view
of human nature, which again extends to himself: he has a
doubtful attitude towards his own actions. The one suggestion
of the potential for Mr Duffy to be more positive in his
attitude to others (and this is developed later in the story) is
that he looks for good qualities in those he meets: *ever alert
to greet a redeeming instinct in others*. However, he is *often
disappointed*. Note how the formality of the language in this
extract (e.g. *abhorred*, *betokened*) reflects the character's
careful, controlled and unemotional approach to life.

Dialogue in prose fiction

Checkpoints

1 Indirect speech is also known as reported speech.
2 Free direct thought: omit *he wondered*. Indirect thought:
   He wondered how she was. Free indirect thought: *How
   was she?* (Note that this is identical to the example of free
   indirect speech on page 83. The difference is that in one
   case we are to imagine the character *thinking* the words,
   whereas in the other he *says* them.)

Exam preparation

Una and Geoffrey Alconbury are a noisy, overpowering
couple. This is partly conveyed by their use of exclamatory
sentences. They embarrass Bridget by loudly announcing
that she took the wrong route (*'She got lost everyone!'* *'Una,
she came off at Junction nineteen!'*). They also make Bridget
uncomfortable by firing questions at her, including the very
personal *'How's your love-life, anyway?'*. Geoffrey interrupts
her. The speech of both characters includes oral signals,
which add to the comedy and increase the general sense
of their loudness: *'Durr!'* *'Hahumph'*. In contrast, Bridget's
own utterances are shorter and clearly said more quietly.

Lexis and imagery

Checkpoints

1 Monosyllabic words have one syllable. Polysyllabic words
   have three or more.
2 The series of clauses connected by the repeated use of
   the simple conjunction *and* reflects the rhythm of natural
   speech. The use of the second person (*you*) similarly
   creates the impression of the narrator speaking to the
   reader.
3 Regional dialect.

Exam preparation

Dickens creates the impression of a town dominated by
industry, which has polluted the town and reduced its
inhabitants to a monotonous, robotic existence. The visual
details in the description contribute to this impression: the

soot-covered buildings, the continually smoking chimneys, the black canal and the purple river. The ceaseless, repetitive movement of the piston, the sameness of the streets and the endless routine of the people's lives suggest a dreary way of life. The imagery is aural as well as visual: the noise of the factories is suggested by *rattling* and *trembling*. There are unusual comparisons, involving the use of metaphor (*interminable serpents of smoke*) and simile (the brickwork *like the painted face of a savage*, the piston moving *like the head of an elephant in a state of melancholy madness*). Together these images create an atmosphere that is sinister and disturbing. The negative connotations of several words convey the ugliness of the town and the miserable existence of its inhabitants: *vast piles of building, unnatural, monotonously, melancholy*. Repetition (*for ever and ever*) evokes a way of life that never changes. This technique is especially evident in the last sentence, which also uses parallelism, syndetic listing and sentence length to emphasise the repetitive cycle of the inhabitants' lives.

Grammar and phonology

Checkpoints

1 The sentence uses parallelism to emphasise the numerous ways the character has suffered.
2 See page 12 for an explanation of these terms.

Exam preparation

Twain creates the narrative voice of an uneducated American boy. The text has a conversational tone and it is as if Huck is speaking naturally to the reader, who is addressed directly using the second person (*You don't know about me*). The lexis includes colloquial expressions such as *lit out*, *a body*, *winds up* and *stretched/stretchers* (meaning exaggeration, or stretching the truth). There is also non-standard spelling, to suggest Huck's unfamiliarity with the word 'civilize' (which becomes *sivilize*). Much of the grammar is non-standard, including double negatives (*I couldn't stand it no longer*), incorrect use of singular and plural verb forms (*There was things*), and non-standard past tense forms (*I never seen*). There are also grammatical constructions that would not appear in standard written English but which suggest the character's speaking voice: *But Tom Sawyer he hunted me up*, *without you have read*.

Analysing prose fiction extracts

Checkpoints

1 A first-person narrator refers to *I* and *me*. A third-person narrator is not a participant in the story and uses third-person pronouns such as *he*, *she* and *they*.
2 This is grammar that does not conform to the grammatical rules of Standard English.

Revision checklist
Prose fiction

By the end of this chapter you should be able to:

1	Outline the main phases in the development of the English novel.	Confident	Not confident. **Revise** pages 74–75
2	Name the main authors associated with these periods.	Confident	Not confident. **Revise** pages 74–75
3	Explain how the setting of a novel might be significant in relation to themes, characters and atmosphere.	Confident	Not confident. **Revise** pages 76–77
4	Explain the difference between first-person and third-person narration.	Confident	Not confident. **Revise** pages 78–79
5	Understand the term narrative voice.	Confident	Not confident. **Revise** page 78
6	Understand the term unreliable narrator.	Confident	Not confident. **Revise** page 79
7	List the main ways of presenting a character in a novel.	Confident	Not confident. **Revise** pages 80–81
8	Understand how to approach the analysis of a character.	Confident	Not confident. **Revise** page 81
9	Identify the main themes in the prose fiction work you are studying.	Confident	Not confident. **Revise** page 81
10	Explain how fictional dialogue differs from genuine spontaneous speech.	Confident	Not confident. **Revise** page 82
11	List the main functions of dialogue in fiction.	Confident	Not confident. **Revise** page 82
12	Recognise the main forms of fictional dialogue, such as direct and indirect speech.	Confident	Not confident. **Revise** pages 82–83
13	Recognise how levels of formality can differ in prose fiction.	Confident	Not confident. **Revise** page 84
14	Understand the significance of connotations.	Confident	Not confident. **Revise** page 85
15	Comment on the effects achieved by different kinds of sentences in prose fiction.	Confident	Not confident. **Revise** page 86
16	Comment on the effects achieved by non-standard grammar.	Confident	Not confident. **Revise** page 87
17	Approach with confidence the analysis of a prose fiction extract.	Confident	Not confident. **Revise** pages 88–89

Drama

The study of plays is included in all the exam board specifications. With several specifications, there is a particular emphasis on the way spoken language is presented in drama, so the use of **dialogue** to reveal characters, relationships and themes is especially significant. When writing about dramatic texts, you should also try to show that you are aware the text was written to be performed on stage. The set, movements and actions by the characters, and the likely reactions of a live audience are all important elements to consider. You may be studying a contemporary play, or one from the past. If you are studying a Shakespeare play, there is a separate chapter on Shakespeare on pages 115–138.

Exam themes

→ Dramatic form and structure.

→ Dialogue in plays.

→ Characters and themes.

→ Performance elements.

Topic checklist

O AS ● A2	OCR	EDEXCEL	AQA A	AQA B	WJEC
Historical overview	●	O●	●	●	●
The structure of plays	●	O●	●	●	●
Key features of drama 1	●	O●	●	●	●
Key features of drama 2	●	O●	●	●	●
Dialogue in plays 1	●	O●	●	●	●
Dialogue in plays 2	●	O●	●	●	●
Characters and themes	●	O●	●	●	●
Specimen texts	●	O●	●	●	●

Historical overview

This introductory section gives a brief overview of the history of English drama. The earliest plays set for study at AS and A2 are usually from the Elizabethan and Jacobean period.

Take note

The earliest English plays date from the Middle Ages. They were performed in the open air by bands of travelling players, on wagons as theatres did not yet exist. The **mystery plays** enacted episodes from the Bible. They were a form of religious instruction, but were also intended to entertain, and included comic scenes and dialogue that incorporated the colloquial language of the time. **Morality plays** developed later, in the late 15th and early 16th centuries. The most admired English example is *Everyman*. The plays use **allegory** to deliver moral lessons. Many morality plays feature the **Vice**, a comic character who is nevertheless the personification of evil. Shakespeare and other later playwrights drew on the traditions of the morality plays, and villains such as Iago in *Othello* have Vice-like characteristics.

Elizabethan and Jacobean drama

Plays of this period were written during the reigns of Elizabeth I (1558–1603) and James I (1603–1625). England's first theatre was built in 1576, and interest in drama escalated in the years that followed. Many famous dramatists belong to this period, which is regarded as the golden age of English drama. **Shakespeare** was the most notable of these dramatists, and his works are discussed in the next chapter (pages 115–138), which also has sections on the historical, social and literary contexts of his plays. Other dramatists of this period include **Christopher Marlowe**, **Ben Jonson** and **John Webster**. Their plays offer penetrating insights into society and the human condition, addressing issues of morality, justice, political discord and social corruption, as well as individual human tragedy. Ben Jonson was a comic **satirist**. In *The Alchemist* he exposes the greed and corruption of a society where people live by material rather than spiritual values.

Restoration comedy

The next important phase in the history of English drama was after the restoration of Charles II in 1660. (In the period immediately preceding this, Charles I had been executed and the Puritans had ordered theatres to be closed.) Restoration comedy was mainly concerned with marriage, sexual desire and infidelity. In many of the plays gullible husbands are duped by their wives and the clever young men they fall in love with. The plays are **comedies of manners**, highlighting the absurdity of much social behaviour. A celebrated example is **William Congreve's** *The Way of the World*. In the 18th century English drama was still mostly comic, though there was less emphasis on sexual intrigue. **Oliver Goldsmith's** *She Stoops to Conquer* (1773) entertainingly ridicules social pretension and general human foolishness.

The jargon

Comedy of manners is a genre associated with the Restoration and the 18th century. Plays of this kind use clever verbal comedy to examine the attitudes and morals of high society.

19th-century drama

The most important 19th-century dramatists emerged towards the end of the century. In particular, the Norwegian playwright **Henrik Ibsen** is generally regarded as the founder of modern drama. His plays broke new ground by addressing contemporary social and political issues. In *A Doll's House*, for example, he examined the social position of married women, portraying a wife who at the end of the play makes the courageous decision to leave her husband. Ibsen is also associated with **naturalism**, a literary movement of the late 19th century which believed in the realistic portrayal of everyday life in novels and plays. Ibsen was an important influence on **George Bernard Shaw**, an Irish-born playwright who lived and worked for most of his life in England. Shaw's first play was produced in 1892, and he continued writing well into the

Checkpoint 1

Can you explain the difference between **naturalistic** and **stylised** dialogue?

20th century. **Oscar Wilde** was another Irish playwright. His works, such as *The Importance of Being Earnest* (1895), are lighter than those of Ibsen and Shaw but their incisive wit is the vehicle for telling social observation.

Modern drama ●●●

The main trend in modern drama has been the rejection of conventional attitudes and beliefs, mirrored in the abandonment of traditional dramatic forms and conventions.

A key figure in the first half of the 20th century was the German dramatist **Bertolt Brecht**. A typical Brecht play has a series of loosely connected scenes, with songs accompanying the action. Brecht rejected the idea that plays should seek to imitate real life, though his works, such as *Mother Courage* (1941), are strongly political.

The Theatre of the Absurd (discussed more fully on pages 98–99) was a movement that emerged in the 1950s. It sought to reflect the absurdity of existence in plays that deliberately confounded audience expectations of a recognisable plot and coherent dialogue. Playwrights associated with this movement, or influenced by it, include **Samuel Beckett** and **Harold Pinter**.

In contrast, the emphasis in British **kitchen sink drama** of the 1950s was domestic realism. Reacting against the drawing-room comedies and middle-class drama of postwar English theatre, dramatists such as **John Osborne** and **Arnold Wesker** focused on the lives of working- and lower-middle-class characters.

Later British drama has continued to address contemporary issues, though from a variety of perspectives. Brian Friel's *Translations* (1980) is partly a historical drama, examining the effects of English rule in Ireland in the mid-19th century, but the play also has clear relevance to the political situation in Northern Ireland in the closing decades of the 20th century. **Feminist theatre** is another development of the late 20th century. Plays by writers such as **Caryl Churchill** (author of *Top Girls*) and **Pam Gems** celebrate women and challenge the values of patriarchal society.

Checkpoint 2

Can you name any plays written by **George Bernard Shaw**?

Take note

The 20th century also saw the rise of **American** drama, which previously had been of little significance. Writers including **Arthur Miller**, **Tennessee Williams** and **David Mamet** found a large international audience for their plays, though the issues they explore are often of particular relevance to American society. Miller's *Death of a Salesman* (1949) concerns the failure of the American dream. *A Streetcar Named Desire* (1947) by Williams reflects the profound social changes occurring in postwar America. Mamet's *Oleanna* (1992) was a controversial response to the vigorous pursuit of political correctness in American universities.

Take note

Although the texts set for AS and A2 study are usually stage plays, it should be noted that most drama is now written for television and film. Like film, television drama encompasses a range of genres, including soap operas, detective dramas and situation comedies. Another distinction is between series and single plays. Early television plays were shot in a studio, but from the 1960s onwards much television drama has been more cinematic. Important writers include **Jeremy Sandford** (who wrote *Cathy Come Home*, a play about homelessness), **Jimmy McGovern** and **Paul Abbott**.

Exam preparation

Carry out a research investigation into the background of the play you are studying, writing up your findings. When was it written and first performed? What other plays were performed around this time? Are there ways in which the play is typical (or notably untypical) of its period? What other plays did the author write? How does this play compare with these other works – how is it similar, and how different?

Examiner's secrets

Useful sources of information might include: the introduction, notes etc. in the edition you are studying; other editions of the play; literature reference books; Internet sources.

The structure of plays

Here we look at the overall organisation of plays: the arrangement of the **plot**, the use of **sub-plots**, and how the division of a play into **acts** and **scenes** can be important.

Structure ●●●

Most plays follow a traditional three-part structure:

→ **Exposition**   The early part of the play introduces the characters, gives us some background information about them and 'sets up' a situation, usually by presenting the central characters with some kind of change or challenge.

→ **Complication**   The middle part of the play develops the initial situation, showing the consequences of change and how characters respond to their altered circumstances.

→ **Resolution**   In the play's closing section (also known as the **denouement**) there is some kind of restoration of order or equilibrium, and characters come to terms with what has taken place.

Brian Friel's play *Translations* (a popular set text) provides an example of how this structure works in practice:

→ **Exposition**   The first Act of *Translations* introduces us to all the characters and to the play's setting: Baile Beag, a small rural community in 19th-century Ireland. The life of the local population is disrupted by the arrival of a party of English soldiers, who are drawing up a map of the area.

→ **Complication**   A romantic relationship develops between Yolland (one of the English soldiers) and Maire (a local woman). Yolland disappears, probably murdered because of his relationship with Maire. In the **climax** of the play, the English react brutally, laying waste houses and farms in their search for the missing soldier.

→ **Resolution**   The Irish characters have to adjust to the reality of English rule, and to what it may mean for the future of Baile Beag.

If you are studying a pre-20th-century play, you are more likely to find that it corresponds quite neatly to the three-part structure outlined above. Contemporary drama is less predictable, with playwrights deliberately breaking conventional structural patterns. The ending of *Translations*, for example, leaves many questions unanswered, so that any sense of 'resolution' is far from complete. The mystery of Yolland's disappearance remains unsolved; we don't know if the further reprisals threatened by the English soldiers are carried out; we know that there are characters who intend resisting the English, but don't know what will happen to them.

The main reason for modern playwrights rejecting orderly, predictable dramatic structures is that they view life itself as unpredictable and disordered, and want their plays to reflect this. **The Theatre of the Absurd** is a term used to describe the work of several European and American dramatists writing in the 1950s and 1960s.

Take note

This structure is also evident in most film and television drama.

Checkpoint 1

What do the words **exposition** and **resolution** usually mean?

Examiner's secrets

If you are answering a question about an extract from a play you have studied, think about the **context** of the extract. Where does it come in the play? What has happened before it, and what happens after it? How significant is this extract to the overall development of the play?

Their plays are characterised by inconsequential storylines and repetitive, apparently meaningless dialogue, suggesting that the world defies rational explanation. Samuel Beckett's *Waiting for Godot* is one of the most influential plays in this tradition. Two tramps, Estragon and Vladimir, spend the play waiting for the mysterious Godot, a character who never arrives. A sense of futility and paralysis pervades the play, each act ending with the exchange *Well, shall we go? – Yes, let's go*, followed by the stage direction *They do not move*.

Plot and sub-plot ●●●

The **plot** of a play is its storyline – 'what happens' in it. *Waiting for Godot* has no plot in the conventional sense, because so little occurs and there is no real sense of progression or development. In contrast, a more traditional play such as Shakespeare's *Othello* has a plot full of action and incident, and moves steadily towards a bloody climax.

A common weakness in examination answers is to describe the plot in too much detail. Nowhere in an answer should you simply 'tell the story' of a text for its own sake. Only refer to details of the plot where they are especially significant, or where they illustrate an argument you are making (for example, about a character or theme).

A **sub-plot** is a secondary plot which runs alongside the play's main plot. It may involve characters who rarely if ever encounter the characters who feature in the main plot. If the play you are studying has one or more sub-plots, you should look for **parallels** and **contrasts** with the main plot. Usually the sub-plot mirrors the themes of the main plot, but presents them from a different perspective (in Shakespeare's plays, for example, the sub-plot is often more comic than the main plot).

Scene divisions ●●●

The division of plays into acts and scenes is another important structural element. You should look for the effects achieved by the **juxtaposition** of scenes, and for contrasts and similarities between particular scenes. Scene divisions can also mark significant lapses of time. In **David Mamet's** *Oleanna* a month elapses between the two acts of the play, both of which show John, a university teacher, in conversation with Carol, a student. During this period Carol makes an official complaint against John, and her manner towards him in the two acts is completely different.

Checkpoint 2

How might television comedy dramas such as *The Office* and *The Royle Family* be said to be in the tradition of the Theatre of the Absurd?

Examiner's secrets

If you are analysing an extract, it might be relevant to explain that it marks a turning point in the plot. If you are arguing that a character has a particular quality (such as courage, or honesty) it would be appropriate to refer to incidents in the play that demonstrate this quality in action.

The jargon

Juxtaposition means positioned next to each other.

Exam preparation (45 minutes)

Analyse the structure of the play you are studying. Does it follow the traditional three-part structure outlined on page 98? If so, how? If not, how does it differ? In what ways does the structure contribute to the overall effectiveness of the play?

Key features of drama 1

The next two sections are mainly concerned with some of the **performance** elements in plays, beginning with the **set** and the playwright's **stage directions**.

The set

Early plays, such as those of **Shakespeare**, contained little or no information about how the plays should be staged. When these plays are performed today, the stage set will reflect the director's interpretation of the play. Modern playwrights, in contrast, often give very detailed descriptions of what the set should look like. These should be studied closely as they can reveal much about a writer's intentions. Sets can be used to reflect aspects of the characters, to create a particular mood or atmosphere, or to suggest a historical period.

Mike Leigh's *Abigail's Party* is a play set in a suburban London home in 1977. The initial description of the set immediately suggests the values and lifestyle of Beverly and Laurence, the married couple who live there:

> *Laurence and Beverly's house, the ground floor. Room divider shelf unit, including telephone, stereo, ornamental fibre-light, fold-down desk, and prominently placed bar. Leather three-piece suite, onyx coffee-table, sheepskin rug. Open-plan kitchen, dining area with table and chairs.*

Laurence is a successful estate agent, and Beverly is a woman of expensive tastes. The modern furnishings suggest a showy, conspicuous display of wealth, reflecting both their prosperity and their materialistic outlook on life.

A Doll's House, written by the Norwegian dramatist **Henrik Ibsen** and first performed in 1879, is also set in the home of a married couple, Nora and her lawyer husband Helmer. Here the furnishings, while reflecting the family's apparent financial security, are more restrained. Ibsen's description begins: *A comfortable room, furnished inexpensively, but with taste.* Unlike Laurence and Beverly, the couple have no desire to flaunt their wealth. As the play develops, we realise that Ibsen's directions also hint at Helmer's carefulness with money.

Props

Props can also be important. In **Tennessee Williams's** *A Streetcar Named Desire* a radio symbolises the power struggle between Stanley and Blanche, his wife's sister. When Blanche turns the radio on, Stanley turns it off; later, when she turns it on again, he hurls it out of a window. In another scene, Stanley rifles through a trunk filled with Blanche's personal possessions. This violation of her privacy is again symbolic, prefiguring his later rape of her.

Stage directions ●●●

As well as providing information about the set, playwrights sometimes include descriptions of the **characters** as well. These are obviously not available to an audience watching the play, but authors include them to guide actors and directors, and they are very useful if you are studying the play. In **Brian Friel's** *Translations* the descriptions of Manus and his brother Owen prepare us for the differences in their characters – Manus the serious-minded idealist, Owen a more worldly, extrovert figure:

> *Manus is in his late twenties/early thirties; the master's older son. He is pale-faced, lightly built, intense, and works as an unpaid assistant – a monitor – to his father. His clothes are shabby; and when he moves we see that he is lame.*

> *Owen is the younger son, a handsome, attractive young man in his twenties. He is dressed smartly – a city man. His manner is easy and charming: everything he does is invested with consideration and enthusiasm.*

Stage directions can also indicate characters' **actions** and **movements**, and these may be significant. Manus's father Hugh shows his son little affection and is quite dismissive towards him, as we see when *He removes his hat and coat and hands them and his stick to Manus, as if to a footman.*

Action point

If the play you are studying does not include character descriptions of this kind, you could try writing your own. The exercise will help to clarify your thoughts about each character.

Links

These descriptions are discussed further on page 102.

Exam preparation (20 minutes)   answer: page 112

Below is Brian Friel's description of the set for his play *Translations*. What impressions of the play's setting do you derive from this passage? (If you are studying the play, write about how the description prepares us for the world we are to encounter in the rest of the play. If you are not, you can still discuss what kind of world you think Friel is trying to create.)

> The hedge-school is held in a disused barn or hay-shed or byre. Along the back wall are the remains of five or six stalls – wooden posts and chains – where cows were once milked and bedded. A double door left, large enough to allow a cart to enter. A window right. A wooden stairway without a banister leads to the upstairs living-quarters (off) of the schoolmaster and his son. Around the room are broken and forgotten implements: a cart-wheel, some lobster-pots, farming tools, a battle of hay, a churn, etc. There are also the stools and bench-seats which the pupils use and a table and chair for the master. At the door a pail of water and a soiled towel. The room is comfortless and dusty and functional – there is no trace of a woman's hand.

Take note

An outline of the plot of *Translations* was included in the previous section (page 98). *Hedge-schools* were unofficial local schools set up in Ireland when it was ruled by the English (the play is set in 1833). Teaching was in Gaelic, unlike in the official national schools, where only English was allowed.

Key features of drama 2

This second section on important features of drama considers some other performance elements, such as how the characters are dressed and the use of lighting and sound effects. The interpretation of a play by its producer and cast is also important, but remember more than one interpretation is usually possible. In fact, one of the characteristics of a great play is that it can be continually re-interpreted. Often new productions of a play will emphasise aspects of the text that are especially relevant to a contemporary audience.

Costume ●●●

Brian Friel's descriptions of Manus and Owen in *Translations* (see page 101) illustrate how dress can be used to **reflect character**.

Manus's *shabby* clothes emphasise his poverty and lack of material ambition. Owen, who left the rural community of Baile Beag in a determined effort to better himself, is in contrast *dressed smartly – a city man*. The military uniforms of the English soldiers separate them from the rest of the characters, making them visibly outsiders, while also symbolising their authority and power.

In *A Streetcar Named Desire* (Tennessee Williams), Blanche is *daintily dressed*, expressing her fragile femininity, while Stanley's *blue denim work clothes* and *bowling jacket* reflect his aggressive masculinity. Blanche is also initially dressed in virginal white, but after her promiscuous past has been exposed she appears dressed in a *scarlet satin robe*.

Lighting, music and sound effects ●●●

A play is an aural and visual experience, and **lighting**, **music** and **sound effects** can make an important contribution to the overall effect. You should consider how they **reflect the mood** at particular points in the play, and how they **reinforce** what is taking place between the characters.

In *Streetcar* Blanche's boyfriend Mitch symbolically turns on a light at the moment he is confronting her with the truth about her past. In contrast, in *Translations* much of the stage is in darkness for the romantic dialogue between Maire and Yolland, enhancing the scene's intimacy. The change in atmosphere for this scene is also marked by music: the loud fiddle playing of the dance that Maire and Yolland have just left fades, and is replaced by gentler guitar music.

Also in *Streetcar*, *blue piano* jazz music is used at the beginning of the play to evoke the atmosphere of New Orleans, and continues to be associated with the life of the city. The music is also linked to Stanley, and as he gains the ascendancy in his battle of wills with Blanche, it grows louder. As the play closes, we hear *the swelling music of the blue piano*. The *Varsouviana*, polka dance music that was played on the night Blanche's husband committed suicide, is associated with her tormented memories. In the final scene, as Blanche descends into madness, the music is heard again, but *filtered into weird distortion*.

Links

The physical appearance of characters, including their dress, can also be significant in prose fiction – see page 80.

Checkpoint 1

What does the word **aural** mean here?

Checkpoint 2

Words such as *symbolically* and *symbolises* appear several times on these two pages. Explain what you understand by **symbolism**.

Other sound effects in *Streetcar* include the occasional roar of a locomotive train, used to reinforce Stanley's role as a character representing the modern industrial age. It also symbolises his menacing strength: in the scene that culminates in Blanche's rape, *The barely audible blue piano begins to drum up louder*, before *The sound of it turns into the roar of an approaching locomotive*.

Performance and interpretation ●●●

However much the playwright tries to control how a play is presented, the way it is **interpreted** by producers and actors – from its overall meaning to decisions about how particular lines should be delivered – is still enormously important. If you see a performance of a play you are studying (or watch a video production), you should note how specific roles or episodes in the play are interpreted.

When answering an exam question, it can strengthen your answer to include brief points about productions you have seen, provided they are relevant to the extract or topic you are writing about.

Role of the audience ●●●

Another crucial element is the presence of a live audience. If the play includes **soliloquies** or **asides**, these may be delivered as if the character is speaking directly to the audience, taking them into his or her confidence. Shakespeare's villains – such as Richard III and Iago – often address audiences in this way, so that we are made to feel like fellow conspirators.

Dramatic irony is a device that exploits the presence of an audience. It hinges on the audience knowing more than the characters: characters say something that has an extra meaning or significance, apparent to the audience but not to the characters themselves.

Translations is a play that makes unusual demands of the audience. All the characters speak in English, but for much of the play we are meant to imagine that the Irish characters are speaking Gaelic, so that their words are not understood by the English soldiers and vice versa. This gives rise to dramatic irony, as when Maire and Yolland struggle to understand each other. The audience, but not the characters, sees that their love masks fundamental differences between them: while Maire wants to leave Baile Beag and pleads *Take me away with you, George*, Yolland is drawn to the place and vows *I'm not going to leave here*.

Dialogue in plays 1

In English Language and Literature courses, the language of literary texts and the language of speech are both major topics. Dramatic dialogue is an especially important aspect of plays because it is an area of study where the two topics overlap.

Dramatic dialogue and real speech

As part of your AS or A2 course you will find that you have to analyse both dramatic dialogue and transcripts of genuine, spontaneous conversation. In the exam you may well find that you have to compare examples of each kind of speech. As we shall see, some dramatists deliberately try to make the **language** their characters use resemble that of everyday speech, and the ways fictional characters **interact** when they are speaking to each other may also resemble what can happen in real conversation. However, there are crucial differences between dramatic dialogue and natural speech, and it is important to be aware of these.

How real speech differs from dramatic dialogue

Natural speech has several features that distinguish it from dramatic dialogue:

→ Most obviously, the **non-fluency features** found in spontaneous speech are generally absent in dramatic dialogue. These include hesitations, pauses, fillers, unintentional repetition, false starts and so on. Even if a playwright incorporates some of these features to make the dialogue seem realistic, the result is still likely to be more coherent than everyday conversation generally is. If a pause is identified in a script, it will have been included for a specific dramatic effect.

→ In real life, people do not speak in neatly constructed sentences, but in plays they often do. Again, a dramatist may use short sentences or non-standard grammar to replicate natural speech, but the proportion of **disjointed** or **incomplete grammatical constructions** will be lower.

→ **Interruptions** and **overlapping speech** (when two or more people speak simultaneously) occur more frequently in natural speech.

→ In real conversation there is more **feedback**. This includes verbal responses (*yeah*, *right* and so on), oral signals such as *mm* and non-verbal responses such as nodding and shaking of the head. In plays characters generally remain silent when another character is speaking.

One of the main reasons the features listed above are found less frequently in dramatic dialogue is that audiences would have difficulty understanding what was being said on stage if speeches were disjointed and full of non-fluency features. They would also be distracted if characters continually spoke over each other and gave as much feedback as they do in natural conversation.

Links

Much of the material in the *Spoken language* chapter (pages 25–48) is relevant to the study of dramatic dialogue.

Checkpoint 1

Explain the difference between **filled** and **unvoiced pauses**.

Checkpoint 2

Do you know a technical term for grammatically incomplete clauses and sentences?

How dramatic dialogue differs from real speech

If we look at the differences from the opposite perspective, focusing on the distinctive qualities of dramatic dialogue, the most important point is that dialogue in plays is **prepared speech**. It is not genuinely spontaneous but has been carefully crafted by a writer. This means it is generally more **organised** and more **coherent** than natural conversation. It will also have a special kind of **intensity** because in good dramatic dialogue not a word is wasted – everything that is said is being said for a **dramatic purpose**. Even when dialogue closely resembles everyday speech it still has this heightened quality.

Another important difference between dramatic dialogue and real conversation is that a play has an **audience**, who hear and observe the conversations between the characters. With most genuine conversations the participants themselves constitute the only 'audience'. As noted on page 103, the presence of an audience can give rise to **dramatic irony**, a literary technique that relies on the audience knowing more than the characters do.

Purposes of dramatic dialogue

These include:

- → It may **reveal character**. For example, the dialogue might shed light on a character's attitudes and values, or reveal something interesting about their past. What is said and how it is said are both significant. A character's **idiolect** – the distinctive features of an individual speaker's language – may be used by a writer to reflect important aspects of the character's personality.
- → It may reveal or develop **relationships between characters**.
- → It may contribute to the development of **themes** and **ideas** that are important to the play as a whole.
- → It may give information that is important to the **plot**, or move the storyline forward in some way (for example, a character might make a significant decision or a key piece of action might occur).
- → It might be intended to generate a specific **reaction from the audience** (e.g. laughter if the dialogue is humorous).

Links

The specific kinds of dramatic purpose that dialogue might serve are discussed below.

Take note

Some spontaneous speech (e.g. radio and television interviews) does have a wider audience, but the speakers are generally aware (and may well adjust their speech accordingly). In drama we are usually meant to imagine that the characters inhabit a self-enclosed world and do not realise an audience is 'listening in'.

> *"In well-constructed dramatic dialogue everything is meant by the playwright, even when it is apparently unintended by the character."*
>
> Mick Short: 'Exploring the language of poems, plays and prose'

Exam preparation (30 minutes) answer: page 112

Text A on page 110 is from the final scene of *Translations* by Brian Friel. Yolland, an English soldier, has disappeared. It is presumed he has been abducted or murdered. Lancey, the English commanding officer, has come to Hugh O'Donnell's school to address members of the local Irish community. We are to imagine that Owen (Hugh's son) translates what Lancey says into Gaelic. Referring closely to Friel's use of language, discuss the dramatic impact of this extract, and the ways the characters of Owen and Lancey are presented.

Dialogue in plays 2

This second section on dramatic dialogue looks at the differences between **stylised** and **naturalistic** dialogue, and offers advice on the analysis of dialogue extracts.

Stylised dialogue

When dialogue has clearly been carefully constructed by a writer, and is very different from the way people naturally speak, it is described as **stylised**. Here is an example from Oscar Wilde's *The Importance of Being Earnest*:

> **Cecily:** It is always painful to part from people whom one has known for a very brief space of time. The absence of old friends one can endure with equanimity. But even a momentary separation from anyone to whom one has just been introduced is almost unbearable.

It is hard to imagine anyone in real life speaking like this. In trying to explain why, the **formality** of the **lexis** might be noted (the repeated use of *one*, the use of *It is* rather than the contraction *It's*), together with the correctness of the **grammar** (sentences are grammatically complete, and *whom* is used rather than *who*).

Naturalistic dialogue

Dialogue that is close to everyday speech is described as **realistic** or **naturalistic**. The example below is from *Our Day Out*, a play by Willy Russell. In the play a group of underprivileged schoolchildren from Liverpool are taken on an outing, which includes a trip to the zoo. Briggs is a teacher; Andrews, Ronson and Girl 1 are pupils.

Briggs and a group of Kids enter and look down into the bear pit.

> **Briggs:** And a brown bear is an extremely dangerous animal. You see those claws, they could leave a really nasty mark.
>
> **Andrews:** Could it kill y', sir?
>
> **Briggs:** Well why do you think they keep it in a pit?
>
> **Ronson:** I think that's cruel, sir. Don't you?
>
> **Briggs:** Not if it's treated well, no. Don't forget, Ronson, that an animal like this would have been born into captivity. It's always had walls around it so it won't know anything other than this sort of existence, will it?
>
> **Ronson:** I'll bet it does.
>
> **Girl 1:** How do you know? Sir's just told you hasn't he? If it was born in a cage an' it's lived all its life in a cage well it won't know any different will it? So it won't want anything different.
>
> **Ronson:** Well, why does it kill people then?
>
> **Andrews:** What's that got to do with it, dickhead?
>
> **Ronson:** It kills people because people are cruel to it. They keep it in here, in this pit so when it gets out it's bound to go mad an' want to kill people. Can't y'see?

Watch out!

If dialogue is stylised, this does not mean it is therefore badly written and ineffective. Many playwrights (especially in previous centuries) did not intend that their dialogue should sound lifelike and realistic.

Checkpoint 1

How does the **overall structure** of the speech also suggest that the dialogue is stylised?

Checkpoint 2

In what ways does the **interaction** between the characters in this extract reflect the fact that Briggs is a teacher and the other characters are pupils?

The **lexis** here is clearly more **informal** than in the Wilde extract. Much of it is monosyllabic, and it includes colloquial expressions (*I'll bet*), contractions (*hasn't*, *it's*), fillers (*Well*) and taboo language (*dickhead*). In terms of **grammar**, the utterances are mostly short, and there are constructions that are generally found in speech rather than writing (e.g. *Not if it's treated well, no*). The use of *y'* rather than *you* suggests the characters' **regional accent**. All of these features contribute to the realism of the dialogue. However, the extract is also **different** from genuine spontaneous speech in important respects. For example, there are few **non-fluency features** and no **overlapping speech**. Moreover, Willy Russell has carefully written the dialogue to serve **dramatic purposes** relevant to the play as a whole. The caged bear, for instance, can be seen as a **metaphor** for the school pupils, who are trapped by their social situation. Briggs is a teacher who at this stage in the play (his attitude later changes) is unsympathetic to the children's plight. He also has an authoritarian teaching style, and believes the pupils should be controlled by strict discipline. These aspects of his **character** are reflected in his comments on the bear.

Analysing dramatic dialogue ●●●

As the Willy Russell extract illustrates, dramatic dialogue often resembles real conversation. Even when the language spoken by the characters is more stylised, there are still similarities. Characters interact with each other, and most of the elements of **conversational interaction** (see pages 32–33) can be found in both dramatic dialogue and genuine conversation. These elements include turn-taking, adjacency pairs, feedback and so on. Speakers can also show dominance in similar ways: for example, by their choice of address forms and by speaking more, controlling the topics of conversation and using imperatives and interrogatives. When analysing dramatic dialogue, you should look for all of these aspects of conversational behaviour and think about how the playwright uses them to reveal characters and relationships. Also look closely at the **language** the characters use, considering **lexis**, **grammar** and **phonology**. How stylised or naturalistic is the language? Is it formal or informal? What does it reveal about individual characters and their attitudes?

Checkpoint 3

Find examples of **complex, polysyllabic** lexis in the Wilde extract on page 106.

Checkpoint 4

What does the Russell extract suggest about **Ronson's** character?

Links

Think also about the **dramatic purposes** served by the Russell extract (see page 105).

Exam preparation (30 minutes)   answer: pages 112–113

Text B on page 111 is from the opening scene of Ibsen's *A Doll's House* (see page 100). Helmer and Nora are husband and wife. What impressions of the characters' relationship are conveyed by the language they use, and the interaction between them?

Characters and themes

Most of the work you do on your set play will relate in some way to characters, themes or both. In preparing for the exam you should ensure you have a good set of notes on the play's characters, and on the main themes.

Types of character

Many traditional plays contain the following types of character:

→ A **hero** or **protagonist**. This is the play's central character. Note that the hero is not necessarily 'heroic' in the sense of being noble and courageous. The hero of Shakespeare's *Richard III* is the cunning, malevolent Richard.
→ An **antagonist**. This is the hero's main opponent. Often the antagonist is also the play's villain.

Othello is an example of a play that conforms to this pattern: Othello is the hero or protagonist, Iago the antagonist and villain.

Ways of presenting characters

If you are writing about how a character is presented in a play, these are some important aspects to consider:

→ How the character is **introduced** by the dramatist. Look at the **stage directions** that accompany the character's first appearance. These may include a description of the character's personality, attitudes or values – for example, Maire in *Translations* is described as *strong-minded*. They might also include information about the character's physical appearance, and how they are dressed (as noted on page 102, external appearance is often used to suggest character).
→ What the character **says**, and how they say it (see *Language and character*, below).
→ How the character **interacts** with other characters, and what is revealed about them by the kinds of relationships they have.
→ **Actions** performed by the character, and their significance. In the opening scene of *A Streetcar Named Desire*, Stanley's raw masculinity is suggested when he enters carrying a parcel of meat, which he tosses to his wife (like a hunter returning home with his kill).
→ How the character **develops** in the course of the play. Do their attitudes and values change? Are their relationships with any of the other characters different in any way?

Language and character

It is very important to consider how **language** is used to reveal character. Try to identify the main features of the character's **idiolect**, looking at lexis, grammar and phonology. In *Abigail's Party* (see page 100), for example, Beverly's working class origins are reflected

---

The jargon

The term **anti-hero** is sometimes used for a protagonist who, while not necessarily evil or villainous, lacks traditional heroic qualities.

Take note

We may be introduced to a character before the character appears. Othello is not present in the opening scene of Shakespeare's play but most of the dialogue is about him.

Checkpoint 1

Explain the difference between **idiolect** and **dialect**.

in her Estuary English accent and her frequent use of informal, non-standard vocabulary: *this bloke, cos, you gonna get changed?, yeah* (one of her verbal mannerisms is the repeated use of this word). In contrast, the formality of her husband Laurence's language suggests his pomposity and pretentiousness: *I find the Mini economical, efficient and reliable*; *I find they have a much wider range of goods there*.

Look also at how **conversational interaction** in the play's **dialogue** reveals character. A feature of Beverly's language towards Laurence is the frequent use of interrogatives to badger and interrogate him: *What happened?*; *How long's all this going to take, please?* Interrogatives are also used to give Laurence orders, so that they function as a form of imperative: *would you like to get the drinks, please?*; *would you like to take Angela's coat, please?*

Importance of characters

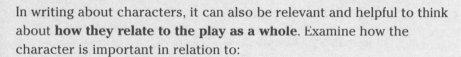

In writing about characters, it can also be relevant and helpful to think about **how they relate to the play as a whole**. Examine how the character is important in relation to:

→ The **plot** – the action of the play.
→ The **themes** – see below.
→ **Other characters** Does the character contrast with another character? Does the character have a relationship that is used by the playwright to reveal something about another character?

Themes

The **themes** of a play are the ideas and issues that run through it. For example, an important theme in *Macbeth* is ambition; a central theme in *Othello* is jealousy. Themes can be expressed through characters, language and plot, and may also be reflected in other dramatic elements such as a play's set, costumes and music. A theme of *A Streetcar Named Desire* is the social change taking place in mid-20th century America. Tennessee Williams uses the characters of Blanche and Stanley to show how one set of values was being supplanted by another. Blanche, fragile and in decline, represents the old American South, while Stanley, strong and confident, represents the new America.

Checkpoint 2

What is **Estuary English**?

Action point

Compile a list of key quotes for each of the characters in your set play. Make sure you include quotations where the character's use of **language** is significant.

Examiner's secrets

It is especially useful to think about the importance of minor characters. Every character is in a play for a purpose – don't dismiss minor characters as insignificant.

Exam preparation (30 minutes)

Choose a secondary character in the play you are studying (that is, someone who would not be regarded as one of the play's central characters). Write about the importance of this character to the play as a whole.

Specimen texts

The texts below are for use with the practice exam questions for this chapter.

The question for this text is on page 105.

Take note

The question for this text is on page 105. If you are studying *Translations*, it is a good idea to compare this passage with a parallel episode in the opening scene, where Owen again translates for Lancey (pages 33–34 in the Faber edition). Owen's approach to the task then was very different.

Text A

Lancey enters – now the commanding officer.

Owen: Any news? Any word?

Lancey moves into the centre of the room, looking around as he does.

Lancey: I understood there was a class. Where are the others?
Owen: There was to be a class but my father ...
Lancey: This will suffice. I will address them and it will be their responsibility to pass on what I have to say to every family in this section.

Lancey indicates to Owen to translate. Owen hesitates, trying to assess the change in Lancey's manner and attitude.

I'm in a hurry, O'Donnell.

Owen: The captain has an announcement to make.
Lancey: Lieutenant Yolland is missing. We are searching for him. If we don't find him, or if we receive no information as to where he is to be found, I will pursue the following course of action. (*He indicates to Owen to translate.*)
Owen: They are searching for George. If they don't find him –
Lancey: Commencing twenty-four hours from now we will shoot all livestock in Ballybeg.

Owen stares at Lancey.

At once.

Owen: Beginning this time tomorrow they'll kill every animal in Baile Beag – unless they're told where George is.
Lancey: If that doesn't bear results, commencing forty-eight hours from now we will embark on a series of evictions and levelling of every abode in the following selected areas –
Owen: You're not – !
Lancey: Do your job. Translate.
Owen: If they still haven't found him in two days' time they'll begin evicting and levelling every house starting with these townlands.

Lancey reads from his list.

Take note

Lancey reads the English versions of Irish place names. Owen gives the names in Gaelic.

Lancey: Swinefort.
Owen: Lis na Muc.
Lancey: Burnfoot.
Owen: Bun na hAbhann.
Lancey: Dromduff.
Owen: Druim Dubh.
Lancey: Whiteplains.
Owen: Machaire Ban.
Lancey: Kings Head.

Owen: Cnoc na Ri.

Lancey: If by then the lieutenant hasn't been found, we will proceed until a complete clearance is made of this entire section.

Owen: If Yolland hasn't been got by then, they will ravish the whole parish.

Lancey: I trust they know exactly what they've got to do.

Text B

Take note

The question for this text is on page 107.
Torvald is Helmer's first name.

Helmer (*from his study*): Is that my little skylark twittering out there?

Nora (*busy opening the parcels*): It is.

Helmer: Scampering about like a little squirrel?

Nora: Yes.

Helmer: When did the squirrel get home?

Nora: Just this minute. (*She slips the bag of macaroons in her pocket and wipes her mouth.*) Come in here, Torvald, and you can see what I've bought.

Helmer: I'm busy! (*A moment later he opens the door and looks out, pen in hand.*) Did you say 'bought'? What, all that? Has my little featherbrain been out wasting money again?

Nora: But, Torvald, surely this year we can let ourselves go just a little bit? It's the first Christmas that we haven't had to economize.

Helmer: Still, we mustn't waste money, you know.

Nora: Oh, Torvald, surely we can waste a little now – just the teeniest bit? Now that you're going to earn a big salary, you'll have lots and lots of money.

Helmer: After New Year's Day, yes – but there'll be a whole quarter before I get paid.

Nora: Pooh, we can always borrow till then.

Helmer: Nora! (*He goes to her and takes her playfully by the ear.*) The same little scatterbrain. Just suppose I borrowed a thousand kroner today and you went and spent it all by Christmas, and then on New Year's Eve a tile fell on my head, and there I lay –

Nora (*putting a hand over his mouth*): Sh! Don't say such horrid things!

Helmer: But suppose something of the sort were to happen . . .

Nora: If anything as horrid as that were to happen, I don't expect I should care whether I owed money or not.

Helmer: But what about the people I'd borrowed from?

Nora: Them? Who bothers about them? They're just strangers.

Helmer: Nora, Nora! Just like a woman! But seriously, Nora, you know what I think about that sort of thing. No debts, no borrowing. There's something constrained, something ugly even, about a home that's founded on borrowing and debt. You and I have managed to keep clear up till now, and we shall still do so for the little time that is left.

Nora (*going over to the stove*): Very well, Torvald, if you say so.

Helmer (*following her*): Now, now, my little song-bird mustn't be so crestfallen. Well? Is the squirrel sulking? (*Taking out his wallet*) Nora . . . guess what I have here!

Nora (*turning quickly*): Money!

Helmer: There! (*He hands her some notes.*) Good heavens, I know what a lot has to go on housekeeping at Christmas time.

Answers
Drama

Historical overview

Checkpoints

1 These terms are explained on page 106.
2 Shaw's plays include *Saint Joan*, *Pygmalion*, *Arms and the Man*, *Man and Superman*.

The structure of plays

Checkpoints

1 An exposition is a comprehensive explanation or description of something. A resolution is a solution to a problem or dispute.
2 The storylines of comedy dramas such as these are often inconsequential. Nothing much appears to 'happen'.

Key features of drama 1

Checkpoints

1 Properties.
2 To prefigure is to anticipate or look forward to.

Exam preparation

The description of the set establishes the material poverty of Baile Beag (the town in 19th-century Ireland where the play is set). As the play develops, we see the contrast between this poverty and the characters' rich cultural heritage. The set also establishes that it is a rural community, but there is a strong sense of decay and neglect: *a disused barn, broken and forgotten implements.* This is significant because Baile Beag is presented as a society stuck in the past, while the world around it changes. Hugh, the schoolmaster, lives alone at the hedge-school with his son Manus, and their difficult relationship is important in the play. Hugh's wife died some years previously, and this is also reflected in the appearance of the room: it is *comfortless and dusty and functional – there is no trace of a woman's hand.*

Key features of drama 2

Checkpoints

1 *Aural* means related to the sense of hearing.
2 Symbolism occurs when something is used to represent something else. For example, Mitch turning on a light in *A Streetcar Named Desire* represents an attempt to reveal and discover the truth.

Dialogue in plays 1

Checkpoints

1 An unvoiced pause is silent. A filled pause is a sound such as *er* or *um*.
2 Ellipsis.

Exam preparation

Lancey is presented as cold and ruthless as he announces his ultimatum and the brutal punishments that will follow if Yolland is not found. The audience would find these shocking. Lancey's manner is brisk and formal, shown by vocabulary such as *suffice*, *address* and *abode*, and by his use of short, direct sentences (*Lieutenant Yolland is missing. We are searching for him.*). He has an attitude of superiority towards Owen, ignoring his opening question, interrupting his second utterance, addressing him by his surname (*O'Donnell*) and using imperatives to give him instructions (*Do your job. Translate.*). His position on the stage is also significant: when he enters, he takes up a commanding position in the centre of the room. Owen translates Lancey's words as asked, but his shock and disapproval are evident in his reactions. He *stares* at Lancey and at one point begins to protest (*You're not – !*). His translation simplifies Lancey's announcement and makes it less formal. For example, Lancey's *we will shoot all livestock in Ballybeg* becomes *they'll kill every animal in Baile Beag.* However, he also uses more emotive language than Lancey, underlining the horror of what is proposed: *we will proceed until a complete clearance is made of this entire section* becomes *they will ravish the whole parish.* (There is a strong contrast with the earlier translation episode in the play. Then Owen, who was collaborating with the English soldiers, softened Lancey's language, making the proposed survey of the area seem less sinister and threatening.) The recitation of Anglicized versions of Gaelic place names, alternating with their Gaelic equivalents, crystallises the political, cultural and linguistic conflicts in the play and the threat to Irish identity that the English military machine represents.

Dialogue in plays 2

Checkpoints

1 The speech has a logical structure not usually found in natural speech. The first sentence puts forward a proposition, which is then clarified and justified in the two sentences that follow. The second and third sentences neatly balance each other.
2 The pupils ask Briggs questions, looking for information and guidance from him. Briggs also asks questions, but he already knows the answers to them. The forms of address also reflect the differences in status between the characters: the pupils address Briggs as *sir*, but Briggs addresses Ronson by his surname.
3 Examples include *equanimity* and *momentary separation*.
4 Ronson is shown to be sensitive, thoughtful and perceptive.

Exam preparation

The relationship is unequal, and Helmer clearly dominates his wife. At first he is unwilling to speak to Nora, responding to her request that he leave his study by saying, *I'm busy*. He uses patronising address forms when speaking to her: *my little skylark, little squirrel, my little song-bird*. The use of the possessive pronoun *my* indicates Helmer's attitude of ownership and control, and the diminutive adjective *little* emphasises his feeling of superiority. The animal images suggest he regards Nora almost as a domestic pet. His criticisms of her show he doesn't credit her with any intelligence: *featherbrain, scatterbrain*. The period of the play, and the patriarchal society in which it is set, are reflected in the chauvinistic comment *Just like a woman!* He sets rules they must follow as a couple (*No debts, no borrowing*). He teases Nora as if she were a child, only giving her money after asking, *guess what I have here?* At this stage in the play (she acts very differently later), Nora accepts Helmer's authority. She briefly argues that they should borrow money, but soon accepts his decision: *Very well, Torvald, if you say so.* Her acceptance of a subordinate position is also shown by her pleading tone (*surely we can waste a little now*) and by her simple, childlike language: *the teeniest bit, lots and lots of money, a big salary.*

Characters and themes

Checkpoints

1 A dialect is a form of language associated with a group of people (often the inhabitants of a particular geographical region).

2 Estuary English is a version of the London accent, initially associated with an area around the Thames estuary. Research suggests it has steadily spread to other parts of the country.

Revision checklist
Drama

1	Outline the main phases in the development of English drama.	Confident	Not confident. **Revise** pages 96–97
2	Name the main dramatists associated with these periods.	Confident	Not confident. **Revise** pages 96–97
3	Understand the terms exposition, complication, resolution and denouement.	Confident	Not confident. **Revise** page 98
4	Explain the difference between plot and subplot.	Confident	Not confident. **Revise** page 99
5	Understand the ways in which the set of a play might be significant.	Confident	Not confident. **Revise** page 100
6	Understand why a playwright's stage directions are important.	Confident	Not confident. **Revise** page 101
7	Recognise the significance of performance elements, including costume, lighting, music and sound effects.	Confident	Not confident. **Revise** pages 102–103
8	Explain the term dramatic irony.	Confident	Not confident. **Revise** page 103
9	Explain how dramatic dialogue differs from real speech.	Confident	Not confident. **Revise** page 104
10	Identify the main purposes of dramatic dialogue.	Confident	Not confident. **Revise** page 105
11	Understand the differences between stylised and naturalistic dialogue.	Confident	Not confident. **Revise** pages 106–107
12	Approach with confidence the analysis of dramatic dialogue.	Confident	Not confident. **Revise** page 107
13	Understand the terms hero, protagonist and antagonist.	Confident	Not confident. **Revise** page 108
14	List the main ways of presenting a character in a play.	Confident	Not confident. **Revise** page 108
15	Identify the ways in which a character might be important to the play as a whole.	Confident	Not confident. **Revise** page 109
16	Identify the main themes in the play you are studying.	Confident	Not confident. **Revise** page 109

Plays by Shakespeare feature on all the exam board specifications, though they are optional on some specifications and compulsory on others. Usually questions require both close analysis of an extract and the discussion of a broader aspect of the play as a whole. The main focus in this chapter is on the distinctive characteristics of Shakespeare's language, and on the strategies you should adopt when examining a Shakespeare extract. The early sections of the chapter give an overview of Shakespeare's plays, and the chapter also includes a section on Shakespeare in performance. You should always remember that Shakespeare wrote his plays to be performed on stage, and if you have the opportunity you should certainly try to see a production of the play you are studying. If that is not possible, an alternative is to watch a video or DVD version.

Exam themes

→ Shakespeare's language.

→ Dialogue in Shakespeare's plays.

→ Context of Shakespeare's plays.

→ Performance elements.

Topic checklist

○ AS ● A2	OCR	EDEXCEL	AQA A	AQA B	WJEC
Shakespeare: an overview	●	○	●	●	●
Shakespeare in context	●	○	●	●	●
Shakespeare's language 1	●	○	●	●	●
Shakespeare's language 2	●	○	●	●	●
Shakespeare's language 3	●	○	●	●	●
Dialogue in Shakespeare	●	●	●	●	●
Analysing Shakespeare extracts 1	●	○	●	●	●
Analysing Shakespeare extracts 2	●	○	●	●	●
Shakespeare in performance	●	○	●	●	●
Specimen texts	●	○	●	●	●

Shakespeare: an overview

This section gives you an initial overview of Shakespeare's plays. It explains how they can be roughly divided into four groups, and looks at the main themes and characteristics of each type of play.

Checkpoint 1

What is a **sonnet**?

Take note

Shakespeare was born in Stratford-upon-Avon in 1564. His father was a glovemaker and prominent local citizen, though he later fell badly into debt. When he was 18 William married Anne Hathaway, who was pregnant with the first of their three children (none of whom survived into adulthood). He moved to London, where he began working in the theatre, initially as an actor. He became the most successful playwright of his day, and by the time of his retirement to Stratford in 1612 was very wealthy. He came out of retirement twice, writing *Henry VIII* and *The Two Noble Kinsmen* (a collaboration with John Fletcher). He died in 1616.

Watch out!

Shakespeare's plays can roughly be divided and grouped as shown on these pages. However, there are not rigid differences between the groups and several plays could be placed in more than one category. For example, *Antony and Cleopatra* is usually considered a tragedy, but it is also in many respects a history play.

Shakespeare's plays

Shakespeare wrote 37 plays, as well as some poetry (notably a collection of **sonnets**). His plays are listed below. They are loosely grouped by genre (**histories**, **tragedies**, **comedies** and **romances**), though this division is sometimes far from clear-cut (see *Watch out!* box on the opposite page). Approximate dates of composition are also given.

Histories

Henry VI Part One (1589–1590)
Henry VI Part Two (1590–1591)
Henry VI Part Three (1590–1591)
Richard III (1592–1593)
King John (1594–1596)
Richard II (1595)
Henry IV Part One (1596–1597)
Henry IV Part Two (1598)
Henry V (1599)
Henry VIII (1612–1613)

Tragedies

Titus Andronicus (1593–1594)
Romeo and Juliet (1595–1596)
Julius Caesar (1599)
Hamlet (1600–1601)
Othello (1604)
King Lear (1605)
Macbeth (1606)
Antony and Cleopatra (1606–1607)
Coriolanus (1607–1608)
Timon of Athens (1607–1608)

Comedies

The Comedy of Errors (1592–1594)
The Taming of the Shrew (1593–1594)
The Two Gentlemen of Verona (1594)
Love's Labour's Lost (1594–1595)
A Midsummer Night's Dream (1595–1596)
The Merchant of Venice (1596–1597)
The Merry Wives of Windsor (1597)
Much Ado About Nothing (1598–1599)
As You Like It (1599)
Troilus and Cressida (1601–1602)
Twelfth Night (1601–1602)
All's Well That Ends Well (1602–1603)
Measure for Measure (1604)

Romances

Pericles (1607–1608)
Cymbeline (1609–1610)
The Winter's Tale (1610–1611)
The Tempest (1611)

Histories

In the early years of his career Shakespeare mostly wrote **histories** and comedies. The majority of his history plays are divided into two groups of four, known as **tetralogies**. The first group includes the three parts of *Henry VI*, and *Richard III*. The second tetralogy comprises *Richard II*, the two parts of *Henry IV* and *Henry V*. Taken together, these plays chart the course of English history from 1400, when Richard II was overthrown, to 1485, when Henry VII (the first Tudor king) came to power.

For much of the period covered by the history plays, England was troubled by rebellion and civil disorder, including the Wars of the Roses. Tudor historians regarded the rightful king as God's representative on earth, and they viewed this turmoil as divine punishment for the removal of Richard II from the throne. According to this account of English history, order was finally restored with the arrival of the Tudor dynasty. When Shakespeare wrote these plays Elizabeth, a Tudor monarch, was on the throne, and it has been argued that Shakespeare's history plays support the orthodox views of his time, and are in effect Tudor propaganda. Other critics identify more subversive elements within the plays, which explore the ruthlessness and self-interest involved in achieving and retaining political power.

Comedies

Shakespeare's **comic plays** are generally romantic comedies in which the characters inhabit a make-believe world where unlikely coincidences, cases of mistaken identity and the wearing of improbable disguises are common. Love relationships are beset by difficulties, but by the end of the play these have usually been overcome and the emphasis is on reconciliation and harmony. However, all of this does not prevent many of Shakespeare's comedies having a serious edge.

Tragedies

The great **tragedies** written in the early years of the 17th century are usually considered the summit of Shakespeare's achievement. It is impossible to give a simple definition of a tragedy, but tragic plays usually have the following elements:

→ The tragic hero reaches a pinnacle of happiness and/or worldly success.
→ He then falls from this height and the play ends with his death.
→ His fall may be due to inner weakness (known as a **tragic flaw**), external circumstances (**fate**), or a combination of these.
→ The character has qualities that are admired by the audience, so that although his downfall may appear inevitable and even deserved, it also leaves us with a sense of loss.

Romances

Shakespeare's last plays are grouped together because they have certain features in common. Characters and settings are less realistic than in earlier plays: the **romances** have a fairy-tale quality, and myth and magic feature strongly. The central characters (such as Leontes in *The Winter's Tale*) are threatened by tragedy, but the plays always end on a lighter, happier note.

Exam preparation (30 minutes)

Which of the following categories does the Shakespeare play you are studying fall into: history, tragedy, comedy, romance? Does the play have elements in it which might be said to belong to one or more of the other categories? Give reasons for your answer.

Examples

Although *The Merchant of Venice* is classified as a comedy, the hatred between the Jews and the Christians in the play is chillingly real, and here as in other plays the 'happy' ending is decidedly ambiguous. In some plays the more disturbing elements are especially prominent, and these have been called **dark** or **problem comedies**: *Measure for Measure*, *All's Well That Ends Well* and *Troilus and Cressida*.

Take note

As a writer of tragedies, Shakespeare was working within a dramatic tradition (which also includes sub-genres, such as **revenge tragedy**), but this does not mean he adhered rigidly to a set of rules and conventions. The basic elements of tragedy may be present, but this does not mean his plays do not have great originality and, in their portrayal of characters, great psychological complexity.

Checkpoint 2

What are plays that combine elements of tragedy and comedy sometimes known as?

Shakespeare in context

This section considers the background to Shakespeare's plays: the historical context, and the literary and dramatic traditions within which he worked. Examiners will give you credit if you show an awareness of how contextual factors such as these influenced Shakespeare's plays.

Historical context

When Shakespeare wrote his plays England was ruled by **Elizabeth I** (who was queen from 1558 to 1603) and **James I** (who reigned from 1603 to 1625). At this time the monarch was still the centre of political power, but during James's rule in particular there was increasing **tension between parliament and the crown**. Eventually this would lead to the Civil War of 1642 and the execution of James's successor, Charles I. **Religion** was another source of division: England was officially a Protestant country but many wanted to restore it to Catholicism. It was a period of plots and conspiracies, such as the rebellion led by the Earl of Essex in 1601 and the gunpowder plot of 1605. This political turbulence and unrest is mirrored in the world of Shakespeare's plays, where **order is repeatedly under threat**. Shakespeare also exposes the weaknesses of those who exercise political power: his kings are not figures of godlike wisdom and authority but flawed individuals, plagued by fears and insecurities and acting in ways that are often morally questionable.

The Renaissance

Shakespeare lived during the **Renaissance**, a period of European history which roughly extends from the 14th to the 17th centuries. 'Renaissance' means rebirth or renewal, and the period is given this name because it was a time of transition between the medieval and the modern world. It was an era of dynamic change: power shifted from the church to the state, new lands were discovered, trade and commerce multiplied. Scientific discoveries and a spirit of restless intellectual enquiry meant that while confidence in a divinely ordered universe grew less, confidence in the energy and potential of the individual increased.

Literary context

The Renaissance was also a period of great artistic achievements. In England, this was especially evident in **literature**. Shakespeare was the most notable in a group of Elizabethan and Jacobean playwrights who, over a period of approximately 50 years straddling the 16th and 17th centuries, created what is usually considered English drama's golden age. Shakespeare's works include numerous features which are typical of the drama of his day. Knowledge of conventions such as these helps our understanding of the plays, but it is of course the use that Shakespeare makes of them that is important – and the ways in which he breaks with tradition.

Checkpoint 1

Explain as fully as you can what you understand by the term **context**.

Checkpoint 1

In Shakespeare's time there was a belief in the **divine right of kings**, though it was an idea that was increasingly questioned. What is meant by this expression?

Examples

Revenge was a recurring theme in the plays of Shakespeare's contemporaries, and is an important element in plays such as *Othello* and *Hamlet*. A stock figure in Jacobean tragedy was the **malcontent**, an embittered character who offers cynical commentaries on the actions of others. Iago in *Othello* is clearly a character in this tradition. There is more discussion of the dramatic conventions of Shakespeare's theatre in the section *Shakespeare in performance* (pages 132–133).

Shakespeare's theatre

The **theatres** of Shakespeare's time differed in many important respects from their modern equivalents. Although a few theatres were enclosed, most (like the **Globe Theatre**, where many of Shakespeare's plays were first performed), were open to the sky. Performances took place during the daytime and there was no artificial lighting. There was also no stage curtain and very little in the way of scenery or props. The actors did however wear rich, elaborate costumes. The rectangular stage jutted out into the body of the theatre and was partially protected from the elements by a canopy. Some of the audience stood around the three exposed sides of the stage; other, wealthier spectators paid extra to sit in one of the three covered tiers or galleries.

Critical approaches to Shakespeare

Since they were first performed, Shakespeare's plays have been interpreted by critics in many different ways. Notable pre-20th-century critics of Shakespeare include **Samuel Johnson** in the 18th century and **Samuel Taylor Coleridge** in the 19th. The major critic of the early 20th century was **A.C. Bradley**, whose approach was very much **character-based**. He wrote sympathetically about Shakespeare's tragic heroes, stressing their nobility of spirit and trying to identify the tragic flaws or weaknesses that led to their downfall. This approach has remained influential, but the main criticisms of Bradley are that he wrote about the characters as if they were real people, and that he ignored other important aspects of the plays.

A major shift in criticism occurred in the closing decades of the 20th century, when there began to be a strong emphasis on the **social, political and historical contexts** of Shakespeare's plays, and on how the plays have **different meanings** for audiences from different times.

One of the critical movements that emerged in the later 20th century was **feminism**. Feminist approaches to Shakespeare focus on the portrayal of women characters in the plays. Elizabethan and Jacobean society was strongly **patriarchal** (male-dominated) and women had limited status and power. Some critics argue that Shakespeare's plays reflect and endorse the view that women are inferior. Other feminist commentators believe Shakespeare is more sympathetic to women, and more critical of traditional sexist attitudes.

New historicism and **cultural materialism** are schools of criticism that emphasise the importance of **historical contexts**, identifying connections between the plays and political events and documents of Shakespeare's time.

Take note

The audience for the plays is likely to have been socially very mixed, from the '**groundlings**' who paid a penny to stand to the more affluent seated spectators. The design of the theatres also meant that the actors were physically very close to the audience, and it is important to remember this when considering some of the dramatic techniques employed by Shakespeare – for example, his use of **soliloquies**.

Links

For more on the performance aspects of Shakespeare's plays, see pages 132–133.

Action point

If you get the opportunity, try to see a Shakespeare production at the reconstructed Globe Theatre in London.

Take note

New historicist criticism is mostly American and usually regards Shakespeare as essentially a supporter of the status quo. **Cultural materialism** is associated with a group of British critics. It focuses more on how the plays demonstrate the vulnerability of those in power, and the existence of resistance to the authority of the state. It also looks at how changes in society cause Shakespeare's plays to be understood and interpreted in different ways.

Exam preparation (30 minutes)

Critics have often commented on the tension between order and disorder in Shakespeare's plays. In what ways is this evident in the play that you are studying?

119

Shakespeare's language 1

Checkpoint 1

Why did the way plays were staged in Shakespeare's day mean that language was especially important?

If you study a Shakespeare play as part of your AS/A2 course, you will be expected to pay particularly close attention to the **language** that Shakespeare uses. Many of the language features discussed elsewhere in the book are found in Shakespeare, but some of the features that are of particular relevance are outlined over the next few pages.

Blank verse

Shakespeare generally writes in **verse**, but parts of his plays use **prose**.

The particular form of verse Shakespeare favours is known as **blank verse**. This consists of unrhymed lines of poetry, with an arrangement of stressed and unstressed syllables known as the **iambic pentameter**. This means there are five pairs of syllables, with the second syllable in each pair stressed – as in the opening line of *The Merchant of Venice*:

> In *sooth* I *know* not *why* I *am* so *sad*

Links

For more on **blank verse** in English poetry, see page 62.

Blank verse was the usual medium for Elizabethan and Jacobean drama, and was the commonest metre in English poetry for several hundred years (it was first used in England in the middle of the 16th century). Shakespeare often uses the pattern of stressed syllables to place **emphasis** on important or emotive words. In the following example, again from *The Merchant of Venice*, Shylock describes the prejudice Antonio has against him because he is a Jewish moneylender; note how the metre stresses the words *spat*, *spurned* and *dog*:

The jargon

In poetic metre, a single metrical unit or group of syllables is known as a **foot** (in the case of the iambic pentameter, this means a pair of syllables).

> Fair sir, you spat on me on Wednesday last,
> You spurned me such a day, another time
> You called me dog

Varying the metre

If Shakespeare kept rigidly to a strict iambic pentameter his plays would sound repetitive and monotonous. Instead, he includes **variations** on the metre. One way of varying the metre is to **alter the expected pattern of stressed and unstressed syllables**. In this line from *Hamlet*, extra stressed syllables help to convey Hamlet's desperation as he wishes that he were dead:

Take note

This line from *Hamlet* has a powerful beginning as it opens with a stressed syllable, immediately reversing the usual pattern. It also has three successive stressed syllables in the middle of the line, before ending with two standard pairs of unstressed–stressed syllables.

> O that this *too too sul*lied *flesh* would *melt*

Another variation is to **alter the expected number of syllables**, by having more or less than ten. This line from *The Tempest* has eleven:

> There's nothing ill can dwell in such a temple

Shakespeare also sometimes breaks the regularity of the metre by **dividing a single line between two or more speakers**, as in this example from *Othello*:

Take note

The reason for dividing a line between speakers so that there is a rapid exchange of dialogue depends on the **context**: it may contribute to a sense of excitement, speed or tension, or may make a passage of conversation seem more natural and spontaneous. In this case, Desdemona's rapid response shows that she is astonished at Emilia's suggestion that she might be prepared to consider committing adultery.

> **Emilia:** Why, would not you?
> **Desdemona:** No, by this heavenly light!

Note how the arrangement of the words on the page (Desdemona's speech begins over to the right) indicates that these speeches make up a single line of verse rather than two lines of prose. When this happens it means that the second speaker responds immediately to the first.

Prose

●●●

Shakespeare's earliest plays, where the language tends to be more formal and artificial, contain very little **prose**, but in his later plays Shakespeare alternates much more frequently between prose and verse. Broadly speaking, there is a tendency for the **aristocratic characters** who feature in the main plots of the play to speak **verse**, while the **lower class characters**, who are more likely to be involved in the less important sub-plots, speak **prose**. In *Measure for Measure*, Angelo, Isabella, Claudio and the Duke usually speak in verse, while Pompey, Mistress Overdone, Elbow, Lucio and Froth usually speak in prose. Prose also tends to be used for **comic scenes** and **informal conversations**, while verse is used for scenes that are more serious and dramatic. However, such generalisations need to be treated with caution. Shakespeare often moves freely from verse to prose and back again, and the same characters can sometimes be speaking prose one minute and verse the next. **Context** is usually key: if you are studying an extract, ask yourself why it might be appropriate for these particular characters to speak in verse or prose in this particular situation.

Shakespeare's lexis

●●●

Because Shakespeare's plays were written 400 years ago, they inevitably contain much **archaic lexis** – that is, expressions that have since fallen out of use. The first 20 lines of *The Winter's Tale*, for example, include words such as *whereon*, *betwixt*, *beseech*, *verily* and *insufficience*. Shakespeare also uses words and expressions that still exist but which over time have acquired **changed meanings**. In the opening scene of *The Winter's Tale*, *unspeakable* means 'too marvellous for words' (the opposite of course of its usual meaning today).

At the same time, Shakespeare's approach to language was innovative and experimental, and many words we are familiar with today have their **first recorded use** in his plays. Examples include *assassination*, *dislocate*, *premeditated*, *reliance* and *submerged*. He also had an inventive attitude towards **word classes**, often turning nouns into verbs, as when Cleopatra dismisses Caesar's promises to her by telling her attendants '*He words me, girls, he words me*'. It is not an exaggeration to say that Shakespeare helped to shape the development of English, not least through the huge number of everyday expressions that originate in his plays: *a tower of strength*, *more sinned against than sinning*, *the long and short of it*, *more in sorrow than in anger*, *it's Greek to me*, *refusing to budge an inch* and many more.

> **Checkpoint 2**
>
> Explain the terms **main plot** and **sub-plot**.

> **Examiner's secrets**
>
> To help your understanding of Shakespeare's language, you should make use of the notes and glossary that are probably included in the edition of the play you are studying. As soon as you have an opportunity, watch a video or stage performance of the play, or listen to an audio recording of it. Audio tapes are useful because you can read the play as you are listening, and the way lines are delivered will add to your understanding of them. You should also begin by trying to get a general grasp of what each scene is about (the plot summaries included in most study guides on the plays can help here), not worrying too much if particular words or lines (or even whole speeches!) leave you puzzled. You can then gradually develop a more detailed understanding of the play as you continue studying it.

> **Exam preparation (45 minutes)**
>
> Write an essay that explores the use of verse and prose in the Shakespeare play that you are studying. Try to explain why certain characters and scenes mainly use verse, while others use prose.

Shakespeare's language 2

This second section on Shakespeare's language considers Shakespeare's use of **imagery**, **repetition** and a variety of **rhetorical techniques**.

Links

For more on imagery, see pages 56–57.

Checkpoint 1

Explain the difference between a **simile** and a **metaphor**.

Examples

In *The Winter's Tale* images of nature and growth mirror the play's themes of regeneration and reconciliation. Images of melting and dissolution in *Antony and Cleopatra* reflect Antony's tragic disintegration: *Authority melts from me, The crown o'the earth doth melt* and so on.

Take note

Also look for words and phrases that have **hidden layers of meaning**. There may be **dramatic irony**, which occurs when what characters say has an additional significance because of something that happens elsewhere in the play; the characters themselves are unaware of the hidden significance. Othello's declaration of love for Desdemona is an example: *Perdition catch my soul/But I do love thee! And when I love thee not,/Chaos is come again.* Othello means that if he ever stopped loving Desdemona, it would be as if the world had returned to the chaos that existed before Creation. What Othello does not realise (though the audience do) is that Iago is about to destroy his love for Desdemona. By the end of the scene Othello has indeed descended into mental and emotional chaos.

Imagery

The term **imagery** is sometimes used to refer to language that appeals to any of our senses, but often it refers more specifically to the use of **similes** and **metaphors** – that is, to language that is **figurative** rather than **literal**. When Othello, planning to kill his wife Desdemona, tells Iago *Get me some poison* he is speaking literally, but when earlier in the play Iago urges Roderigo to wake up Brabantio and *poison his delight*, the word *poison* is used figuratively. When imagery occurs you should consider its effect – why has Shakespeare used this comparison? In this case, the *poison* image confirms that Iago is a malign, destructive influence, the enemy of order and goodness.

As well as considering the effect of individual images, you should look for **patterns** in the imagery of the play you are studying. It is likely that certain images are repeated. It may be that a **character** is strongly associated with a particular kind of image. In *Othello*, Iago often uses animal imagery when describing the other characters, emphasising his contempt for humanity. Repeated (or **recurring**) images can also reflect important **themes** in the play. Images of darkness recur in *Macbeth*, suggesting the evil that overtakes Scotland after Macbeth's murder of Duncan.

Repetition of key words

Another feature of Shakespeare's style is that in any one play there are likely to be certain **words** that occur with unusual frequency. In *Othello*, for instance, the words *lie*, *honest* and *jealous* occur repeatedly. Often, as here, the words have a clear link to the central themes of the play, but as they are repeated they can also acquire different shades of meaning. Another example is the repetition of the word *world* in *Antony and Cleopatra*. On one level this reminds us that Antony and Caesar are rulers of a great empire, and that the power struggle they become engaged in is of momentous political significance. At the same time, the word is used to assert the magnificence of Antony and Cleopatra's love, as when Antony proclaims he wants *the world* to know *we stand up peerless*.

Rhetoric

Rhetoric is the art of speaking or writing persuasively. From the 12th century onwards books on literary composition were written, advising writers on literary conventions and techniques they should use. Shakespeare and his contemporaries were very much aware of these techniques, and made use of them in their works. They include:

Parallelism

Many rhetorical techniques involve some kind of repetition – of sounds, individual words and grammatical structures. When grammatical structures are repeated, this is known as **parallelism**. An example occurs when Othello describes to the Senate the stories he told Desdemona during their courtship:

> Wherein I spoke of most disastrous chances,
> Of moving accidents by flood and field,
> Of hairbreadth scapes i'th' imminent deadly breach

The parallelism is created here by having a series of noun phrases beginning *of* . . .

Antithesis

This is the contrasting of direct opposites. Here is an example from *Romeo and Juliet*:

> Why then, O brawling love, O loving hate,
> O any thing, of nothing first created:
> O heavy lightness, serious vanity

Wordplay

As the term itself suggests, **wordplay** involves playing around with the sounds or meanings of words. Wordplay involving meaning produces **puns**, as in Mercutio's macabre joke as he is dying in *Romeo and Juliet*:

> Ask for me tomorrow, and you will find me a grave man

Hyperbole

This is the use of exaggeration. *Antony and Cleopatra* has numerous examples, such as Cleopatra's description of Antony:

> His legs bestrid the ocean, his rear'd arm
> Crested the world

The difference between Shakespeare and many of his contemporaries is that whereas they often used these techniques mechanically, as if they were merely following the rules of fine writing, Shakespeare (especially in the middle and later plays) *used* the techniques because they served his artistic purpose. Mercutio's pun, for example, is suited to his character because from the beginning of the play he is presented as a rather self-consciously clever and witty character. Shakespeare was aware that rhetoric could seem artificial and contrived, and in some of his plays he parodied those who used it excessively. He also grew less dependent on conventional rhetorical techniques as his career developed, though he never abandoned them completely.

Links

Examples of rhetorical devices involving sound include **alliteration**, **assonance** and **onomatopoeia**. For more on these devices see page 65.

Checkpoint 2

What impression of Antony is created by this description of him?

Examples

There are examples of rhetoric in Shakespeare's last major play, *The Tempest*. Ferdinand describes Miranda as *Admired Miranda,/Indeed the top of admiration, worth/What's dearest to the world!* Here Ferdinand begins by playing on the similar sounds of *Miranda* and *Admired*, then uses hyperbole to continue his praise of her. The stylised language suits the portrayal of Ferdinand as someone who is gracious and courteous.

Exam preparation (30 minutes)

Identify and discuss patterns in the imagery of the Shakespeare play you are studying. What kinds of images tend to recur, and why?

Shakespeare's language 3

This final section on the distinctive features of Shakespeare's language considers **grammar** and **phonology**. The role of language in portraying **character** is also discussed.

Grammar

Syntax

One of the difficulties the modern reader has in understanding Shakespeare is that sentences are often **longer** and more **complex** than we would usually find today. Another barrier to understanding is that **syntax** is sometimes very **compressed**, with constructions that dispense with conjunctions and prepositions. **Word order** can also be a problem: the elements that make up a sentence are often in an unexpected sequence. This is partly because Shakespeare moved words around in order to conform to the pattern of stressed and unstressed syllables demanded by the **iambic pentameter**, and partly because in Shakespeare's time word order was in any case freer than today.

There are also grammatical constructions in Shakespeare which have since become **archaic**. An example is **putting an adjective after a noun** rather than the other way round. When Othello speaks of the vast caves and empty deserts he has encountered on his travels, he refers to *antres vast and deserts idle*, not to 'vast antres and idle deserts'. This construction is no longer in use today, though it survives in a few traditional expressions such as *little boy blue*. Shakespeare also used the adjective–noun construction that we are more familiar with: in the very next line Othello refers to *Rough quarries*.

Another archaic construction commonly used by Shakespeare involves **placing a modifier before a determiner**. In *The Winter's Tale* Hermione addresses Leontes as *Gentle my lord*, not *My gentle lord*.

Thou and *you*

Another archaic feature of Shakespeare's language is his use of the **second person pronoun *thou***. In earlier English *thou* had been singular and *you* plural, but by Shakespeare's time *you* was also in use as a singular pronoun. However, there was an important difference in how these singular pronouns were used. *Thou* was more intimate and informal, and was also used towards those of lower rank, whereas *you* was more formal and respectful. In *The Merchant of Venice* Portia always addresses her maidservant Nerissa as *thou*, while Nerissa always addresses Portia as *you* – a clear indication of their difference in status. Sometimes the choice of pronoun can be revealing: when in *The Winter's Tale* Paulina announces the apparent death of Hermione she shows her anger towards Leontes by addressing him as *thou*, even though he is her king.

Links

The **iambic pentameter** was explained on page 120.

Take note

In time you will get used to some of these unusual ways of constructing phrases and sentences. You should also of course make use of the notes in your edition, which will usually explain the more difficult parts of the text. You may find it reassuring (or the opposite!) to know that there are many passages in Shakespeare whose exact meaning continues to be hotly disputed.

Archaic inflections

Inflections are grammatical word endings. Shakespeare uses some that have now generally disappeared from English, such as the *-th* and *-st* endings in *hath* and *hast*, and *doth* and *dost*. The modern forms *has* and *does* were increasingly being used in Shakespeare's time, and this is reflected in his plays, where they are used alongside the older forms.

Phonology

You should never forget when studying Shakespeare's plays that the language was written to be **heard**. As a result, **phonological features** such as those described earlier in the book (see pages 64–65) are especially important. Shakespeare makes regular use of devices such as **alliteration**, **assonance**, **sibilance** and **onomatopoeia**. **Rhythmic effects**, **stress** and **intonation** are also important (see the earlier discussion of blank verse in Shakespeare, page 120). Shakespeare used **rhyme** quite sparingly (except in the earlier plays), though it sometimes features in more formal set-piece speeches (such as prologues and epilogues to the plays). **Rhyming couplets** are also sometimes used at the ends of scenes, to create a sense of concluding a phase of the action.

Language and character

Shakespeare uses language to give his characters **distinctive individual voices**. We have already in this chapter noted one or two examples of this – Mercutio's enjoyment of wordplay in *Romeo and Juliet*, Iago's use of animal imagery in *Othello*. As well as noting the particular features of language that are associated with specific characters, you should also consider how character **change** and **development** is expressed through language. When Leontes in *The Winter's Tale* is seized by an irrational jealousy, his language becomes agitated and confused:

> There have been,
> (Or I am much deceiv'd) cuckolds ere now,
> And many a man there is (even at this present,
> Now, while I speak this) holds his wife by th'arm,
> That little thinks she has been sluic'd in's absence

When the death of his son Mamillius, and the supposed death of his wife Hermione, shock him into repentance, his language becomes quieter and more measured:

> Once a day I'll visit
> The chapel where they lie, and tears shed there
> Shall be my recreation.

Links

For more on **inflections**, see page 18.

Take note

It has been suggested that *has* and *does* were less prestigious, and consequently tended to be used by Shakespeare in the speech of comic, lower class characters, but the evidence for this is not completely convincing.

Checkpoint 1

What is a **rhyming couplet**?

Checkpoint 2

What is the term for the way language is used by a particular individual?

Exam preparation (20 minutes)   answer: page 136

Text A on page 134 is from *Othello*. Iago and Cassio are discussing Othello's recent marriage to Desdemona. In what ways does the language of the two speakers suggest differences in their characters?

Dialogue in Shakespeare

Although **soliloquies** are an important feature of Shakespeare's plays (see page 130), most of the text of each play is made up of **dialogue**. This section identifies some important points to consider when you are studying passages of Shakespearean dialogue.

Shakespeare's dialogue and real conversation

Differences

At some point in your AS or A2 course you will study transcripts of real-life conversation. It will soon become obvious to you that there are many differences between **scripted dialogue** and genuine **spontaneous conversation**. In conversation there are far more hesitations, repetitions, pauses, interruptions and simultaneous or overlapping speech. Grammatical constructions are often disjointed and may occasionally be incoherent. Even when dialogue is intended to sound realistic (as is often the case with film and television scripts), it is likely to be more organised and more polished than actual speech. Scripted dialogue also has an **intensity** usually lacking in everyday conversation, because the writer will have chosen the words spoken by characters with deliberate care, using the dialogue to reveal something significant about the characters, their relationships or their situations.

Rhetorical features

The above points apply especially to Shakespeare, who was writing at a time when dialogue was not expected to be naturalistic (true to life). For one thing, many of Shakespeare's speeches are in **blank verse**. Also, as explained on pages 122–123, Shakespeare and his contemporaries employed a range of **rhetorical devices** in their writing. This sometimes results in dialogue that is obviously far removed from real conversation (see the example from *Romeo and Juliet* alongside). This kind of rhetorical patterning appears less frequently in Shakespeare's middle and later plays, but the important point to be aware of is that dialogue does not need to be realistic to be effective. Shakespeare used (and also stretched and remoulded) the conventions of his day to produce dialogue of tremendous dramatic power.

Similarities

Of course, there are also respects in which scripted dialogue *does* resemble genuine conversation. Speakers question, order, exclaim, dominate and so on. There are also passages in Shakespeare where he is clearly trying to capture the rhythms and vocabulary of natural speech. This means that many of the features you might look for if you were analysing a transcript of spontaneous conversation remain relevant if you are analysing a Shakespeare extract.

Links

The similarities and differences between scripted dialogue and real conversation are also discussed on pages 104–107.

Checkpoint 1

What broad term is used for interruptions to the flow of a person's speech (hesitations, repetitions etc.)?

Example

This example of rhetorical patterning in dialogue is from *Romeo and Juliet*:

Juliet: I have forgot why I did call thee back.

Romeo: Let me stand here till thou remember it.

Juliet: I shall forget, to have thee still stand there,
Remembering how I love thy company.

Romeo: And I'll stay, to have thee still forget,
Forgetting any other home but this.

Links

For more on the elements of conversation, see pages 32–33.

Analysing Shakespearean dialogue: a checklist

Listed below are some of the key aspects that might be relevant if you are examining dialogue from a Shakespeare play.

Context

Begin by considering the **context** the conversation has in the play:

→ **When** does it take place? (What has led up to it? Is this some kind of turning-point in the play?)
→ **Where** does it take place? (Is the location significant? Is the conversation private or are there onlookers?)
→ **Who** is involved in the conversation? (What is their relationship? Are their differences of status?)
→ **What** are the speaker's purposes in the conversation? (Do their purposes conflict? Is one speaker trying to persuade or deceive the other?)

Interaction

Here you can consider aspects of conversational behaviour you will have studied elsewhere in the course:

→ How do the speakers **address** each other? (Do the modes of address used reflect their feelings towards one another? Or differences in status?)
→ How is **turn-taking** managed? (Does one character control or dominate the conversation? If so, how? Do they speak the most, initiate and change topics, use imperatives, ask questions?)
→ How do the characters **respond to each other**? (Do they contradict, misunderstand or ignore each other?)
→ Is there any **rhetorical patterning**? (What are the effects?)
→ How does the conversation **begin**, **develop** and **end**? (Note that you may only be looking at part of a conversation – but you can still consider how the mood or direction of the dialogue changes.)

Other aspects

It is important not to overlook all the other elements that are relevant to the study of any extract, whether it involves dialogue or not. In other words, you need to think about the **characters** and **themes** of the play and how these are created through the use of **language** (lexis, grammar, and so on). These additional elements are discussed in the sections on *Analysing Shakespeare extracts* (pages 128–131).

Links

Again, the sections on conversation earlier in the book should be helpful here. See pages 32–37.

Checkpoint 2

Explain why characters' use of *thou* or *you* to address each other might be significant.

Exam preparation (20 minutes)   answer: page 136

Text B on page 134 is from *The Winter's Tale*. In the extract, Paulina brings to Leontes the baby daughter that his wife Hermione has just given birth to. Hermione has been imprisoned by Leontes because he suspects her of adultery. Write an analysis of the conversation, explaining how Shakespeare uses dialogue to portray Leontes, Paulina and the relationship between them at this point in the play.

Analysing Shakespeare
extracts 1

In AS/A2 exams, questions on Shakespeare often involve the close analysis of extracts. The next two sections offer advice on answering extract-based questions.

Types of question ●●●

Depending on the specification you are taking, you may be asked to:

→ Comment closely on one or more extracts, showing in the course of your answer how they relate to the rest of the play.
→ Show how in given extracts Shakespeare transforms the characteristics of everyday talk to produce dramatic effects.
→ Select your own extracts for close comment, relating them to the play as a whole.

Most of the advice that follows is relevant to all these types of question, but in the exam you will obviously need to take careful note of what the question specifically asks you to do.

Context ●●●

Usually a good way to get started is to consider the **context** of the extract in relation to the play as a whole. Ask yourself *When*, *Where*, *Who* and *What*:

→ **When** in the play does the extract occur? What has led up to it? In broad terms, what is its importance to the development of the play's plot, characters or themes?
→ **Where** is the extract set? This is not necessarily significant, but it may be. In *Othello*, for example, there are important differences between the scenes set in Venice and the scenes set in Cyprus. Venice is associated with civilisation and order, whereas in Cyprus there is disorder and confusion. In *Antony and Cleopatra* the settings of Rome and Egypt contrast.
→ **Who** is speaking? Use your knowledge of the characters to help your understanding of the extract. If more than one character speaks, what kind of relationship do the characters involved have? Are there characters who do not speak but who are also present?
→ **What** is the extract about? You obviously need to understand what is going on at a very simple level (e.g. 'Leontes is asking Polixenes to extend his stay in Sicilia'), but you also need to consider the extract's deeper meaning and significance (see the advice on *Interpretation*, p. 131).

Using the language frameworks ●●●

You will be expected to comment closely on the **language** of the extract. To help you do this you should make use of the four key language frameworks: **lexis**, **grammar**, **phonology** and **discourse structure**.

Watch out!

Make sure you know the kind of question you are going to be set.

Links

The previous section on *Dialogue in Shakespeare* (pages 126–127) is especially relevant to the second of these three question types.

Examiner's secrets

A brief paragraph summarising these contextual elements is often a good way to begin an answer.

Links

Broader contextual aspects may also be relevant – see *Interpretation*, page 131.

Lexis

→ How does the vocabulary that is used reflect the personalities of individual **characters**, and the way they are feeling at this particular point in the play? In *Othello*, for instance, there is a contrast between the grand, elevated diction of Othello and the blunt, coarse language often associated with Iago.

→ What **imagery** (similes/metaphors) is present? What effect does it have? Are there links between any of the images that are present and the imagery found elsewhere in the play?

→ What about the effects achieved by **individual words**? What connotations do these words have? Are they shocking, evocative, revealing, powerful?

→ Are any **key words** present – words that are important because they occur repeatedly in the play as a whole (e.g. the word *honest* in *Othello*)?

→ Are any **rhetorical** devices used, such as repetition, antithesis, wordplay and hyperbole?

→ Is there any **dramatic irony**? Is anything said that has an extra significance, which the character speaking the words is unaware of?

→ How do the characters **address** each other? Are these modes of address significant or revealing?

→ Does the lexis in any way **echo** vocabulary found somewhere else in the play? Or are there **contrasts**?

Links

See pages 122–123 for more on the rhetorical devices found in Shakespeare.

Grammar

→ What **types of sentence** are used? Declarative, imperative, interrogative, exclamatory? How does this reflect the moods or attitudes of the speakers at particular points in the extract?

→ How **long** are the sentences? Are any especially long, or especially short? If so, what effect does this have?

→ Are any effects achieved by **word order**? Are any particular words or phrases foregrounded (made to stand out), for example by placing them at the beginning or end of lines and sentences?

→ Is there any kind of **rhetorical** patterning in the way sentences are organised – for example, parallelism?

→ How do any of these grammatical elements reflect **themes** of the play, or aspects of the **characters** who are speaking? In *The Tempest*, for instance, Prospero is a figure of authority and as a result often uses imperative sentences.

Checkpoint 1

Words and phrases can also be foregrounded by **inverted syntax**. What is inverted syntax?

Checkpoint 2

Explain the term **parallelism**.

Exam preparation

There are two specimen Shakespeare extract questions at the end of the next section, on page 131.

Analysing Shakespeare extracts 2

This second section on Shakespeare extract questions looks at two other language frameworks (**phonology** and **discourse structure**), at what you might say about the **staging** of an extract, and at other factors to consider when you offer your **interpretation** of the extract.

Phonology

Checkpoint 1

Explain the terms **assonance** and **sibilance**.

→ Are any **phonological devices** such as alliteration, onomatopoeia, assonance and sibilance used? (Remember you should only mention these if you are confident they have a particular effect, and you can explain what this effect is.)

→ Is **blank verse** used? If so, does the metre cause significant words to be stressed? Is the metre disturbed or altered at any point, and if so why does this happen? If the metre is steady and regular, why might this be appropriate?

Checkpoint 2

What collective term is used for spoken language features such as intonation, pace and volume?

→ How would **intonation** influence the effect that the extract has? With what tone of voice should particular words or lines be delivered? Are there lines that could be said in different ways? In *The Winter's Tale*, when Hermione succeeds in persuading Polixenes to stay in Sicilia, her husband Leontes comments, *At my request he would not.* Depending on how it is delivered, this could appear a straightforward observation or a line suggesting deep suspicion.

→ Is **pace** significant at any point? Are particular lines said especially quickly or slowly? Are there any changes in pace?

→ If the extract were heard in performance, what part would **volume** play? Would some lines be shouted, or said especially quietly?

Discourse structure

The jargon

Discourse structure refers to the overall form and structure of the extract.

→ Is the extract a passage of **dialogue**, a single **speech** by a character (with other characters present), or a **soliloquy** (a speech delivered by a character alone on stage)?

→ If it is **dialogue**, how do the characters **interact**? (For more on this, see *Dialogue in Shakespeare*, pages 126–127.

→ If it is a **soliloquy**, what is revealed about the character's innermost thoughts? What kind of relationship does the character have with the audience? Often soliloquies make the audience feel closer to the character concerned.

Example

Iago's soliloquies in *Othello* make us aware of his villainous intentions, but we are also likely to admire his wit and his incisive intelligence.

→ Are there any **asides**? These occur when a character says something the other characters do not hear. They can serve a variety of purposes: characters may share private jokes with the audience, reveal what they are secretly thinking or make candid observations about what is taking place on stage.

→ Is the extract **prose** or **poetry**, or a mixture of the two? You may be able to comment on the likely reason for this (see page 121).

→ How does the extract **start**, **develop** and **end**? Are there any changes of mood or atmosphere? Does the extract build to a climax?

Staging

→ How would the extract be **presented on stage**? Try to visualise it (if you have seen a performance or watched a video of the play, this will obviously help).

→ Are there any **stage directions**? Note that sometimes characters' actions are indicated by what is said rather than by explicit stage directions.

→ Are the characters' **actions** in any way significant? What impact do they have on the audience?

→ Where are the characters **positioned** on stage? What does this tell us?

→ Do **sound effects** (such as music) play a part in the scene?

Interpretation

Here are some additional points you should bear in mind when interpreting the meaning and significance of the extract:

→ Don't just 'tell the story'. You need to **comment** on the characters' words and actions.

→ Focus on how the **language** of the extract develops our understanding of **characters and their relationships**, and of the **themes** in the play.

→ Consider the **dramatic effect** that an extract has. Note that 'dramatic' here doesn't have its everyday sense of exciting and out of the ordinary. It refers to the effects that are achieved when the play is performed in front of an audience.

→ Remember to **make connections with the rest of the play**, especially if the question you are answering specifies that you should do this. Look for similarities and contrasts with other parts of the play, and think about the significance of the extract in relation to what has preceded it and what happens later.

→ Are any aspects of the extract open to **alternative interpretations**? It might be possible (if relevant) to refer to one or more of the **critical approaches** to Shakespeare outlined on page 119.

→ It is important to consider the **context** the extract has within the play as a whole (see page 128). However, it may also be relevant to refer to the play's broader social, political or historical **contexts** (see page 118).

Exam preparation (45 minutes)   answer: page 137

Texts C and **D** on page 135 are from *The Tempest* and *Measure for Measure* respectively. Choose one of the extracts and answer the following question on it:

Comment closely on Shakespeare's use of language in this extract. Develop your answer by discussing the significance of the extract in relation to the play as a whole.

Examiner's secrets

The main focus of your answer should usually be on the **language** of the extract, but you will also be given credit if you show you are aware the extract was written to be performed on stage.

Watch out!

Remember that when you are writing about plays you should refer to the *audience* rather than to the *reader*.

Examples

The main dramatic effect of an extract might be to cause amusement, build a sense of anticipation, create an atmosphere of conflict or confusion and so on.

Take note

If you are not studying either of these plays, you could still attempt an analysis of the language of Text C, which is the beginning of *The Tempest*. Develop your answer by commenting on the effectiveness of the extract as an opening to a play.

Shakespeare in performance

Links

See page 119 for more on the theatres of Shakespeare's day.

Although you will rightly spend much of your time reading your Shakespeare text, it is important to remember that Shakespeare's plays were written to be performed on stage. This section considers how the plays were influenced by the performance conventions of Elizabethan and Jacobean theatre, and also how producers and performers today are able to offer contrasting interpretations of individual plays.

The importance of language

As explained on page 119, theatres in Shakespeare's time did not have artificial lighting and also made very little use of scenery or props. In contrast, today's dramatists can if they choose achieve effects through the use of lighting and elaborate stage sets, as well as technological devices such as revolving stages, back-projection and computer-generated images. Because these resources were not available to Elizabethan dramatists, **language** was crucial to the creation of mood, atmosphere and a sense of location.

You should look out for examples of this in the play you are studying. In *The Tempest*, for instance, the island where the play is set is created in our imaginations by the **visual imagery** of passages such as this:

> So I charmed their ears,
> That, calf-like, they my lowing followed, through
> Toothed briers, sharp furzes, pricking goss, and thorns,
> Which entered their frail shins. At last I left them
> I' th' filthy-mantled pool beyond your cell,
> There dancing up to th'chins, that the foul lake
> O'erstunk their feet.

Checkpoint 1

Apart from our sense of sight, what other senses does this description appeal to? What are these kinds of image known as?

Visual and aural effects

Although Elizabethan theatres made limited use of scenery, visual effects could still be achieved by the characters' **costumes** and by their **actions**. Shakespeare's plays are often enlivened by dynamic events such as swordfights, battle-scenes, dances and processions. Sometimes actions are understated but still powerful, as in the chilling moment when Othello and Iago kneel together and commit themselves to vengeance on Desdemona and Cassio. The main sound effect was the use of **music** (again *The Tempest*, where music helps to create the island's magical atmosphere, is a good example of this).

Examiner's secrets

Although in writing about Shakespeare your primary focus will usually be on the language of the plays, you will also be given credit if you show an awareness of effects that are dependent on the play being seen in performance.

Dramatic conventions

Some other dramatic conventions of Shakespeare's time are worth noting:

→ The use of **soliloquies** and **asides**. The closeness of spectators to the stage meant that characters could share jokes with the audience, and give the impression of confiding in them.

Checkpoint 2

Explain the difference between a **soliloquy** and an **aside**.

→ The occasional use of **prologues** and **epilogues** to begin and end plays.

→ The use of **blank verse** and **rhetoric** – dialogue was generally not meant to appear realistic (see pages 120 and 122–123).

→ The use of certain stock **character types**, such as the tragic hero, the revenger and the malcontent. Shakespeare drew on tradition and convention here, but still created characters who are individuals rather than stereotypes.

→ The **absence of act or scene divisions**. These did not exist in the versions of Shakespeare's plays printed during his lifetime. The divisions inserted by later editors mark natural breaks in the action, but contemporary productions of Shakespeare's plays would have been faster and more free-flowing than we are used to today.

→ The exclusive use of **male actors**, even for female roles. It is thought that women's parts were usually played by apprentice actors in their early teens (though mature characters such as Lady Macbeth and Cleopatra were probably played by older apprentices).

Performance and interpretation

Although you should try to imagine how the play you are studying would first have been presented, you should also think about the effects achieved by more recent productions. Try to see a performance of the play, ideally in a theatre but alternatively on video. You should consider how the producer and the actors have **interpreted** the play, and particular roles within it. Shakespeare's plays contain many passages that are **ambiguous**, where the nature of what occurs, or the response Shakespeare intended us to have, is open to debate.

The closing scene of *Measure for Measure* is an example. The Duke proposes to Isabella, who says nothing and remains silent for the rest of the play. Clearly a wide range of possible non-verbal reactions are available to the actress playing Isabella – should she look pleased, uncomfortable, angry?

More broadly, a producer can aim for specific effects by setting the play in a particular historical period (including the present day) or by emphasising particular aspects of it. Productions of *Othello*, for example, sometimes see the hero as primarily a victim of a racist society, and highlight this by changing the play's setting.

Links

See page 119 for more on how Shakespeare's plays are open to a variety of interpretations.

Exam preparation (45 minutes)

Write an essay on the opening scene of the Shakespeare play you are studying, discussing how the staging of the scene might contribute to its overall effect. You might refer to productions you have seen, or to how you would choose to stage the play yourself.

Specimen texts

Take note

The question for this text is on page 125.

The texts below are for use with the practice exam questions for this chapter.

Text A

Cassio: Welcome, Iago. We must to the watch.

Iago: Not this hour, lieutenant; 'tis not yet ten o'th'clock. Our general cast us thus early for the love of his Desdemona; who let us not therefore blame. He hath not yet made wanton the night with her, and she is sport for Jove.

Cassio: She's a most exquisite lady.

Iago: And, I'll warrant her, full of game.

Cassio: Indeed, she's a most fresh and delicate creature.

Iago: What an eye she has! Methinks it sounds a parley to provocation.

Cassio: An inviting eye; and yet methinks right modest.

Iago: And when she speaks, is it not an alarum to love?

Cassio: She is indeed perfection.

Iago: Well, happiness to their sheets!

Take note

The question for this text is on page 127.

Text B

Paulina: Good my liege, I come,
And I beseech you, hear me, who professes
Myself your loyal servant, your physician,
Your most obedient counsellor, yet that dares
Less appear so in comforting your evils
Than such as most seem yours: I say, I come
From your good queen.

Leontes: Good queen!

Paulina: Good queen, my lord, good queen; I say, good queen;
And would by combat make her good, so were I
A man, the worst about you.

Leontes: Force her hence.

Paulina: Let him that makes but trifles of his eyes
First hand me: on mine own accord I'll off;
But first I'll do my errand. The good queen,
For she is good, hath brought you forth a daughter:
Here 'tis; commends it to your blessing. [*Laying down the child.*]

Leontes: Out!
A mankind witch! Hence with her, out o'door:
A most intelligencing bawd!

Paulina: Not so;
I am as ignorant in that as you
In so entitling me, and no less honest
Than you are mad; which is enough, I'll warrant,
As this world goes, to pass for honest.

Text C

On a ship at sea. A tempestuous noise of thunder and lightning heard.
Enter a Shipmaster *and a* Boatswain *severally.*

Master: Boatswain!

Boatswain: Here, master: what cheer?

Master: Good, speak to the mariners: fall to't yarely, or we run
ourselves aground: bestir, bestir. [*Exit.*]

Enter Mariners

Boatswain: Heigh, my hearts! Cheerly, cheerly, my hearts! Yare, yare!
Take in the topsail. Tend to the master's whistle. – Blow,
till thou burst thy wind, if room enough!

Enter Alonso, Sebastian, Antonio, Ferdinand, Gonzalo, *and others.*

Alonso: Good boatswain, have care. Where's the master? Play the
men.

Boatswain: I pray now, keep below.

Antonio: Where is the master, boatswain?

Boatswain: Do you not hear him? You mar our labour: keep your
cabins: you do assist the storm.

Gonzalo: Nay, good, be patient.

Boatswain: When the sea is. Hence! What cares these roarers for the
name of king? To cabin: silence! Trouble us not.

Take note

The question for this text is on page 131.

Text D

Angelo: What's this? What's this? Is this her fault or mine?
The tempter or the tempted, who sins most? Ha!
Not she; nor doth she tempt: but it is I,
That, lying by the violet in the sun,
Do as the carrion does, not as the flower,
Corrupt with virtuous season. Can it be
That modesty may more betray our sense
Than woman's lightness? Having waste ground enough,
Shall we desire to raze the sanctuary,
And pitch our evils there? O, fie, fie, fie!
What dost thou, or what art thou, Angelo?
Dost thou desire her foully for those things
That make her good? O, let her brother live!
Thieves for their robbery have authority
When judges steal themselves. What! do I love her,
That I desire to hear her speak again,
And feast upon her eyes? What is't I dream on?

Take note

The question for this text is on page 131.

Answers
Shakespeare

Shakespeare: an overview

Checkpoints

1 A sonnet is a poem of 14 lines, usually conforming to a set rhyme scheme.
2 Tragicomedies.

Shakespeare in context

Checkpoints

1 On one level, the context of an extract (e.g. from a Shakespeare play) means such things as where it comes in the play, what has led up to it, what follows it, and how it is similar to or different from other parts of the play. At the same time, the context of a literary work refers to such external influences as the historical period in which it was produced, the kind of society that existed at the time, the life of the author and so on.
2 This is the belief that the king derived his authority from God, and in effect was God's chosen representative. Rebellion against the rightful king was therefore a challenge to divine order.

Shakespeare's language 1

Checkpoints

1 The absence of scenery meant that language was correspondingly more important in terms of evoking a setting and creating an appropriate atmosphere.
2 The main plot is the main storyline of a play. The sub-plot is another storyline running alongside it, usually involving a group of subsidiary characters.

Shakespeare's language 2

Checkpoints

1 A simile is a comparison that uses the words *like* or *as*. A metaphor is a comparison that goes one stage further and implies that something actually *is* something else – what is said is not literally true.
2 The description has connotations of grandeur and magnificence. It reflects Antony's status as a leader of the Roman Empire, but also Cleopatra's belief that as a human being he was extraordinary and without equal. Antony has a genuine heroic stature in the play, but he is also flawed and Cleopatra's hyperbolic description has an element of unreality. A few lines later, she asks Dolabella, *Think you there was, or might be, such a man/As this I dream'd of?* Significantly, Dolabella replies, *Gentle madam, no.*

Shakespeare's language 3

Checkpoints

1 A pair of rhymed lines.
2 Idiolect.

Exam preparation

Iago speaks coarsely and salaciously about Desdemona and her relationship with Othello: *He hath not yet made wanton the night with her, she is sport for Jove, full of game, happiness to their sheets*. He seems to be goading Cassio, trying to get him to cast his civilised, gentlemanly attitude aside and descend to Iago's vulgar level. Instead Cassio maintains a sense of decorum and, while agreeing with Iago's compliments, expresses them in a more courteous and elegant manner: *most exquisite, most fresh and delicate, right modest, perfection*.

Dialogue in Shakespeare

Checkpoints

1 Non-fluency features.
2 As a singular pronoun, *you* was more respectful. *Thou* was used towards those of lower rank, but could also imply intimacy and informality. See page 124.

Exam preparation

Paulina begins by speaking respectfully to Leontes, addressing him as *Good my liege* and *my lord*. She describes herself as a *loyal servant* and *most obedient counsellor*, and politely asks Leontes to listen to what she has to say (*I beseech you*). Her mood becomes more defiant when Leontes scornfully rejects her description of Hermione as a *good queen*. She repeats the phrase three times in one line, then a few lines later uses it again, emphasising her point with a supportive subordinate clause: *The good queen,/For she is good*. When Leontes orders her to be removed, she shows strength and spirit by threatening anyone who dares lay a hand on her. In her last speech in the extract she is directly critical of Leontes, calling him *ignorant* and *mad*. Leontes is initially dismissive of Paulina, echoing her but in a mocking, disbelieving tone (*Good queen!*), and using an abrupt imperative to order her removal (*Force her hence*). When she stands her ground and presents him with his newborn daughter he erupts, the exclamatory sentences showing his fury. He viciously insults Paulina, calling her a *witch* and a *bawd*.

Analysing Shakespeare extracts 1

Checkpoints

1 This occurs when the usual grammatical order of words is reversed. See page 13.
2 This occurs when two or more phrases or sentences have a similar grammatical pattern or structure. See page 13.

Analysing Shakespeare extracts 2

Checkpoints

1 Assonance occurs when the vowel sounds within two or more words rhyme. Sibilance is the repetition of *s*, *sh*, *z* and soft *c* sounds.
2 Prosodic features.

Exam preparation

(**Text C** – *The Tempest*)

The play opens with a storm that, on a literal level, is the 'tempest' that gives the play its title. But the storm is also a metaphor for the chaos and disorder which are to overwhelm the characters before harmony and equilibrium are restored at the end of the play. In the extract there is an atmosphere of noise and confusion, created by exclamatory sentences, short, urgent utterances and a succession of exits and entrances. The social order that would have existed in Naples disintegrates in the turmoil of the storm, again prefiguring what is to happen in the play. The Boatswain angrily dismisses the King (Alonso) and his courtiers, using a series of imperatives to order them to return to their cabins: *Keep your cabins, Hence! To cabin: silence! Trouble us not*. The King's authority is meaningless in the face of hostile natural elements: *What cares these roarers for the name of king?* After the shipwreck the King and his courtiers will find themselves in an alien environment, where the certainties of Naples are overturned. The play's dramatic opening prepares us for this.

(**Text D** – *Measure for Measure*)

Angelo's soliloquy after his first meeting with Isabella is a key speech in the development of his character and of the play as a whole. He has considered himself above sexual desire and has punished licentiousness in others. Now he finds himself attracted to Isabella. The broken rhythms of the speech, and the interrogative and exclamatory sentences, show his inner turmoil. He is bewildered by his own feelings and racked by guilt and self-disgust. He believes it is Isabella's purity that, ironically, tempts him and makes him *desire her foully*. Lexis with connotations of goodness runs through the speech, alongside contrasting lexis suggestive of corruption: *virtuous*, *sanctuary*, *modesty*, *sins*, *evils*. The use of imagery is an important feature of the speech, especially the complex image of the *violet* and the *carrion* (decaying animal flesh). In this metaphor Isabella is the violet, the beautiful flower which thrives naturally in the sun, while Angelo is the carrion, which exposed to the same heat grows rotten and *corrupt*.

Shakespeare in performance

Checkpoints

1 The extract also appeals to these senses: hearing (auditory imagery); touch (tactile imagery); smell (olfactory imagery).

2 An aside is a brief speech by a character, which is not heard by some or all of the other characters present. It may be addressed to another character, or to the audience. A soliloquy is a longer speech, in which a character appears to be thinking aloud. The character is usually alone on stage.

Revision checklist
Shakespeare

By the end of this chapter you should be able to:

1	List the four types of play written by Shakespeare.	Confident	Not confident. **Revise** page 116
2	Explain the main characteristics of each type of play.	Confident	Not confident. **Revise** pages 116–117
3	Explain in broad terms key elements in the historical and literary contexts of Shakespeare's plays.	Confident	Not confident. **Revise** page 118
4	Outline the main critical approaches to Shakespeare.	Confident	Not confident. **Revise** page 119
5	Understand the terms blank verse and iambic pentameter.	Confident	Not confident. **Revise** page 120
6	Explain possible reasons for parts of Shakespeare's plays being in verse, and parts in prose.	Confident	Not confident. **Revise** page 121
7	Identify rhetorical techniques used by Shakespeare.	Confident	Not confident. **Revise** pages 122–123
8	Understand the differences between *thou* and *you* in Shakespeare's plays.	Confident	Not confident. **Revise** page 124
9	Identify differences between Shakespearean dialogue and real conversation.	Confident	Not confident. **Revise** page 126
10	Identify similarities between Shakespearean dialogue and real conversation.	Confident	Not confident. **Revise** page 126
11	Approach with confidence the analysis of Shakespearean dialogue.	Confident	Not confident. **Revise** page 127
12	Explain what is meant by the context of a Shakespeare extract.	Confident	Not confident. **Revise** page 128
13	Approach with confidence the analysis of a Shakespeare extract.	Confident	Not confident. **Revise** pages 128–131
14	Explain the main dramatic conventions of Shakespeare's day, and why they are significant.	Confident	Not confident. **Revise** pages 132–133
15	Understand how different interpretations of a Shakespeare play are possible.	Confident	Not confident. **Revise** page 133

Non-literary texts

As well as studying plays, poetry, novels and short stories, all of the exam board specifications require you to study non-literary texts. The kinds of non-literary texts you are likely to come across include newspaper articles, advertisements, leaflets, website pages and so on. There are also **genres** (such as autobiography or travel writing) which cannot be neatly classified as literary or non-literary, but which you may again be asked to study. Different genres have different conventions relating to format, structure and use of language and you should always consider these when analysing a non-literary text, looking at how they have influenced the text in question. As with all texts, you should also think carefully about the audience the text is aimed at, the purpose it has and how these elements are evident in the language that is used.

Exam themes

→ Differences between literary and non-literary texts.

→ Genre conventions of non-literary texts.

Topic checklist

○ AS ● A2	OCR	EDEXCEL	AQA A	AQA B	WJEC
What are non-literary texts?	○●	●	○●	○●	○●
Advertisements	○●	●	○●	○●	○●
Newspaper articles	○●	●	○●	○●	○●
New technology texts	○●	●	○●	○●	○●
Specimen texts	○●	●	○●	○●	○●

What are non-literary texts?

This first section on non-literary texts considers the problematic question of how we distinguish between literary and non-literary texts. It also lists some examples of non-literary genres and outlines some general principles to bear in mind when you are analysing non-literary texts.

Literary and non-literary texts

Although some texts (a play by Shakespeare, for example) are obviously **literary**, while others (such as a passport application form) are equally obviously **non-literary**, the division between the two kinds of writing is not always so clear-cut. The private diary, for instance, is usually considered a non-literary genre, but many would argue that Samuel Pepys's famous 17th-century diaries are a work of literature. In terms of language, many of the features we associate with literature (such as the use of simile and metaphor) can be found in non-literary texts as well. So the list below of common ways of distinguishing between literary and non-literary texts should be read with caution – many texts are hard to categorise, and no definition of what we mean by 'literature' is completely secure.

→ Literary texts can be divided into three broad genres: **poetry**, **drama** and **prose fiction**. This is the most useful criterion; texts that fall outside these genres can usually be described as non-literary.

→ Literary texts are usually **imaginative** rather than **factual**, while the opposite is true of non-literary texts.

→ Literary texts **use language creatively**, and compared to non-literary texts are more likely to include such features as imagery, onomatopoeia, parallelism, rhyme and so on.

→ Literary texts are generally **more valued** than non-literary texts, and appreciation of them may be more lasting. Many non-literary texts are intended to be only of temporary use.

→ Literary texts usually have an **artistic** purpose, while non-literary texts often have a clear **practical** purpose.

Types of non-literary texts

Some examples of non-literary texts are shown below. You will encounter many or even all of these during your AS/A2 course, but the list is not exhaustive. Also remember that as explained above there is not a rigid distinction between literary and non-literary texts: there are examples of travel writing, for example, that might be described as literature.

Newspaper articles
Magazine articles
Advertising/promotional material
New technology texts (websites, e-mails, text messages)
Biographical/autobiographical writing
Diaries and journals
Letters

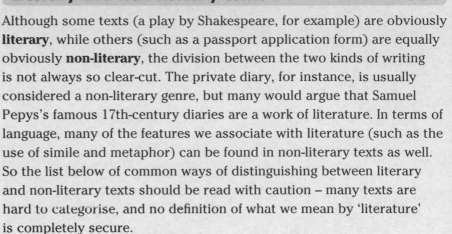

Checkpoint 1

Explain why you think diaries are usually considered non-literary texts.

Links

Later in this chapter there are sections on the specific features of **advertisements** (pages 142–143), **newspaper articles** (pages 144–145) and **new technology texts** (pages 146–147).

Informative, instructional and educational texts
Travel writing
Scientific writing
Historical writing
Leaflets, brochures
Legal documents
Spontaneous, unplanned speech (e.g. conversations)
Speeches

Analysing non-literary texts ●●●

In many ways your approach to analysing any kind of text – whether literary or non-literary – should be the same. Essentially, you try to identify the **effects** the writer or speaker wishes to have, and then look at how **language** is used to achieve these effects. In analysing the language you can make use of five language frameworks: **lexis**, **grammar**, **phonology**, **graphology** and **discourse structure**.

Another key principle that applies to all text analysis answers is that a typical analytical 'point' will have three elements to it:

→ Identification of a **language feature**, using appropriate **terminology**.
→ One or more **examples**, in the form of **quotations** from the text.
→ **Comment** on the **effects** achieved or intended, or on the **reasons** for the language feature being present.

With many non-literary texts, your understanding of what writers or speakers are trying to achieve, and of how they use language, will be increased if you give careful consideration to **purpose**, **genre** and **audience**:

→ **Purpose**   As mentioned earlier, non-literary texts often have a very clear purpose. The primary purpose of advertisements, for example, is usually to persuade, while entries in dictionaries and encyclopaedias are obviously intended to inform. These purposes will influence the type of language that is used.
→ **Genre**   Particular genres have specific conventions relating to language use, and you should be alert to these when analysing texts. Diaries, for instance, often have a compressed, telegraphic style, with the use of abbreviations and grammatically incomplete sentences.
→ **Audience**   Many non-literary texts target very specific audiences (magazines are an obvious example), and again this will have an influence on language.

> **Watch out!**
>
> The three elements listed here do not always have to be in this order. Often it is sensible to describe an effect first, then explain and illustrate the language features that achieve this effect.

> **Watch out!**
>
> Texts can have more than one purpose. The primary purpose of an advertisement might be to persuade, but it might also aim to inform and entertain.

> **Checkpoint 2**
>
> In what ways does the language used in a dictionary reflect the fact that the purpose of the text is to inform?

> **Exam preparation (20 minutes)**   answer: page 150
>
> **Text A** on page 148 is an extract from a diary kept by a soldier during the First World War. Analyse the writer's use of language, commenting in particular on how the language of the extract reflects the fact that it is a diary.

Advertisements

The next few sections look at some specific types of non-literary text that you might encounter: **advertisements**, **newspaper articles** (pages 144–145) and **new technology texts** (pages 146–147).

Advertiser, audience, purpose

If you are analysing an advertisement, it is helpful to start by establishing the following:

→ Who is the **advertiser**?
→ Who is their **target audience**?
→ What is their **purpose**?

The identity of the **advertiser** can be important. For example, is it a commercial organisation driven primarily by the need to make a profit, or an advertiser with different motives, such as a charity or government agency? Advertisers usually have a very specific **audience** in mind, and you should try to work out who this is. Think about gender, age group and socio-economic status (social class). The basic **purpose** is often to persuade the audience to buy a particular product or service, but think more deeply about how the advertisement is trying to persuade the audience to view the product. Does it want people to think the product is indispensable, good value, fashionable, prestigious?

Lexis

Aspects of lexis worth looking for when analysing advertisements include:

→ **Brand names**, and the associations that these have.
→ **Slogans** and **catchphrases** (e.g. Tesco's *Every little helps*).
→ Use of **positive lexis**, often in the form of **pre-modifiers**. **Comparatives** (*faster*, *cleaner*) and **superlatives** (*fastest*, *cleanest*) are common.
→ Words that suggest the product is **unique** or **exclusive** (e.g. *only*, *special*).
→ **Conversational lexis**, which may address the reader familiarly and create a sense of informality.
→ **Puns** and **wordplay**, intended to make the advertisement humorous and memorable.
→ **Technical** or **scientific vocabulary**, used to impress the reader.
→ **Non-standard spellings**, which can make the advertisement seem lively and unconventional.

Grammar

Grammatical features associated with advertisements include:

→ Use of **short sentences** and of **ellipsis** (grammatically incomplete sentences). These may make the message of the advertisement clear, concise and direct. They can also help to give an advertisement an informal, conversational tone.

Take note

Another common purpose of advertisements (e.g. those issued by government departments or agencies) is to **inform**.

Checkpoint 1

What is a **pre-modifier**?

→ Use of the **second person** (*you*) to speak directly to the reader.
→ Use of **imperatives**. These again address the reader directly and are often used to urge and persuade (as in *Go on, spoil yourself*).
→ Use of **interrogatives**. Another way of interacting with the reader.
→ Use of the **first person plural** (*we, us*) to refer to the advertiser. This can be part of an attempt to make a large organisation seem less impersonal.

Address to reader ●●●

As noted above, an advertisement may speak very directly to the reader. Think about the **tone** or **attitude** towards the reader – is it respectful, familiar, ironic? Note also any **interactive features**, such as forms to complete.

Phonology ●●●

Look for devices such as **rhyme**, **alliteration** and **onomatopoeia**.

Discourse structure and content ●●●

→ Advertisements frequently begin with a **hook** – the initial piece of attention-seeking language used to draw the reader in. Often this takes the form of a question.
→ The bottom-line summary that often appears at the end of an advertisement is known as the **signature line**.
→ The advertisement may adopt the **form of another genre**. For example, junk mail advertising often adopts the form of a personal letter. Food advertisements sometimes incorporate recipes.
→ The advertising copywriter may have created a 'voice' for the advertisement – a **narrator**. For example, we may be asked to believe that an ordinary housewife, a famous celebrity or a cartoon character is speaking to us.
→ Advertisements may reflect and reinforce social and cultural **stereotypes** (e.g. the assumption that household cleaning should be carried out by women and men are hopeless at it). More sophisticated advertisements may challenge these stereotypes, or use them as the basis for humour.

Graphology ●●●

→ Look for **typographical variations** (e.g. use of bold print, italics, upper and lower case letters) and for the use of **logos**, **illustrations** and **colour**. Never simply describe these visual elements – always comment on the effects that they have.
→ How is the **written text** organised and presented? Is it broken up, for example by using boxed sections and short paragraphs?

Checkpoint 2

What is a **logo**?

The jargon

The written text in an advertisement is sometimes known as the **copy**.

Exam preparation (20 minutes)   answer: page 150

Text B on page 148, which advertises airline cabin crew vacancies, is from an easyJet in-flight magazine. Consider how the text uses language to appeal to the reader.

143

Newspaper articles

This section outlines some of the important language features of newspaper articles, focusing in particular on the key differences between **broadsheet** and **tabloid** newspapers.

Broadsheets and tabloids

Broadsheet newspapers include such papers as *The Times* and *The Guardian*. Examples of **tabloid** newspapers are *The Sun* and the *Daily Mirror*. The **content** of tabloids tends to be quite lightweight, with stories about celebrities and extensive coverage of television, pop music and other forms of entertainment. In the broadsheets, serious news stories such as those involving politics and foreign affairs are covered in more detail, and there is more reporting of the arts and 'highbrow' culture (for example, there are more reviews of books and plays).

Tabloids and broadsheets have different **audiences**. Broadsheet readers tend to be educated, middle class and in professional occupations. Tabloids tend to have a mainly working-class readership.

There are important differences in the **language** that is used by broadsheets and tabloids. These can be examined more closely by looking at the following aspects of newspaper language: **headlines**, **lexis**, **grammar**, **discourse structure** and **graphology**.

Headlines

→ Usually a headline **summarises** the content of the story – e.g. SNOW CAUSES TRAFFIC CHAOS. Broadsheet headlines are sometimes more detailed, and therefore more informative, than tabloid headlines.

→ Other **purposes** of headlines can include: arousing interest by creating a sense of **drama** and **excitement**; seeking to entertain through the use of **humour**; influencing the reader's point of view by the use of a headline that is **biased**. These purposes tend to be more obviously apparent in tabloid headlines, but can also be present in broadsheet newspapers.

→ **Linguistic features** of newspaper headlines include the use of **simple** and **informal** lexis; **journalese** (see *Lexis* below); **puns**; **ellipsis** (compressed, grammatically incomplete sentences); **noun phrases** (e.g. PETROL PRICE RISE SHOCK, that is a single noun phrase); **present-tense verbs** (which create a sense of immediacy, so readers feel they are reading the very latest news); **phonological** devices such as onomatopoeia and alliteration. Again most of these features occur more often in tabloid headlines.

Lexis

→ In tabloids, the lexis tends to be **simple** and direct. Vocabulary in broadsheets is more **complex** and sophisticated, with greater use of **polysyllabic** words.

→ Tabloid lexis also tends to be **less formal**. Conversational expressions are often present, and individuals who feature in stories may be referred to familiarly (for example, by their first names).

Checkpoint 1

Give some more examples of **broadsheet** and **tabloid** newspapers.

Take note

The terms **broadsheet** and **tabloid** refer to page size, and for many years the most obvious difference between the two types of newspaper was that broadsheets had larger pages. However, in 2003 broadsheet newspapers such as the *Independent* began to produce tabloid-sized editions.

Take note

Newspapers such as the *Daily Mail* and the *Daily Express* occupy a kind of middle ground between the traditional broadsheets and tabloids. They are sometimes known as **middle market newspapers** or **upmarket tabloids**.

Checkpoint 2

Comment on the way language is used in this headline:
CRANE PLUNGE HORROR (The story reported how several building workers were injured when a crane collapsed.)

Take note

In addition to present-tense verbs, headlines often use **infinitive verbs** to refer to the future, as in QUEEN TO VISIT CHINA.

- **Journalese** is more common in tabloids. These are newspaper clichés – words that occur repeatedly in newspapers, such as *storm, soar, row, probe, boost*.
- Lexis in tabloids is often more obviously **emotive**, **dramatic** and **sensational**. Modifiers often have an emotional impact (e.g. *tragic, brave*). Broadsheets tend to be more factual and informative.
- **Bias** tends to be more obvious in tabloids. Words often have connotations that are clearly positive or negative. In broadsheets the tone may be more neutral, or bias may be expressed more subtly.

Grammar ●●●

- Tabloids use a large number of **short sentences**, which are often **simple** or **compound**. In broadsheets sentences tend to be **longer**, making more demands upon the reader. **Complex** sentences, often with two or more subordinate clauses, occur more frequently.
- **Fronted conjunctions** (which occur when sentences begin with a conjunction such as *And* or *But*) are more common in tabloids.
- Tabloids often rely on **simple connectives** (especially *and, but, now*) to achieve **cohesion**. In broadsheets a wider range of cohesive devices is employed.

Discourse structure ●●●

- The **opening paragraphs** of news reports usually summarise the key facts.
- In tabloids, **paragraphs** are generally **short** and often only one sentence long. In broadsheets, paragraphs tend to be **longer**, and articles as a whole tend to be more **detailed**.
- **Closing paragraphs** are often used to provide background information or to give the latest available news.

Graphology ●●●

- In tabloids there is more extensive use of **graphological features**, to make the text eye-catching and accessible.
- Tabloids avoid too much **dense text**. Articles are usually short and paragraphs are also brief.
- In tabloids there is more **typographical variation**, with the use of bold print, italics etc.

Links

Modifiers are explained on page 10.

Links

Cohesion is explained on page 14.

Watch out!

Graphological features are also important in broadsheets, but the use of graphology is more restrained. Written text is more prominent than in tabloids.

Exam preparation (30 minutes)   answer: pages 150–151

Text D on page 149 is an editorial from the *Daily Mirror*. **Text E** is part of an editorial from *The Observer*. Compare the use of language in these texts.

Take note

On page 149 there is also information on the background to these two editorials.

New technology texts

The AS/A2 specifications require you to study texts of different types and from different periods, so you should be familiar with the language features of the new types of text that are emerging as a result of developments in technology. This section looks at three examples: **websites**, **e-mail** and **text messages**.

Websites

Some websites only differ from traditional written texts in that printed material is presented on a screen rather than on a page, but others have features that make websites a distinctive form of text:

→ The way material is **organised** and **presented** is influenced by the dimensions of the screen. Text that runs along the top or bottom of the screen, or down the margins, is common.

→ Much of the text is **non-linear**. Traditional linear text is read progressively from the top of the page to the bottom, but on websites separate sections of text occupy different parts of the screen, and we do not read them in a fixed sequence (there is some similarity here with a page in a newspaper). There may be a main body of text, but additional material, such as advertisements and links to other pages or sites, is also usually present.

→ Partly because of the size of the screen, information is **broken down** into manageable segments. Headings, lists and summaries are common, and paragraphs are generally short.

→ **Graphological features** are important, with the use of colour, animation and visual images. In written text colour coding or underlining may be used to indicate hypertext links.

→ Websites are much more **interactive** than traditional written texts. If you are buying goods or booking a flight, for example, you will be asked to provide information in a set sequence. More proactively, you might choose to enlarge or transfer visual images from a site.

E-mail

As with websites, not all e-mails differ significantly from their traditional written equivalents: some are very similar to letters. However, it is also the case that many e-mails do have distinctive linguistic characteristics. In particular, the **informality** of e-mail, together with the **interactive** relationship between senders and receivers (especially evident in Internet chatrooms), makes it a form of written communication that is in many ways close to **spoken** language. Significant features of e-mail language include:

→ **Lexis** is often **conversational**, with the frequent use of colloquialisms and contractions. There is more tolerance of **spelling errors** than in traditional texts: messages are typed out quickly, and are not usually checked for errors (some non-standard spelling may be deliberate – see below).

Checkpoint 1

Can you think of any other genres that feature **non-linear** text?

Take note

New technology has created a huge number of **neologisms** (new words and expressions), sometimes known collectively as **cyberspeak** or **netspeak**. Here are just a few examples:

→ **WAP**   An acronym from 'wireless application protocol', referring to technology that enables mobile phones and other radio devices to be connected to the Internet.

→ **ISP**   An initialism, short for 'Internet Service Provider'.

→ **Clickthrough**   The number of visitors to a site.

→ **Silver surfer**   A retired person who uses the Internet frequently.

→ **Yettie**   A young person who makes money from the Internet (an acronym derived from 'young entrepreneurial technocrat').

Checkpoint 2

What are **contractions**?

→ **Greetings** and **farewells** illustrate the informality of the medium. *Hi* has become a standard way of opening messages, though sometimes greetings are dispensed with altogether as the names of sender and receiver automatically appear at the top of the message.

→ **Grammatical features** include **loosely constructed sentences**, which resemble the natural flow of speech. In order to type messages more quickly, some **punctuation marks** may be omitted, and **lower case letters** used where standard grammar would usually require capitals.

→ Various methods are used to suggest the **prosodic features** of speech, such as stress and tone of voice. These include upper case letters to indicate emphasis, non-standard spelling to suggest pronunciation and multiple punctuation marks (especially exclamation marks) to convey intonation:

> I was SOOooo PLEASED to see you last night!!!

→ A large number of **abbreviations** are used in e-mails, Internet chatrooms and mobile phone text messages. Examples include *BBL* ('be back later'), *MYOB* ('mind your own business') and *JK* ('just kidding').

→ **Emoticons** (also known as **smileys**) are graphical symbols used to represent facial expressions and body language:

> :-) smile
> :-(anger, displeasure
> {} a hug

Text messages ●●●

The main influence on text messaging style is the need to keep messages as short and concise as possible. The small screen size (which usually accommodates about 160 characters) and the small keypad encourage compression, and shorter messages also take less time to compose. In addition to **abbreviations** and **emoticons** (see above), linguistic features found in text messages include:

→ **Words are shortened**, as in *TXT* (for 'text') and *TLK* (for 'talk'). As these examples illustrate, it is often vowels that are dropped.

→ **Phonetic spelling**, as in *LUV* (for 'love') and *NE* (for 'any').

→ **Letter homophones**, as in *C* (for 'see') and *U* (for 'you').

→ **Number homophones**, as in *2* (for 'to') and *4* (for 'for').

→ **Grammatical compression** Determiners, auxiliary verbs etc. are often omitted from sentences, and punctuation marks may also be missing.

> **Take note**
>
> The stylistic features of text messages are not entirely new. Telegrams made use of grammatical compression, and the Phoenicians (one of the first civilisations to develop writing) used an alphabet made up entirely of consonants, with no vowel sounds.

> **Take note**
>
> On Valentines Day in 2003, an estimated 70 million text messages were sent in Britain. This far exceeded the number of Valentine cards received on the same day.

Exam preparation (15 minutes)   answer: page 151

Text C on page 149 is a series of messages from an Internet chatroom.
Comment on the use of language in these messages.

Specimen texts

The texts below are for use with the practice exam questions for this chapter.

Text A

Take note

The question for this text is on page 141. Private Horace Bruckshaw fought at Gallipoli during the First World War, and the diary entries are from this period. On a visit home he left the diaries with his wife. Later in the war he fought in France, where he was killed in 1917.

Sunday, 9 May 1915. Spent a rotten night of it. This is a terrible place simply infested with snipers. Nine of us went out with Capt. Andrews hunting them during the morning. Could find nothing however although we were sniped at every step we took. Luckily we all got safely back to our trench. Chapman wounded in chest this morning just as he got up to go to the assistance of another wounded man. It made us a wee bit nervous as he was sitting against me. After dark we went over the back of the trench to a point about a mile back to fetch rations up. We had just returned when the Turks greeted us with a fusillade of rapid fire. This they kept up all night.

Monday, 10 May. Things went quieter by breakfast time but the snipers kept very busy. We laid pretty low all day. We have lost nearly all our officers with these blessed snipers. Captain Tetley is the latest victim having been hit in both legs while leading a party sniper hunting. Very few of them got back again. Heavy firing commenced at dusk and continued all night.

Text B

Take note

The question for this text is on page 143. The complete advertisement features a photograph of a woman in an EasyJet uniform talking to another womam on a train.

So I'm on this train, right? Wednesday morning. Going to work. I start chatting to this girl sitting opposite me. She saw my uniform and, like a lot of people, started to ask me a few questions about my work. It's usually the same thing they want to know – people always think that you just wear loads of makeup, flirt with pilots and do 'that thing' with your arms before take off! So I set her straight. There's a lot more to working for **easyJet** than that. We're there to make sure every single passenger on every single aircraft has exactly the flight they want. Sometimes they just want to read. Sometimes they just want a reassuring word or smile. And, on occasion, when we've got a group of lads off on a stag do, they'll want a little more than that! The one thing they all have in common is that my fellow Crew and I are responsible for them. And working for **easyJet**, unlike some other airlines, we get more of a chance to be ourselves. And if there's anything orange about us, it's our uniforms, not our make up . . .

To find out more about the role and how to apply for a position at our London Stansted, Gatwick and Luton bases, visit the cabin crew jobs page at www.easyJet.com/en/jobs

Text C

Take note

The question for this text is on page 147.

>>JillyB<JillyB@postchat.co.uk wrote:
>>>how have the holidays been treating everyone?
>>>lots of lounging about I trust.

Jimbo@postchat.co.uk
>>Lounging and some blowing-of-the-gift-money shopping today. And
>>I don't have to be back at work until January 5!

Geoff<Geoff@postchat.co.uk wrote:
>I am doing the very same! I got a new BOOK! Off to read it!
>Jimbo, What day you wanna hang out? Tues, Wed or Thurs? Not free Fri or Sat or Sun!!!

Text D

DON'T GIVE SICK KILROY A PLATFORM

For anyone to write about Arabs as Robert Kilroy-Silk did would be damn stupid.

For a well-known BBC presenter to do it was absurd.

Newspaper columnists enjoy being provocative but that is not the same as being downright offensive, insulting and racist.

Ever since the terrible events of 9/11, responsible people throughout the West have tried to explain that not all Arabs are terrorists. It is ridiculous to suggest they are – and to do so displays the same narrow-minded, blinkered view of the world which is the hallmark of fanatics.

Robert Kilroy-Silk had a special responsibility. As the BBC has learnt, its leading presenters are seen as speaking for the Corporation – although they obviously are not – and some countries will even believe that what they say is sanctioned by the BBC or government.

Yet Kilroy-Silk heaped mindless, disgraceful abuse on all Arabs.

Unbelievably, the Sunday Express fully supports him, insisting what he said is not racist, thus confirming that their editor is a complete idiot.

The BBC, though, has rightly suspended Kilroy. He has no place on our screens while he spouts such dangerous, nasty nonsense.

Take note

The question for this text is on page 145. In January 2004 the television presenter Robert Kilroy-Silk was suspended by the BBC after he made controversial comments about Arab countries in an article he wrote for the *Sunday Express*. **Text D** is an editorial from the *Daily Mirror*, giving the newspaper's views on the matter. **Text E** is part of an editorial from *The Observer*.

Text E

KILROY-SILK IS AN ASS. SO IS THE BBC

IT IS IMPOSSIBLE to defend Robert Kilroy-Silk's views about the Arab world. They are crass, racist and ill-informed – the kind of stuff heard at the nineteenth hole from people who drink too much pink gin and live into late middle-age without learning the difference between Arabs and Iranians, as has Kilroy-Silk.

Yet, whatever we feel about the coarseness of Kilroy-Silk's intellect, however much we shudder at his pointless good looks and the daftness of his effusions on daytime television, there is something deeply disturbing about the BBC's response which has been to shelve Kilroy-Silk's programme pending an investigation. Given that the man has apologised and the circumstances of how the column was mistakenly reprinted are now understood, we wonder what there is to investigate, particularly since the original article was read by millions nine months ago without raising a murmur.

Answers
Non-literary texts

What are non-literary texts?

Checkpoints

1 Some diaries are simply a record of events and may not be especially creative or imaginative.
2 The language is precise, clear and unambiguous. A dictionary gives definitions in a dry, factual manner – there is no attempt to interest or entertain the reader. The style is plain, concise and abbreviated, with no embellishment.

Exam preparation

The main stylistic feature typical of diaries here is the frequent presence of ellipsis. Sentences are kept short and are often grammatically incomplete, as in *Spent a rotten night of it*, which omits the subject (*We* or *I*), and *Chapman wounded in chest this morning*, which omits the auxiliary verb (*was*). Even when sentences are complete they are often short, simple sentences: *We laid pretty low all day*. The extract is still moving and powerful, the stark simplicity of the sentences leaving the reader to imagine the full horror of what is being described: *Very few of them got back again*.

The discourse structure is also characteristic of diaries, with dated entries and a chronological narrative that records the events of each day. As the writer is describing his own experiences, first person pronouns are used, though they are all plural: *we, us, our*. This reflects the fact that the writer is a member of a military unit and conveys a feeling of solidarity with his fellow soldiers.

The lexis is simple and often monosyllabic (*This they kept up all night*), confirming that this is not a carefully crafted literary text. In places the lexis is also quite informal: *a wee bit nervous, pretty low*. Two of the informal expressions now sound quite archaic, reflecting the text's period: *these blessed snipers, a rotten night*. There is a semantic field of warfare: *Heavy firing, rations, fusillade of rapid fire*. Some of this field-specific lexis evokes the nature of fighting in the First World War: *trench, snipers*. The vocabulary is occasionally emotive (*a terrible place*), but generally the brutality of war and the fear it must have caused are described in a restrained, understated way: the shooting of a man sitting alongside him makes the writer *a wee bit nervous*. The factual, declarative sentences are generally left to speak for themselves: *We have lost nearly all our officers*.

Advertisements

Checkpoints

1 Words that come before the head word in a phrase and give us more information about it. See page 10.
2 A symbol or small design used to represent an organisation, often appearing on signs, letterheads etc.

Exam preparation

This advertisement uses the device of an imaginary female cabin crew member talking about her job. The fictional scenario places her on a train, speaking casually to another passenger. The text has a conversational opening: *So I'm on this train, right?* The conjunction *So* implies she is in mid-conversation, and the use of a contraction (*I'm*) and a discourse marker (*right*) replicate natural speech. The informal register is maintained as the text develops: *chatting, loads, lads off on a stag do*. The presence of ellipsis (*Wednesday morning. Going to work*) and of short, simple sentences (*Sometimes they just want to read*) strengthens the impression of natural speech. Fronted conjunctions (several sentences begin with *And*) keep the sentences short and have a similar effect. Also typical of genuine conversation is the way the speaker switches between present and past tense as she narrates her story: *I start chatting to this girl . . . She saw my uniform*. Occasional exclamatory sentences suggest the speaker's intonation and animated delivery.

The advertisement challenges the sexist stereotype of air hostesses simply wearing *loads of makeup* and flirting with pilots. The speaker emphasises the responsibility of her job, and her pride in her work is conveyed by the use of intensifiers and of parallelism: *We're there to make sure <u>every single passenger</u> on <u>every single aircraft</u> has <u>exactly</u> the flight they want*. The speaker is also used to make the job sound appealing by stressing its variety and the interaction with a range of people, from quiet passengers who simply want to read to *lads off on a stag do*. The job is also presented as offering an opportunity for individual self-expression, unlike the implied conformity imposed on their employees by other airlines: *working for **easyJet**, unlike some other airlines, we get more of a chance to be ourselves*.

The advertisement ends with a separate, more formal section advising readers how they can obtain more information about cabin crew jobs. Imperatives are used to address the reader directly (*To find out more . . . visit the cabin crew jobs page*). Throughout the advertisement the name of the company, *easyJet*, is foregrounded by the use of bold print.

Newspaper articles

Checkpoints

1 Other broadsheet newspapers include *The Daily Telegraph, The Independent, Financial Times, The Observer, The Sunday Times, The Sunday Telegraph, The Independent on Sunday*. Other tabloid newspapers include *The Star, News of the World, Sunday Mirror, The People*.
2 CRANE PLUNGE HORROR is a noun phrase and an example of ellipsis. It uses journalese (*plunge, horror*) and is also dramatic.

Exam preparation

The noun phrase *sick Kilroy* in Text D's headline immediately indicates the article's hostile attitude towards the television presenter. The headline is also a forceful imperative, expressing the *Daily Mirror*'s view that the BBC was right to suspend him. The negative lexis continues in the main body of the article: *absurd, mindless, disgraceful, dangerous, nasty*. Intensifiers make the tone of this criticism more aggressive and emphatic: <u>*damn*</u> *stupid*; <u>*downright*</u> *offensive, insulting and racist*. The editor of the *Sunday Express* is branded a *complete idiot* for supporting Kilroy-Silk.

Text D is from a tabloid newspaper and this is reflected in the use of simple, monosyllabic vocabulary (*He has no place on our screens*) and informal lexis (*damn stupid, downright, spouts*). However, the lexis is occasionally more formal and more complex: *sanctioned, provocative, special responsibility*. The discourse structure is typical of tabloid newspapers in that paragraphs are short and often a single sentence long. Short, simple sentences occur frequently: *Robert Kilroy-Silk had a special responsibility*. A variety of graphological features is used to make the text accessible and visually interesting: upper case letters, bold print, italics and underlining. Often these also give additional emphasis to particular points, as when the concluding comment is italicised and underlined.

The attitude expressed in Text D is clear, simple and unambiguous. The stance of Text E, from a broadsheet newspaper (*The Observer*), is more complex. While the article condemns Kilroy-Silk, it is also critical of the BBC, and questions the decision to suspend the presenter. As in Text D, the headline is used to summarise this viewpoint and present it in plain, simple language. Also as in Text D, negative lexis is used in the article to refer to Kilroy-Silk's views (*crass, racist, ill-informed*), though there is less of it and the tone is not as aggressive. The phrase *the kind of stuff* is dismissive, and the article also distances itself from Kilroy-Silk by referring to him as *the man*. The vocabulary is occasionally more complex than in Text D: *the coarseness of Kilroy-Silk's intellect, effusions*. More noticeable are the differences in sentence structure. The article begins with a short, direct sentence (*It is impossible to defend . . .*), but the rest of the extract is made up of just three long, complex sentences, each containing several subordinate clauses. There is also much less attempt to give the text visual impact, though the opening words of the article are in upper case.

New technology texts

Checkpoints

1 Leaflets often feature non-linear text.
2 These are abbreviated forms such as *don't, I've, it's* etc.

Exam preparation

The text has the informality associated with chatroom messages and in this and other ways resembles speech. Informal lexis includes *hang out, lots of lounging about*, the abbreviations *Tues, Wed* etc. and the heavy, non-standard pre-modification of *blowing-of-the-gift-money shopping*. Grammatical informality includes ellipsis (*Off to read it!*) and fronted conjunctions (*And I don't have to be back at work*). There is also non-standard punctuation, with lower case letters used to begin sentences (in JillyB's message) and multiple punctuation marks (in the last sentence of Geoff's message). The prosodic features of speech are suggested in a variety of ways. Non-standard spelling suggests pronunciation (*wanna*), while upper case letters indicate stressed words (*BOOK*). Exclamatory sentences suggest intonation. Interrogative sentences have a similar effect, and also reflect the interactive nature of the text. The discourse structure, with the text made up of a series of short messages, also resembles spoken interaction. The layout (use of headers etc.) has features typical of e-mail texts.

Revision checklist
Non-literary texts

By the end of this chapter you should be able to:

1 Explain the differences between literary and non-literary texts.	Confident	Not confident. **Revise** page 140
2 List some common types of non-literary texts.	Confident	Not confident. **Revise** pages 140–141
3 Approach with confidence the analysis of non-literary texts.	Confident	Not confident. **Revise** page 141
4 Recognise the importance of identifying the advertiser, the target audience and the purpose when analysing advertisements.	Confident	Not confident. **Revise** page 142
5 List lexical features commonly associated with advertisements.	Confident	Not confident. **Revise** page 142
6 List grammatical features commonly associated with advertisements.	Confident	Not confident. **Revise** pages 142–143
7 Understand how to analyse the discourse structure and content of advertisements.	Confident	Not confident. **Revise** page 143
8 Explain the differences between broadsheet and tabloid newspapers.	Confident	Not confident. **Revise** page 144
9 Identify the main linguistic features of newspaper headlines.	Confident	Not confident. **Revise** page 144
10 List lexical features commonly associated with newspaper articles.	Confident	Not confident. **Revise** pages 144–145
11 List grammatical features commonly associated with newspaper articles.	Confident	Not confident. **Revise** page 145
12 Identify aspects of discourse structure commonly associated with newspaper articles.	Confident	Not confident. **Revise** page 145
13 Explain the distinctive linguistic features of website pages.	Confident	Not confident. **Revise** page 146
14 Explain the distinctive linguistic features of e-mail messages.	Confident	Not confident. **Revise** pages 146–147
15 Identify the language features of text messages, using appropriate terminology.	Confident	Not confident. **Revise** page 147

Writing and adapting texts

This chapter focuses on your own writing skills, looking at two kinds of writing you are likely to be asked to undertake: **original writing**, and adapting (or '**transforming**') texts written by others so that they are suited to a specified audience and purpose. The precise nature of these writing tasks varies from one examining board to another, so it is important that you familiarise yourself with the requirements of the specification you are studying. With original writing assignments you often have considerable freedom of choice, and it is important that you think carefully about what you want to do. You should aim to choose a topic that engages your interest and that will enable you to write well. You also need a clearly defined audience and purpose. When you are adapting texts written by others, you need to produce a text that is genuinely different from the source material and that is internally consistent (in other words, it reads as a coherent whole and is not obviously made up of ideas from different sources patched together). Original writing tasks and text transformation exercises both usually require accompanying **commentaries** (where you analyse your own writing), and this chapter also has advice on writing these.

Exam themes

→ Original writing tasks.

→ Transformation of one or more texts.

→ Commentaries.

Topic checklist

O AS ● A2	OCR	EDEXCEL	AQA A	AQA B	WJEC
Original writing 1	O	O	O	O	O
Original writing 2	O	O	O	O	O
Adapting and transforming texts 1	●	●	●	●	●
Adapting and transforming texts 2	●	●	●	●	●
Writing commentaries	O●	O●	O●	O●	O●
Specimen texts	●	O	●	●	●

Original writing 1

Original writing assignments give you the opportunity to write creatively and about topics that interest you. However, they require careful thought and planning. In particular, you need to have a clear understanding of your **audience**, your **purpose** and the characteristics of your chosen **genre**.

What you have to do

For most specifications original writing pieces are **coursework** assignments rather than exam tasks. Usually you are asked to write a minimum of **two** pieces. You will probably find that compared to GCSE English you have much more freedom of choice regarding the kinds of assignment you undertake, although depending on the specification there may be some restrictions. For example, the two pieces might have to be from different **genres**, or written for different **purposes**, and one might have to be primarily for a **reading audience**, while the other is for a **listening audience**. The required **word length** varies, but is often around 750–1,000 words for a single piece.

If your specification requires you to complete a creative writing assignment under **examination** conditions, you will not have so much choice, but the task will probably be accompanied by **stimulus material** to give you ideas.

All specifications usually require at least one of your pieces to be accompanied by an **analytical commentary** (see pages 162–163).

Some ideas

Here are some ideas for original writing assignments. You will need of course to choose a topic that meets the requirements of the specification you are taking. It is also advisable to check with your teacher that your idea is suitable before you begin working on it.

- A short story
- The beginning of a novel
- A newspaper article
- A magazine feature
- A sports report
- A book review
- A film review
- An album review
- A review of a live performance (e.g. a play or a concert)
- A guide to a local amenity
- A beginner's guide to . . . (buying a car, playing the drums etc.)
- Autobiographical writing
- Biographical writing
- A guide for new students at a school or college
- A handbook for new employees of a business or organisation
- An educational text (e.g. a study guide or study pack)
- Travel journalism
- CD liner notes

Watch out!

Make sure you are familiar with the particular requirements of your specification.

Checkpoint 1

Can you think of any types of text that might have both a reading audience and a listening audience?

Watch out!

Creative writing assignments for which stimulus materials are provided should not be confused with assignments which require you to **adapt** or **transform** source materials (see pages 158–161).

A charity appeal (e.g. in the form of a leaflet or advertisement)

An instruction booklet

A leaflet giving health advice or information

Publicity material for a drama group, sports club etc.

An Internet text

A radio talk

A radio play

A script for a film or television drama (probably an excerpt)

A script for a radio advertisement

A comedy sketch for radio or television

A script for an audio guide (e.g. for an art gallery or museum)

A speech on a controversial issue

Genre, audience, subject, purpose ●●●

During the planning stage, you should give careful consideration to:

→ **Genre** What *type* of text are you intending to produce? Try to be as precise as you can. If it is a magazine article, what kind of magazine might publish it? Try to think of an actual publication where you could imagine seeing your article in print. If you are thinking of writing a short story or part of a novel, to which genre of fiction will it belong – detective fiction, fantasy, horror?

→ **Audience** An understanding of who you are writing for is crucial. Again you need to be as precise as possible: you should be able to define your audience with reference to such characteristics as age, gender, experience, knowledge, education, interests, attitudes etc.

→ **Subject** What will you be writing about? Do you know enough about it? If not, do you know where you can find the information you need? Does your original idea for the subject need to be extended, or cut back? For example, if you intend to write a magazine article about Spain, it might be more sensible to focus on a particular city or region rather than attempting to write about the whole country.

→ **Purpose** Finally, you need a clear sense of purpose. The main purposes of written and spoken texts are: to persuade, to inform, to entertain and to instruct. The primary purpose of your text is likely to be one of these, but the text as a whole may have a combination of purposes. For example, the main purpose of an educational text written for children will be to inform, but it may try to do this in an entertaining way.

Checkpoint 2

How many other fiction genres can you think of?

Examiner's secrets

Thinking ahead in this way will not only improve the quality of your assignment, it will also make writing a **commentary** much easier (see pages 162–163).

Take note

If you are completing a coursework assignment, you should also have time to carry out some **research**. In particular, you might find it helpful to investigate more fully your **genre** and your **subject**. It is a good idea to find **style models** – examples of the kind of text you are going to produce. While you should not slavishly imitate these, they can give you ideas about layout and presentation, and about the kind of language you should use. Investigating your subject will be necessary if you need to find out information. Try to gather information from more than one source, and think carefully about how you need to **adapt** the information to serve your purposes (the sections on *Adapting and transforming texts* should be helpful here – see pages 158–161).

Exam preparation (15 minutes)   answer: page 166

Sort the topics listed under *Some ideas* above into four groups, according to their purpose: to persuade, to inform, to entertain or to instruct. Where you think an idea might have more than one purpose, decide what you think the primary purpose would probably be.

Original writing 2

This second section on original writing assignments mainly focuses on how you should ensure you have used **language** appropriately.

Getting the language right

When your original writing piece is marked, the main thing your teacher or examiner will be trying to assess is whether you have used language effectively and appropriately. You will be much more likely to have done this if (as suggested on page 155) you have given careful thought to your genre, audience, subject and purpose. The language you use should be influenced by all four of these elements:

→ **Genre**   The language should be appropriate to the genre. Tabloid and broadsheet newspaper articles, for example, have different language features.
→ **Audience**   Your language needs to appeal to your target audience, and should be accessible to them.
→ **Subject**   The language used should demonstrate knowledge of your subject, and should incorporate relevant semantic fields, but should not be too technical for your audience.
→ **Purpose**   Your language should help you to achieve your purpose. In other words, where appropriate it needs to be persuasive, informative, entertaining or instructional.

All of this can be summed up by saying that your text needs to have an appropriate **register**. This in turn can be explained more fully by looking at the main language frameworks: **lexis**, **grammar**, **phonology**, **graphology** and **discourse structure**. Below is a checklist of language features to consider when checking your work, arranged under these five headings.

Lexis

→ Is there a suitable level of **formality**?
→ Is the lexis **simple** or **complex** as appropriate?
→ Do words have relevant **connotations**, and are they drawn from relevant **semantic fields**?
→ If appropriate, have you used **literary features** such as similes and metaphors?

Grammar

→ Are appropriate **types of sentences** used – declarative, imperative, interrogative, exclamatory?
→ Is the mix of **simple**, **compound** and **complex** sentences suitable?
→ Are **first**, **second** and **third person** used appropriately and consistently?
→ Is the use of **tense** effective and consistent?
→ If appropriate, have you used **stylistic features** such as parallelism and foregrounding?

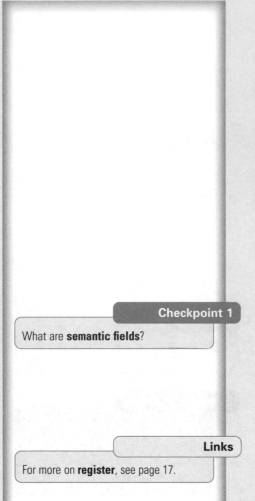

Checkpoint 1

What are **semantic fields**?

Links

For more on **register**, see page 17.

156

Phonology

(Phonological features will be especially significant if you are writing for a **listening audience** – see below.)

→ If **phonological devices** such as onomatopoeia and alliteration have been used, are they appropriate and effective?

Graphology

→ Are the **layout** and other **visual features** appropriate to the genre, and are they effective?

(Computer software packages can greatly improve the presentation and appearance of coursework pieces. Remember though that the assessment will mainly be based on the other language frameworks.)

Discourse structure

→ Is the text **well organised**?
→ Is it **coherent**, and does it **develop** in a clear, consistent way?
→ Are the different sections of the text of an appropriate **length** in relation to each other?
→ If you have created **fictional characters**, are they sufficiently developed and is the portrayal of them consistent?
→ If you have written a **story**, are the **beginning** and **ending** effective? Is there an appropriate balance between **description**, **action** and **dialogue**?

Writing for a listening audience ●●●

Original writing pieces are most commonly written texts, but spoken texts are also possible, and one of the specifications stipulates that one piece must be primarily for a **reading audience** and another primarily for a **listening audience**. Again it is important that the language you use reflects the nature of the task:

→ **Phonological features** will be especially important. It might be appropriate to indicate **stress** on particular words, **intonation**, **pauses**, **sound effects** and so on. Other devices such as **repetition** and **parallelism** might also be used.
→ Depending on the genre of the piece, different ways of **involving** and **addressing the audience** can be used. For example, if you are addressing a live audience you might involve them by the use of **first person plural pronouns** (*we, our*).
→ **Deictic expressions** might be appropriate – for example in an audio guide, where they can be combined with **imperatives** (*Look to your right and you will see ...*).

Checkpoint 2

What are **deictic expressions**?

Exam preparation (20 minutes)

Imagine your teacher has asked you to prepare a leaflet promoting AS English Language to GCSE English students. Make notes on the kind of language you would use, referring to the language frameworks of lexis, grammar, phonology, graphology and discourse structure.

Adapting and transforming texts 1

As explained below, **text transformation** exercises are found on all Language and Literature specifications. They take various forms and are sometimes known as **text adaptation** or **editorial writing**.

What you have to do

All of the specifications include **text transformation** of some kind, either as **coursework** assignments or **exam** tasks.

With **exam questions** you're usually provided with a collection of **source material** on a particular topic, then asked to produce a **new text** based on this material. Depending on the specification, the material will either be provided in advance of the examination or in the exam itself. The amount of source material also varies – there might be a pre-release booklet containing several texts, or just two or three shorter texts included in the exam paper. The material, and the text you are asked to produce, can be literary or non-literary. For instance, you might be given a group of texts on Ireland (a poem, and extracts from a guide book and an encyclopedia), then asked to write a script suitable for use on a radio travel programme.

With **coursework** assignments you usually have more freedom of choice. You will probably be able to choose your own source material and decide how you want to adapt it. One of the AQA specifications stipulates that you must choose a literary text and change all or part of it into a different genre (see page 161).

For all text transformation tasks you are usually asked to write an accompanying **analytical commentary**, in which you compare your text with the original source material (see pages 162–163).

Understanding the task

Whether you have been set a task, or have devised one yourself, it is essential that, as with other writing assignments (see page 155), you begin with a clear understanding of these key elements: **genre**, **audience**, **subject**, **purpose**.

→ **Genre**   What *type* of text have you been asked to produce? You will need to use language in a way that is appropriate to the genre. Think about the conventions and characteristics of the genre you will be working within. A particularly common failing in exam answers is that students who have been asked to produce a text for a listening audience instead create a conventional written text, which would be much more suitable for a reading audience.

→ **Audience**   Exam questions will usually explain who your audience are. This information is very important, as the age, background etc. of your audience should influence the kind of language you use.

→ **Subject**   This is especially important in an exam. What exactly have you been asked to write about? The source material will almost certainly contain ideas and information that are irrelevant to the task, and you do not want to include any of this material by mistake.

Watch out!

Remember to ask your teacher or check your specification so you are clear about what you have to do.

Examiner's secrets

The acronym **GASP** may help you to remember these four elements.

Checkpoint 1

List a few of the ways in which a text for a **listening audience** might be different from a text for a **reading audience**.

→ **Purpose** Remember the four main purposes of texts are to persuade, inform, entertain and instruct. Which one of these is your primary purpose? Does your text have other purposes as well? Again the purpose of your text should be reflected in the language that you use.

Reading the source material ●●●

As mentioned earlier, with some specifications the source material is distributed in advance of the examination, with others it is not. In either case, it is important that you read the material **actively** rather than passively. Here are some important general principles:

→ **Annotate** the texts as you read them. Highlight key words, phrases, dates, statistics etc. If you know the task, have the key elements of genre, audience, subject and purpose in your mind all the time as you study the texts. If the source material is in a pre-release booklet, you will have more time to annotate in detail – but don't over-annotate so that in the exam you are faced with a mass of highlighted and underlined text!
→ Remember **you don't need to use all of the source material**. Once you know the task, try to decide quickly which parts will be of no use to you.
→ At the same time, if you are given several texts, **try to draw information and ideas from a range of them** – don't just base your answer on one or two.

More detailed advice on making use of the source material follows below and on pages 160–161.

Looking at context and content ●●●

→ Think about the **context** of each text. Who wrote it, and who were their audience? Does this influence the point of view that is expressed, or the way the topic is approached? What purpose does the text have?
→ Think about **content**. What is the text about? What aspects of the topic does it focus on? What are its key points? Often it is helpful to try to summarise the content of each text in a few sentences.

Examiner's secrets

If you are given a **pre-release booklet**, make good use of the time. Read each text through several times, so you don't need to do too much re-reading in the exam.

Checkpoint 2

Can you think of any other aspects of a text's **context** that might be significant?

Exam preparation

There is a text transformation question at the end of the next section (page 161).

159

Adapting and transforming texts 2

This section has further advice on how you should read and adapt the source material, and also has some tips on transforming literary texts.

Looking at language and style ●●●

As you read the source material, as well as looking for ideas and information you can use, you need to study the **language** of the original texts and consider how it needs to be changed. Focus on the main language frameworks: **lexis**, **grammar**, **phonology**, **graphology** and **discourse structure**. Listed below are examples of the kinds of questions you should ask.

Lexis

→ Does the lexis need to be made more or less **formal**?
→ Is the lexis too **complex**? Are there technical terms that need to be explained more simply?
→ Is the tone generally too dry and abstract – does it need to be made more **emotive** and **persuasive**? Or the other way round?

Grammar

→ Do your sentences need to be **shorter**, or **longer**?
→ Do you need to use different **types of sentences** (e.g. interrogatives and imperatives)?
→ Does the text use the **third person** when you need to use the **first person**, or the other way round? Do you need to involve the reader by making more use of the **second person**?

Phonology

→ Do you need to convert a written text into a **spoken text**, or the other way round? Do spoken language features need to be added, or removed?

Graphology

→ Would it be appropriate for you to make more – or less – use of **visual devices** such as illustrations, boxed text, bullet points etc.?
→ Are there ideas or information that could usefully be **presented** in a different way?

Discourse structure

→ Are **paragraphs** too short, or too long?
→ Does the material need to be **ordered differently**?

Using the source material ●●●

Although you need to change the source material, your new text has to be based on it so there will also be parts of it you want to use. Here are some guiding principles:

Watch out!

Remember that as well as language that you need to change, the source material may also include features you could profitably make use of – see *Using the source material* below.

Examiner's secrets

If you are asked to produce a spoken text, never forget you are writing something that will be **listened** to. Make sure your use of language reflects this.

Watch out!

It might well be appropriate to make use of graphological features such as those mentioned here, but don't get too carried away. Remember you will mainly be assessed on how you have used **language**.

→ Don't copy out large chunks of material. If there are short passages you want to repeat word-for-word, make it clear that they are **quotations**.

→ As far as possible, try to put points, ideas etc. from the source material into **your own words**.

→ There is nothing wrong with repeating **dates**, **statistics** etc. – in fact this is usually a good idea.

→ Often it is appropriate to **summarise** parts of the source material.

→ There may also be **language features** that you wish to make use of – for example, persuasive lexis or direct address to the reader. Be careful here to **adapt** these techniques to your purposes and make the wording of your new text as original as you can.

Your own text ●●●

Much of the advice in the earlier sections on *Original writing* (especially pages 156–157) is applicable to the writing of an adapted or transformed text. Essentially, you should try to ensure that:

→ You produce a genuinely '**new**' text.

→ Your text '**works**' in that it is a convincing example of the relevant genre, and is suitable to its audience and purpose.

→ Your text is well structured and has **cohesion**. Although possibly based on several different sources, the 'joins' should be invisible and there should be a consistent tone and register.

Transforming literary texts ●●●

A particular kind of text transformation you may be asked to undertake is the transformation of all or part of a literary text into another genre. The basic principles outlined over the last four pages still hold true: you need a clear sense of genre, audience and purpose and should aim to produce a text that is convincing, consistent and genuinely different from the original source. If you are working with an older text and adapting it for a modern audience, some other considerations also apply. As well as updating the language, you may need to change the setting and the social backgrounds of the characters. You may also want to examine the attitudes and values within the original work and decide if you want to modify them.

Checkpoint 1

Paraphrasing is an important skill when adapting and transforming texts. What is paraphrasing?

Take note

Think about the 'voice' of your text. It needs to be consistent and appropriate.

Checkpoint 2

What is **cohesion**?

Exam preparation (30 minutes)   answer: pages 166–167

Imagine you have been invited to take part in a current affairs radio programme. Each week the programme looks at a different issue. Speakers are asked to give a short talk, presenting their views to a studio audience, then a wider discussion follows. As a school or college student, you have been invited to contribute to a programme on education. The specific issue being addressed is, 'Should schools try to change pupils' regional accents, or should they leave them alone?' Making use of the ideas and information in the extracts on pages 164–165, write the script for the talk that you would give. Write about 300 words.

Writing commentaries

For both original writing and text transformation tasks you are usually asked to write an accompanying **commentary**, in which you explain and illustrate the significant features of your own texts.

What you have to do

If the commentary accompanies an **original writing** task, you will be commenting closely on your own use of language, drawing attention to features of your text and explaining why you included them. If the commentary is part of a text transformation assignment, you will also be doing this, but there will be an additional **comparative** element, as you will probably be asked to compare your own text with the source texts, explaining how and why you have changed them (see *Comparative commentaries* on the next page).

Planning an answer

In many ways, you should approach the commentary as you would the analysis of any text; the only difference is that you're the writer of the text you are analysing rather than someone else. As in other kinds of text analysis, most of the points you make should have **three parts** to them:

→ **Identify a feature** (such as 'emotive vocabulary').
→ **Quote** one or more examples.
→ **Comment** on reasons/effects – why did you include the feature, and what effect do you think it has?

If you carefully planned the writing of your text, the commentary should not be difficult. This is because you will already have made deliberate decisions about what kind of language to use, and now simply need to explain what these decisions were. In fact it is sensible to **have the commentary in the back of your mind** as you write your text. Make a mental note of features you will be able to refer back to when you write the commentary.

Listed below are some features you might have made use of, and which could therefore be mentioned in the commentary. You need, however, to take into account what you've been asked to cover in the commentary, and how long it needs to be. Some specifications require commentaries of 500+ words, others much less than this. In shorter commentaries you will obviously not be able to comment on as many features. However, it is usually a good idea to cover a **range** of language features (e.g. you shouldn't just write about lexis and nothing else).

Introductory points

You might begin by outlining your **genre**, **audience**, **subject** and **purpose**. If any of these have already been identified in the examination question, you do not need to repeat them. If, however, it is an original writing coursework assignment, they will need careful explanation (see page 155). Once you have established these four elements you can regularly refer back to them during your commentary, explaining

Examiner's secrets

As suggested here, the secret is consciously to include language features you will later be able to discuss in the commentary.

Watch out!

Make sure you know the kind of commentary your specification requires you to write, including how long it should be.

Examiner's secrets

Reading examination questions carefully is essential, but in your answers you should not waste time by repeating (especially at length) information contained in the question.

how aspects of the language you have used are appropriate (e.g. you might say, *I have used complex, polysyllabic vocabulary because the text is aimed at a mature, educated audience*).

Lexis
This includes use of: **informal** vocabulary (e.g. **colloquial** expressions, **contractions**); **formal** vocabulary; **simple** (possibly **monosyllabic**) or **complex** (possibly **polysyllabic**) vocabulary; **semantic fields**; words with **positive** or **negative connotations**; words with specific **connotations**; **emotive** vocabulary; **pre-modifiers** and **post-modifiers**; **repetition** of key words; **similes** and **metaphors**; **visual**, **auditory**, **tactile**, **gustatory** and **olfactory imagery**; **deictic** expressions; **puns** and other kinds of **humour**.

Checkpoint 1

Explain the differences between **visual**, **auditory**, **tactile**, **gustatory** and **olfactory imagery**.

Grammar
Use of: **declarative**, **interrogative**, **imperative** and **exclamatory** sentences; **simple**, **compound** and **complex** sentences; **short** and **long** sentences; **ellipsis**; **parallelism**; **foregrounding**; **syndetic** and **asyndetic** listing; **first**, **second** and **third person**; **past**, **present** and **future tense**.

Checkpoint 2

Explain the difference between a **simple** and a **compound** sentence.

Phonology
Use of: **onomatopoeia**; **alliteration**; **rhyme**; **rhythmic effects**, **stress** and **intonation**; **pauses**; **repetition**; **sound effects**.

Discourse content and structure
Includes discussion of: how you've **started**; how you've **organised** your points (e.g. **order**, use of **paragraphs**); how you've **finished**; what you've **included**, and what you haven't; how you've achieved **cohesion**; in stories, **development** of **plot** and **character**, and balance of **description**, **action** and **dialogue**.

Graphology
Use of **layout** and **visual features**.

Watch out!

Students often write too much on graphology. Be careful not to do this.

Comparative commentaries ●●●

In **comparative commentaries**, you include points such as those listed above, but develop the points further by explaining how your text **compares** with the source texts, commenting in particular on the **differences** and on the **reasons** for any changes you have made. In the commentary it is usually appropriate to **quote** from the source texts as well as from your own text, in order to illustrate the points made.

Exam preparation (40 minutes)   answer: page 167

Write a commentary of approximately 400 words to accompany your answer to the text transformation exercise on page 161.

Specimen texts

The texts below are for use with the practice exam questions on pages 161 and 163.

Take note

Text A is an abridged version of an article by Colin Cottell that appeared in *The Guardian* newspaper on 20 December 2003.

Text A

It ain't what you do, it's the way that you say it

Some people will do whatever it takes to get ahead in their career. Change job, move house, ingratiate themselves with their boss. Even change their accent.

'I want to neutralise my accent,' says Victoria Hardy, an image consultant. She moved to Glasgow after a childhood spent in the north-east. Now Ms Hardy is taking lessons from Derek Rogers, a language and accent specialist from Glasgow.

'I am doing it for career purposes really, to achieve maximum impact when I speak so everyone understands what I am saying,' she says.

You might think that Ms Hardy is paranoid or insecure. But a recent study by the Aziz Corporation, a firm of image consultants, suggests otherwise. It found that 46% of company directors believe that having a strong regional accent is considered a disadvantage to business success.

It also showed that some accents are more unequal than others. Liverpudlian, Brummie, West Country and Cockney accents came out worst. But Home Counties' and Scottish accents are seen as career assets.

The study confirmed previous research, which showed that having the wrong type of accent can affect your career. It also added credence to the belief that the 'acceptability' of local accents is a key factor in companies' decisions about where to locate.

'I think it is blind prejudice,' says Khalid Aziz, chairman of the Aziz Corporation. 'It seems to be pretty general. It is not just that southerners don't like people from the north; traditionally the Scots don't like the English. It works all ways round. The fact is that it is not what you say, but the way that you say it.'

Jenni Hunt, a lawyer from Wimbledon, and originally from Worksop, used to speak with a south Yorkshire accent. But after leaving her home town 16 years ago, she says she ditched her twang. 'I wanted to be taken seriously and to take myself seriously. I am pretty sure that it has helped my career,' she says.

In an attempt to boost her other career performing voiceovers she is having one-to-one sessions with Frances Parkes, a speech coach, and head of www.makethemostofyourvoice.com.

'When I ring up agents I speak with my lawyer's voice, the one I use for meetings,' says Ms Hunt.

People make assumptions about you based on your accent, says Ms Hardy. 'Every accent has a stigma attached to it in various ways. I don't want people to think about my accent. I want them to focus on what I am actually saying.'

Text B

Inquiries? Now the accent is on profit

Bin the brogue and adopt a cut-glass Home Counties voice. That was once the best advice for ambitious Celts and northerners. But now, amid the chaos of directory inquiry deregulation, comes victory for regional accents.

Traditional southern English is no match for a Scottish lilt, charming Irish chirp or warm Welsh warble when dealing with irate callers, and most inquiries to the controversial new 118 numbers are being handled by centres in northern England and the Celtic fringe. You may not be told the price of the call, you may not even get the right number, but at least you will be greeted by a dulcet tone.

The dominance of regional accents in call centres may be put down to the establishment of operations in areas where land is cheaper and jobs harder to come by than in the South-East, but telecoms bosses admit that accents played a part in determining where they settled.

Cable and Wireless, the biggest operator of new numbers coming on stream from today, said its research showed callers preferred to be greeted by northern and Scottish accents. It operates its services from three main centres, two of which are in Glasgow.

Philip Cheal of C&W said: 'Some accents are consistently more popular and trusted. The main thing is that calls are taken by someone with a clear voice who speaks politely to the customer. People are not turned down for a job on the grounds of their accent.'

The Number has launched its 118 118 directory service from a call centre in Cardiff and last week announced it had created 2,000 jobs. Its decision to locate in Wales was partly driven by the accent. 'The accents of people living near our call centres do lend themselves to this type of work,' said a spokesman.

The southern accent has also lost ground in broadcasting. Younger presenters including the BBC's Brummie Adrian Chiles, Welshman Huw Edwards and Scotswoman Kirsty Wark have not had to go all Cholmondeley-Warner to get ahead in the game. In recent years there have even been howls from some sectors within the BBC that plummy accents were proving a barrier to promotion.

The BBC has made a conscious move to diversify accents on Radios 3 and 4 in the past decade, admitting it had lagged 'a little behind the sound of the nation – beginning to sound a bit antique.'

However, callers to the new numbers say they are less interested in the telephonists' voices than in their ability to find the right numbers. Sheila MacMillan, 35, a Glasgow teacher, said yesterday: 'I phoned a 118 line for the number of a charity's head office in London. The operator had a pleasant accent but proved useless at finding the number. I ended up speaking to a shop assistant in Bromley. She had a nice accent, too, but it was a waste of 10 minutes and £2.'

Take note

Text B is an abridged version of an article by Stephen Khan that appeared in *The Observer* newspaper on 24 August 2003.

Answers
Writing and adapting texts

Original writing 1

Checkpoints

1 Stories written for young children are one type of text that might have both a reading audience and a listening audience.
2 Other fiction genres include: romantic fiction, historical novels, war stories, ghost stories, epistolary novels (stories told in the form of letters).

Exam preparation

To persuade: Charity appeal; publicity material; radio advertisement script; speech on a controversial issue.

To inform (note that in some cases the primary purpose of the following might be to persuade or to entertain): Newspaper article; magazine feature; sports report; book review; film review; album review; review of a live performance; guide to a local amenity; beginner's guide; autobiographical writing; biographical writing; guide for new students; handbook for new employees; educational text; travel journalism; CD liner notes; health information leaflet; Internet text; radio talk; audio guide script.

To entertain: Short story; beginning of a novel; radio play; film or television script; comedy sketch.

To instruct: Instruction booklet.

Original writing 2

Checkpoints

1 Groups of words with meanings linked to a particular field or topic.
2 These are sometimes known as 'pointing' words. They only make sense if they are related to the immediate situation or context – e.g. *now, yesterday, here, there.*

Adapting and transforming texts 1

Checkpoints

1 The audience might be addressed more directly (e.g. by the use of interrogatives and of the second person). The text might incorporate phonological/prosodic features.
2 When the text was written might be important. The circumstances in which the text was intended to be read or listened to might also be significant.

Adapting and transforming texts 2

Checkpoints

1 To paraphrase is to express the same meaning in different words.
2 This refers to the various techniques used to link the different parts of a text together. See page 14.

Exam preparation

In tackling this question you initially need to make sure you have a clear understanding of the four GASP elements (genre, audience, subject, purpose). The genre is prepared speech. The fact that you are being asked to produce a *spoken* text has important implications for the kind of language you will need to use. The immediate audience are in the studio, but there is also a wider audience of radio listeners. In both cases they are likely to have an interest in current affairs and to be aged from late teens upwards. The subject is regional accents and whether schools should seek to change them. The purpose is partly to inform the audience about the topic, but mainly to persuade them to share your views.

You should also think about language features that could be included in your answer. These will need to be appropriate to the four GASP elements. For example, lexical features might include: a generally formal register (to reflect the context – a current affairs radio programme); occasional informality (to achieve a rapport with the audience); relevant semantic fields (such as education and regional accents); monosyllabic words (to make clear, direct statements); polysyllabic words (to reflect the seriousness and complexity of the topic); persuasive, positive lexis (used to present views you agree with); negative lexis (used to present views you disagree with); emotive vocabulary (to move and persuade the audience). Possible grammatical features include: declarative sentences (to present your views); use of second person and of interrogative sentences (to address and involve the audience); occasional use of short sentences (to make points clearly and forcefully); rhetorical techniques such as parallelism, repetition, contrast and tripling (to achieve emphasis and rhythmic effects). Phonology will be important as the text is for a listening audience. Use of different types of sentence will help to give the talk varied intonation, and as mentioned rhetorical techniques can be used to achieve a strong sense of rhythm. In the script pauses for effect and stress on particular words might also be indicated. The discourse structure will partly depend on the points you intend to include (see below). You need to think about how to introduce and conclude the talk, and the rest of it needs to have a logical structure.

Two texts are provided as source material. You should read through these carefully, looking for ideas and information you can use. It is important to make use of *both* texts, even if one appeals to you more than the other.

Here is a specimen answer to the question:

If you think you have a good ear for regional accents, you might be surprised to hear that I'm a student at a college in Liverpool. However, if you think you can detect the unmistakable vowel sounds of a north Londoner you'd actually be quite right, because I grew up in Camden Town. I've lived in Liverpool for four years now and I'm pleased to say that in all that time none of my teachers has made any attempt to modify my accent. They've also not tampered with the accents of my classmates, even though there have been surveys suggesting Scouse and Cockney accents are both pretty low down the popularity league.

Of course there are those who will tell you that changing your accent is the key to getting on in life. Research by the

Aziz Corporation found that many company directors think regional accents are a disadvantage in the world of business. But do you know who the Aziz Corporation are? (Pause) A firm of <u>image consultants</u>. Do you detect an element of vested interest here? In fairness to Mr Aziz, the company's chairman, he himself says the attitudes revealed in his survey are 'blind prejudice'.

But the evidence that regional accents are a handicap is in any case mixed to say the least. It's been reported that call centres positively favour telephone operators with regional accents. Research by Cable and Wireless has found that callers like to hear northern and Scottish accents.

In my English class at college there's the expected complement of Liverpudlians, but also Sue from Wales, Scott from Birmingham and Sarah from Newcastle. And our teacher's from Northern Ireland! I believe diversity should be celebrated, and I'm pleased that the BBC, traditionally the preserve of upper class Home Counties accents, has made a positive effort to employ presenters with regional accents.

I'm sure I speak for the great majority of young people when I say to those in charge of our education system: leave our accents alone please, they're part of what we are and we're proud of them.

Writing commentaries

Checkpoints

1 Each of these five types of imagery appeals to a different sense: visual – sight; auditory – hearing, tactile – touch; gustatory – taste; olfactory – smell.
2 A simple sentence has only one clause. A compound sentence is two simple sentences joined together by and, but or so.

Exam preparation

Here is a specimen commentary to accompany the earlier answer to the question on page 161:

The genre for my text is prepared speech, so it was important that I produced a text suitable for a listening audience. I am addressing a studio audience, but also a wider audience of radio listeners. I have assumed these would be people with an interest in current affairs, aged from approximately 16–17 upwards. The purpose of my talk is to persuade the audience to share my view that schools should not attempt to change pupils' accents.

As the talk is for a current affairs radio programme, the register is often quite formal. This is reflected in the use of complex lexis ('vested interest'), some of which is polysyllabic ('modify', 'diversity'). However, in order to establish a rapport with the audience much of the language used is quite informal. This includes the use of contractions ('I'm', 'you'd') and conversational expressions such as 'pretty low', 'getting on in life' and 'to say the least'.

It was important to engage the audience by speaking to them directly. I achieved this from the very beginning by the use of the second person ('If you think you have a good ear'), which continues to be a recurring feature of the text. I have also involved the audience by using interrogative sentences: 'But do you know who the Aziz Corporation are?' This question is followed by a pause, which gives greater emphasis to my answer, which also stresses the words 'image consultants'. I am making the point here that the company has a clear interest in persuading people to want to change their accents.

The inclusion of questions also helps to give the talk varied intonation, as my voice would rise when asking them. Similarly, there is an exclamatory sentence which would be delivered with a rising intonation and which I hope would produce laughter in the audience: 'And our teacher's from Northern Ireland!' Other phonological features include the use of alliteration, parallelism and tripling, which would all have a rhythmic effect: 'Sue from Wales, Scott from Birmingham and Sarah from Newcastle'.

I have begun the talk by telling the audience about my background, which I hope would engage their interest. I also make my viewpoint clear from early on. I then look critically at the case for changing pupils' accents, before presenting the opposing view. I have tried to give the talk a powerful conclusion, by ending with a strong imperative.

Revision checklist
Writing and adapting texts

By the end of this chapter you should be able to:

1 Understand the original writing requirements of your exam board specification.	Confident	Not confident. **Revise** page 154
2 Recognise the importance of considering genre, audience, subject and purpose when planning an original writing assignment.	Confident	Not confident. **Revise** page 155
3 Understand the importance of using an appropriate register in original writing assignments.	Confident	Not confident. **Revise** page 156
4 List key considerations relevant to the lexis used in original writing assignments.	Confident	Not confident. **Revise**page 156
5 List key considerations relevant to the grammatical features of original writing assignments.	Confident	Not confident. **Revise** page 156
6 Identify phonological devices you might use in original writing.	Confident	Not confident. **Revise** page 157
7 Understand why graphological features might be important in original writing.	Confident	Not confident. **Revise** page 157
8 List key considerations relevant to the discourse structure of original writing assignments.	Confident	Not confident. **Revise**page 157
9 Explain the differences involved in writing for a reading audience and a listening audience.	Confident	Not confident. **Revise** page 157
10 Understand the text transformation requirements of your exam board specification.	Confident	Not confident. **Revise** page 158
11 Recognise the importance of considering genre, audience, subject and purpose when approaching text transformation exercises.	Confident	Not confident. **Revise** pages 158–159
12 Understand how to approach the reading of source material, and recognise the importance of reading actively.	Confident	Not confident. **Revise** page 159
13 List key considerations relevant to the production of your own text in text transformation exercises.	Confident	Not confident. **Revise** page 161
14 Understand the importance of thinking ahead to the commentary when you are writing the text on which the commentary will be based.	Confident	Not confident. **Revise** page 162
15 Approach with confidence the writing of a commentary.	Confident	Not confident. **Revise** pages 162–163

As with other A2 subjects, the Unit 6 English Language and Literature exam is known as the **synoptic module**. This means it is broader than the other modules, as it is intended to test a range of knowledge and skills acquired over the two years of the course. For all of the exam board specifications you are required to analyse and compare a selection of unseen literary and non-literary texts and extracts. 'Unseen' means you will not have studied the extracts before (i.e. they are not taken from any of your set texts), though you might find you are taking a specification where the texts are included in a pre-release booklet given to you a few days before the exam. You need to be prepared to analyse texts from a variety of literary and non-literary genres, and spoken as well as written texts. The texts will also be drawn from different historical periods. You should make sure you have a workable strategy for answering questions of this type. This chapter offers some practical advice on constructing answers, and you will also of course receive guidance from your teacher.

Exam themes

→ Analysis and comparison of texts of different types, and from different periods.

→ Evaluation of the relevance and usefulness of the approaches you have taken.

Topic checklist

○ AS ● A2	OCR	EDEXCEL	AQA A	AQA B	WJEC
The synoptic module	○●	○●	○●	○●	○●
Constructing an answer 1	○●	○●	○●	○●	○●
Constructing an answer 2	○●	○●	○●	○●	○●
Specimen texts	○●	○●	○●	○●	○●

The synoptic module

This section outlines the content of the synoptic module, and some guiding principles you should have in mind when approaching the exam.

What you have to do

There are strong similarities in the Unit 6 examinations set by the various examination boards. All of them ask you to **analyse** and **compare** texts of **different types** and from **different historical periods**. Usually you are also required to **evaluate** your own analysis, commenting on the approaches you have taken and how useful they were in relation to the specific texts you looked at.

Differences between the specifications include:

→ The **number of texts** you are asked to analyse varies, though usually it is **three or more**.

→ Usually all the texts are **unseen** (that is, you do not see them before the examination), but you may be taking a specification that provides some of the texts in a **pre-release booklet** distributed about three days before the exam. Even here though you will be given additional unseen texts to study in the exam itself.

→ Often there is **no choice** of question and you must analyse all the texts, but if you have a pre-release booklet you may be able to **select** the texts to write about.

→ The **evaluation** may be a separate question, but in some specifications the analytical comparison and the evaluation are combined in a single question.

Types of texts

As mentioned above, the texts will be of different types and also from different periods. Some specifications are a little more precise. For example, one states that every year there will be a literary text, a non-literary text and a spoken text. Another states that the texts will be from specified genres, such as travel writing, reportage and speeches. Essentially, however, you should be prepared to encounter almost any type of text, including:

→ Literary texts, e.g. poetry, drama, prose fiction.

→ Non-literary texts, e.g. newspaper articles, advertisements – for a fuller list, see pages 140–141.

→ Texts that are not easily classified as literary or non-literary, e.g. diaries and autobiographies.

→ Spontaneous speech, e.g. transcripts of conversation.

→ Prepared speech, e.g. public speeches.

Usually you will find there is a **thematic link** of some kind between the texts. You might for instance be given a collection of texts about childhood, or about family relationships.

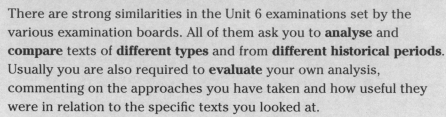

Watch out!

Make sure you are familiar with the format of the Unit 6 paper you will be taking.

Take note

Again, be sure to check your specification.

Ways of comparing texts

The next sections look at how you might construct an exam answer (pages 172–175), but it is important to grasp from the outset that you are required to **compare** the texts. This means you need to be alert to the kinds of similarities and differences that might exist between texts. You should be looking for these as you study the texts, and they should form the core of your answer. The main **points of comparison** between the texts include (note that some of these overlap):

→ Genre and mode **Genre** refers to the *type* of text – for example, one text might be scripted dialogue from a **play**, while another might be a passage of dialogue from a **novel**. **Mode** essentially means whether the text is **spoken** or **written**.
→ Audience.
→ Purpose.
→ Subject and theme.
→ Attitudes and values.
→ Period – this might for example be reflected in the language or form of a text, or in the attitudes expressed in it.
→ Form and structure.
→ Context – see *Getting started* below.
→ Language and style – this is one if the most important. In your answer you should closely analyse the language of the texts, and point out similarities and differences.

Getting started

As you read each text for the first time, try to get as clear an idea as you can about the following:

→ The **genre**, **audience**, **subject** and **purpose**. (**GASP** is an acronym that will help you remember this.) It is sometimes difficult to be precise about the audience of a text, but look for clues that might suggest – for example – the likely age, gender or educational background of readers.
→ The **period**.
→ The **attitudes** and **values** expressed. What views are implicit or explicit in the text? What feelings, ideas, beliefs etc. are considered valuable and important?
→ The **context**. This means all the factors that might have influenced the text, including: the author and his or her background or personal circumstances; the period it was written or spoken, including social, political and economic conditions, literary conventions and prevailing attitudes and values; the audience it was intended for, and the circumstances in which they would have read or heard it; the genre; the purpose.

Checkpoint 1

Give some simple examples of how the form and structure of two texts might differ.

Watch out!

Remember that a text can have more than one audience: the primary audience for an educational text might be schoolchildren, but the text might also be intended to appeal to parents and teachers. Similarly, texts can have more than one purpose.

Checkpoint 2

Explain the difference between **explicit** and **implicit**.

Examiner's secrets

Students often overlook the information about the texts provided on the examination paper. This often includes important contextual details.

Exam preparation

A practice synoptic module examination question is on page 173.

Constructing an answer 1

The next two sections give detailed advice on the planning and writing of answers to synoptic module questions.

Alternative approaches

There is no single method for answering questions of this kind that can be considered clearly superior to all other methods. Partly this is because the different specifications require slightly different approaches. This is reflected in the wording of the questions, which often contain some suggestion of the approach you should take. It is also because you need to have some flexibility, and to construct an answer that approaches the texts in a way that is appropriate to their particular features and characteristics.

Broadly speaking, however, there are two main ways of answering the question. Both can be successful, and while both also have possible pitfalls these can be avoided if you are aware of them. The approaches are:

1 After an introduction, you focus in turn on **points of comparison** between the texts. For example, you might have a paragraph comparing the lexis of each text, another comparing the grammatical features and so on. The points of comparison (which are the **frameworks** of your analysis) will be those that are most relevant to the texts you are analysing. The answer ends with a conclusion. The advantage of this approach is that the answer is clearly **comparative**. A danger is that an understanding of the 'whole' of each text – that is, an understanding of the overall meaning and effect – may not be conveyed.

2 After an introduction, you **analyse each text in turn**, pointing out the similarities and differences between the texts as you go along. Again you utilise relevant **frameworks** (such as lexis and grammar), and again you end with a conclusion. The advantage of this approach is that you give a **coherent overall account** of each individual text. A danger is that you may not compare the texts enough.

The choice is yours. What is important is that through practice, and with the guidance of your teacher, you develop a strategy that allows for some flexibility and which you can apply with confidence.

Making analytical points

Whichever approach you adopt, the detailed analytical points you make should usually have **three parts** to them:

→ Identification of a **literary or linguistic feature**, using appropriate terminology. Often this will involve a comparative reference to other texts (e.g. *Text B has more imagery than the other texts*).
→ The feature is illustrated, usually by giving one or more **quotations**.
→ The **effects** achieved by the feature, or the **reasons** it is present, are explained (e.g. *This is partly because Text B is a literary text*).

Checkpoint 1

How might an introduction to an answer reduce the danger referred to in Approach 1?

Take note

Answers following either of these approaches can be **introduced** and **concluded** in similar ways. See *Introductory overview* on the next page, and *Concluding an answer* on pages 174–175.

Examiner's secrets

This is very important – go into the exam with a clear idea of how your answer will be organised.

Take note

You should be used to this three-part structure by now! It is relevant to all kinds of text analysis, and also to commentaries on your own writing.

Note that these elements do not always have to be in this order. For example, you might write *Unlike the other texts, Text B is a literary text and one indication of this is the extensive use of imagery*.

Introductory overview ●●●

It is also generally the case that with any approach it is a good idea to begin with an **introductory overview** of the texts. You do not want to spend too long on this but should aim to write a substantial paragraph. It is an opportunity for you to show the examiner that you have a broad understanding of the texts, and of the key similarities and differences. See *Getting started* on page 171 for aspects of the texts that might be outlined in an introductory paragraph. In particular, it is useful to identify the **genre**, **audience**, **subject** and **purpose** of each text. You can also state the **frameworks** you will be using for your analysis (see below).

Analytical frameworks ●●●

Your analytical frameworks are the **points or areas of comparison** you will be looking at when examining the texts. Some are listed under *Ways of comparing texts* on page 171. There needs to be some flexibility here as the frameworks you choose should be ones that are relevant to the particular texts you are analysing. However, it is important to include some **language frameworks**, as much of your answer should be devoted to the close analysis of the language of the texts. The main language frameworks are: **lexis**, **grammar**, **phonology**, **discourse structure** and **graphology**. The next section (pages 174–175) gives advice on applying these frameworks.

Checkpoint 2

You should be especially careful not to write too much on one of these frameworks. Which one?

Exam preparation (2 hours)   answer: pages 178–179

Read **Texts A**, **B** and **C** on pages 176–177. Compare the attitudes and values expressed in the texts, and the ways in which these are conveyed. Your answer should include discussion of the following:

→ the influence of variations in genre and context;

→ similarities and difference in the use of language;

→ any other aspects which you consider important to an understanding of these texts.

Take note

On pages 176–177 you will also find important background information on the three texts. You will find it easier if you attempt this question after you have read the next section (pages 174–175).

Constructing an answer 2

This second section on constructing a Unit 6 answer lists some aspects of language and style that might be examined in an analytical comparison. It also offers advice on writing an **evaluation** of your analysis.

Language frameworks

With all these language frameworks you should look for how aspects of the language of each text reflect similarities and differences of **context**, **themes**, **attitudes** and so on. Some specific stylistic features that you might be able to comment on are listed below.

Lexis

Look for comparative points involving such features as: levels of formality; non-standard vocabulary; complexity; archaisms; neologisms; dialect; semantic fields; connotations; modification (pre- and post-modifiers); emotive vocabulary; imagery (including similes and metaphors); repetition of key words; puns; ambiguity.

Grammar

Types of sentence (declarative, interrogative, imperative, exclamatory; also simple, compound, complex); non-standard grammar; archaic constructions; ellipsis; parallelism; foregrounding; syndetic and asyndetic listing; first, second and third person; tenses.

Phonology

Devices such as onomatopoeia, alliteration, assonance and sibilance. In poetry, effects of rhyme, rhythm and metre. In spoken texts, effects of pauses, repetition, stress, intonation. In prepared speech, use of such techniques as parallelism and antithesis. In spontaneous speech, evidence of non-fluency features.

Discourse structure

Organisation and development of each text; literary form (e.g. sonnet, ballad); methods of organisation (e.g. stanzas, paragraphs); degrees of cohesion and how they're achieved; narrative point of view; interaction between speakers in dramatic dialogue or transcripts of conversation.

Graphology

Layout and visual features.

Concluding an answer

With some specifications, you need to conclude your answer with an **evaluation** of the approaches you have used in the analysis of the texts. With others the evaluation is a separate question. Advice on writing an evaluation is given below. One effective way of concluding the actual analysis of the texts is to consider **how successful** the texts are in terms of achieving their purposes and appealing to the reader or listener. You

Checkpoint 1

Explain the difference between an **archaism** and a **neologism**.

Checkpoint 2

Explain the difference between **assonance** and **sibilance**.

can give your own opinion here, but should try to justify your views by referring back to what you have said about the texts in the main body of your answer.

Evaluating your analysis

Most Unit 6 examination papers ask you to evaluate your own analysis of the texts. Usually the question is phrased something like this:

> Explain the methods you chose to examine the texts, and evaluate how useful they were.

Or:

> Say briefly how your knowledge of literary and linguistic approaches has helped you to analyse the texts.

You need to identify the approaches you have used in analysing the texts, and comment on how relevant and productive they were. Some of the approaches you are likely to have used are listed under *Ways of comparing texts* on page 171, and under *Language frameworks* opposite. You might for example say that discussing the likely **audience** for each text helped you to account for some of the differences in the language that was used (you would then go on to explain this more fully). Or you might refer to the usefulness of specific **language frameworks**, writing something along the lines of:

> Text A contained very few significant phonological features, but as Text B was a spoken text phonological effects were much more evident. The speaker used many of the techniques associated with public speeches, such as parallelism, tripling and repetition, all of which had a rhythmic effect. Stress and intonation also made an important contribution to the persuasiveness of the speech. It was again helpful to consider phonology when analysing Text C, because . . .

You will find it much easier to write an effective evaluation if your analysis of the texts is coherent and structured. If you examined the texts using a set of clear and appropriate analytical frameworks, the evaluation should be relatively straightforward.

Take note

Usually the evaluation does not need to be very long, but you should check this by asking your teacher or looking at past exam papers.

Examiner's secrets

There is a similarity here with writing commentaries; the hard work is essentially done beforehand (see page 162).

Exam preparation (30 minutes)   answer: page 179

After you have answered the question on page 173, explain the approaches you used in analysing and comparing the texts, and comment on their relevance and usefulness.

Specimen texts

The texts below are for use with the practice exam questions on pages 173 and 175.

Text A

The Schoolboy

Take note

Text A, *The Schoolboy*, is by **William Blake**. It was first published in 1794.

I love to rise in a summer morn,
When the birds sing on every tree;
The distant huntsman winds his horn,
And the skylark sings with me.
Oh! what sweet company.

But to go to school on a summer morn,
Oh! it drives all joy away;
Under a cruel eye outworn,
The little ones spend the day
In sighing and dismay.

Ah! then at times I drooping sit,
And spend many an anxious hour,
Nor in my book can I take delight,
Nor sit in learning's bower,
Worn through with the dreary shower.

How can the bird that is born for joy
Sit in a cage and sing?
How can a child, when fears annoy,
But drop his tender wing,
And forget his youthful spring?

Oh! father and mother! if buds are nipped,
And blossoms blown away,
And if the tender plants are stripped
Of their joy in the springing day,
By sorrow and care's dismay,

How shall the summer arise in joy,
Or the summer's fruits appear?
Or how shall we gather what griefs destroy,
Or bless the mellowing year,
When the blasts of winter appear?

Text B

Take note

Text B is an extract from *The Rainbow*, a novel by **D.H. Lawrence**, first published in 1915. The novel is set in Nottinghamshire and follows the lives of three generations of the Brangwen family. The extract is about Ursula Brangwen's plans to become a teacher.

On Friday her father said there was a place vacant in Brinsley Street school. This could most probably be secured for her, at once, without the trouble of application.

Her heart halted. Brinsley Street was a school in a poor quarter, and she had had a taste of the common children of Ilkeston. They had shouted after her and thrown stones. Still, as a teacher, she would be in authority. And it was all unknown. She was excited. The very forest of dry, sterile brick had some fascination for her. It was so hard and ugly, so relentlessly ugly, it would purge her of some of her floating sentimentality.

She dreamed how she would make the little, ugly children love her. She would be so *personal*. Teachers were always so hard and impersonal. There was no vivid relationship. She would make everything personal and vivid, she would give herself, she would give, give, give all her great stores of wealth to her children, she would make them *so* happy, and they would prefer her to any teacher on the face of the earth.

At Christmas she would choose such fascinating Christmas cards for them, and she would give them such a happy party in one of the classrooms.

Text C

Why am I the first Kinnock in a thousand generations to be able to get to university? Why is Glenys the first woman in her family in a thousand generations to be able to get to university?

Was it because *all* our predecessors were 'thick'? Did they lack talent – those people who could sing, and play, and recite and write poetry; those people who could make wonderful, beautiful things with their hands; those people who could dream dreams, see visions; those people who had such a sense of perception as to know in times so brutal, so oppressive, that they could win their way out of that by coming together?

Were those people not university material? Couldn't they have knocked off all their A levels in an afternoon?

But why didn't they get it?

Was it because they were weak? – those people who could work eight hours underground and then come up and play football?

Weak? Those women who could survive eleven childbearings, were they weak? Those people who could stand with their backs and their legs straight and face the people who had control over their lives, the ones who owned their workplaces and tried to own them, and tell them, 'No. I won't take your orders.' Were they weak?

Does anybody really think that they didn't get what we had because they didn't have the talent, or the strength, or the endurance, or the commitment?

Of course not. It was because there was no platform upon which they could stand; no arrangement for their neighbours to subscribe to their welfare; no method by which the communities could translate their desire for those individuals into provision for those individuals.

And now, Mrs Thatcher, by dint of privatisation, and means test, and deprivation, and division, wants to nudge us back into the situation where everybody can either stand on their own feet, or live on their knees.

Take note

Text C is an extract from a speech delivered during the 1987 General Election by **Neil Kinnock**, who was then leader of the Labour Party. Early in the extract he makes a brief reference to Glenys, his wife. He also refers to his opponent in the election, Margaret Thatcher, who was Prime Minister and leader of the Conservative Party.

Answers
Comparing unseen texts

The synoptic module

Checkpoints

1 A text might for example take the form of a poem, a prose passage or a piece of dramatic dialogue. The text might be complete or an extract from a larger text. One text might have longer paragraphs than another. One text might have a more clearly recognisable beginning, middle and end.

2 Explicit means openly expressed or stated. Implicit means hidden or implied.

Constructing an answer 1

Checkpoints

1 If an introduction gives an overview of each text, this gives you the opportunity to show you have a grasp of each text's overall meaning and effect.

2 Graphology.

Exam preparation

An answer to this question might begin with an introductory paragraph which gives an overview of the three texts and outlines the approach you will take to analysing them. Text A is by the Romantic poet William Blake. The Romantic poets of the late 18th and early 19th centuries were noted for their interest in the workings of the individual consciousness. They often wrote about childhood, because they believed children possessed a natural wisdom and understanding which as they grew up was restricted and repressed by society. These attitudes are reflected in *The Schoolboy*, which associates education with suppression of the child narrator's instinctive love of life. Text B contrasts with Text A, not only because it is a prose fiction text from a later period, but also because it views education from the perspective of a young woman about to enter teaching, describing her idealistic belief in what she will be able to achieve. Text C is different again, and again this is in part a difference of genre and period. It is closer to the present day, and is a public speech delivered by a politician. In it Neil Kinnock argues that for generations large sections of society were denied the opportunity to fulfil their potential by continuing their education beyond the school-leaving age. He warns that the policies of his opponents in the election threaten a return to this.

An approach to the analysis of the texts might be to focus on the differing perspectives on education offered by a fictional schoolboy, a fictional teacher and a real-life politician. The aim of the analysis would be to establish through this the views of the writers of the text, and how these are conveyed by the language that they use. Relevant areas of language to explore include lexis, grammar and phonology.

The narrator of Text A is a child whose natural joy and spontaneity are crushed by school. The language of the poem is notably simple and direct, with a large number of monosyllabic words and a regular rhyme scheme. This is a feature of the verse of many Romantic poets (including Blake), but here it is especially appropriate because it helps to suggest the voice of a child. Natural imagery is another important stylistic feature of the poem. It is used to suggest that the forced education of children is *un*natural.

The first stanza expresses the child's love of life and delight in nature. Auditory imagery creates a world full of happy sounds – singing birds, the huntsman's horn. Words with positive connotations (*love, sweet*) convey the narrator's pleasure, as does the exclamatory *Oh!* The conjunction *But* at the beginning of the next stanza immediately indicates a change in mood. School is portrayed as a joyless place where children toil under the eye of a *cruel* schoolteacher. The lexis now has negative connotations, and in place of the happy sounds of the opening stanza there is *sighing and dismay*. In the first line of the third stanza, word order foregrounds *drooping* (*I drooping sit* instead of *I sit drooping*), emphasising the child's dejection. The pre-modifiers *anxious* and *dreary* suggest unhappiness and boredom. Ironically, the boy is in fact eager to learn. He longs to take *delight* in his book and to sit in *learning's bower*, a metaphor which suggests the bliss of private, solitary learning – in contrast to the misery of enforced, institutionalised education.

The second half of the poem is a series of rhetorical questions, addressed to the child's parents and to the reader. More natural images are used: the child is like a caged bird, or a young plant not allowed to grow and flourish. Passive verbs present the boy as a helpless victim (*buds are nipped, tender plants are stripped*). Exclamations convey feelings of urgency and distress: *Oh! father and mother!* In the closing stanza, parallelism (the repetition of *Or . . .* and *How shall*) gives the questioning increased intensity. The poem argues that if we do not have the freedom to enjoy life when we are young, we shall be unhappy in later life: unable to cope with loss (*gather what griefs destroy*) and unable to accept and embrace the passing of time (*bless the mellowing year*). In this last verse the changing of the seasons is used to represent the cycle of life.

Text B is another literary text, though it is from a different genre and views education from the perspective of a teacher rather than a pupil. In contrast to the first-person narrator of Text A, Text B has a third-person omniscient narrator, a device often employed in prose fiction. Much of the extract uses the technique of free indirect thought to present Ursula's hopes and plans to the reader (*She would be so personal*). In some ways the extract shares Text A's negative view of conventional education, associating it with cold, mechanical relationships between teachers and pupils: *Teachers were always so hard and impersonal. There was no vivid relationship.* However, Ursula is convinced she can be different and is *excited* about the future. Words with positive connotations are used as she imagines the close, caring relationship she will have with her pupils: *personal, vivid, happy, fascinating.* Metaphor is used to suggest the deep knowledge and wisdom she will pass on to her pupils: *her great stores of wealth.* Her enthusiasm is stressed by the use of intensifiers (*so happy, such fascinating Christmas cards*) and repetition (*she would give, give, give*). Syntactic parallelism has a similar effect: *She would make . . . she would give . . . she would give . . . she would make . . .*).

However, Lawrence hints in a variety of ways that her hopes are unrealistic. *She dreamed* suggests this, as does the hyperbole of *they would prefer her to any teacher on the face of the earth*. There is also her initial trepidation, conveyed by the short sentence describing her immediate reaction to the news that there is a vacancy at Drinsley Street: *Her heart halted*. The social class divisions of the time are reflected in her misgivings about the children of the area: they are *common* and *ugly*. So although Text B presents more positive attitudes towards education than Text A, these are the attitudes of a character within a novel, and we sense that the author is undermining them and exposing their naivety.

There is less ambiguity about Text C. The speaker, Neil Kinnock, clearly values education, and he decries the fact that for generations the opportunity of further and higher education was denied to millions of ordinary working class people. Unlike Texts A and B, Text C is not a literary text and the attitudes expressed are more straightforwardly those of the speaker as they are not mediated through a fictional character. It is also a spoken rather than a written text, and has many of the rhetorical features associated with public speeches. It is about post-compulsory education, whereas Texts A and B both evoke the world of school. A further difference is that the previous texts focused on the attitudes and experiences of characters directly involved in education (a pupil and a teacher), while Text C is more about the merits of those who were denied a university education, and why this happened. The speech has a political purpose, and seeks to persuade listeners to support Labour at the General Election.

Text C engages more directly with its intended audience than the other texts, and much of the extract is made up of interrogative sentences. Another rhetorical feature is syntactic parallelism, used to stress the talents of the ordinary people of previous generations, and also their strength of character and powers of endurance: *those people who could sing . . . those people who could make wonderful, beautiful things . . . those people who could dream dreams*. This parallelism gives the speech a powerful, emphatic rhythm, as does the use of heavily syndetic listing, which in this quotation forcefully condemns the policies of Kinnock's opponent, Margaret Thatcher. *Mrs Thatcher, by dint of privatisation, and means test, and deprivation, and division*. Phonological variety is achieved by alternating the long sentences that have these repetitive grammatical structures with short, emphatic sentences: *Of course not*.

Constructing an answer 2

Checkpoints

1 An archaism is a word or expression that has fallen out of use. A neologism is a new word or expression.
2 Assonance occurs when vowel sounds within words rhyme. Sibilance is the repetition of *s*, *z*, *sh* and soft *c* sounds.

Exam preparation

In answering this question you should explain and comment on the approach you used when analysing the three texts on pages 176–177. In your introduction to the analysis you might well have outlined the approach you were taking, and this will give you a starting point. You might, for example, comment that it was useful to examine the different perspectives on education: each text approaches the topic from a different direction (the imagined experiences of a pupil and a teacher in Texts A and B, and the views of a politician in Text C). The attitudes expressed also differ. You should also identify the language frameworks you have used. Examination of lexis and grammar is especially relevant to an analysis of Texts A and B, while as Text C is a speech rhetorical techniques are the most significant linguistic feature.

Revision checklist
Comparing unseen texts

By the end of this chapter you should be able to:

1	Understand the synoptic module requirements of your exam board specifications.	Confident	Not confident. **Revise** page 170
2	Distinguish between different types of text you might be required to analyse.	Confident	Not confident. **Revise** page 170
3	List the main aspects of texts that might be compared.	Confident	Not confident. **Revise** page 171
4	Recognise the importance of clarifying the genre, audience, subject and purpose of each text.	Confident	Not confident. **Revise** page 171
5	Understand the need to consider the historical period of each text.	Confident	Not confident. **Revise** page 171
6	Understand the importance of considering the attitudes and values expressed in each text.	Confident	Not confident. **Revise** page 171
7	Explain what is meant by the context of a text, and why it is important.	Confident	Not confident. **Revise** page 171
8	Explain how you would approach the comparison of unseen texts.	Confident	Not confident. **Revise** page 172
9	Identify the three elements that make up an analytical point.	Confident	Not confident. **Revise** pages 172–173
10	Identify the main language frameworks, and list the key features within each framework.	Confident	Not confident. **Revise** page 174
11	Approach with confidence the comparison of unseen texts.	Confident	Not confident. **Revise** pages 172–175
12	Explain how you would approach writing an evaluation of your analysis.	Confident	Not confident. **Revise** page 175

This chapter offers some final information and advice as you prepare for your AS or A2 exams. The first section lists and explains the **assessment objectives** used by examiners to determine your grade. Students are often unaware of these, but knowing what the examiner is looking for is clearly advantageous if you are trying to maximise your mark. There is also a checklist of literary and linguistic terms. Failure to include relevant terminology is a common failing in weaker answers. You should make sure you know these terms, and take care to use them accurately. Finally, there is a selection of 'tips for success' – some practical advice on coursework, revision and writing effective exam answers.

Exam boards

It is useful to have a copy of your exam specification. You can obtain one from the board's publications department or by downloading the specification from the board's website. The boards also supply copies of past exam papers.

→ AQA (Assessment and Qualifications Alliance)
   Publications Department, Stag Hill House, Guildford, Surrey
   GU25XJ – www.aqa.org.uk
→ EDEXCEL
   One 90 High Holborn, London WC1V 7BE –
   www.edexcel.org.uk
→ OCR (Oxford, Cambridge and Royal Society of Arts)
   1 Hills Road, Cambridge CB2 1GG – www.ocr.org.uk
→ WJEC (Welsh Joint Education Committee)
   245 Western Avenue, Cardiff CF5 2YX – www.wjec.co.uk

Topic checklist

○ AS ● A2

	OCR	EDEXCEL	AQA A	AQA B	WJEC
How you're assessed	○●	○●	○●	○●	○●
Terminology checklist	○●	○●	○●	○●	○●
Tips for success	○●	○●	○●	○●	○●

How you're assessed

This section outlines the structure of AS/A2 English Language and Literature courses, and how you will be assessed. In particular, it explains the eight official **assessment objectives**, which examiners use to calculate your marks.

Coursework and exams

Take note

As with other subjects, your AS marks account for 50% of your total A-level mark and are carried forward into your A2 year. You can though re-sit individual units (modules) before finishing the course in order to improve your final grade.

Depending on the specification you're taking, and the options chosen by your school or college, you may be assessed by exam only or by a combination of exams and coursework. If the assessment is purely exam based, you'll probably sit three exam papers in your AS year and another three in your A2 year. If coursework is part of your assessment, you're likely to find that coursework assignments replace one AS paper and one A2 paper. Coursework (if taken) is worth 30% of the AS assessment and 30% of the A2 assessment, which means that when the marks are added together it is also worth 30% of the full A-level.

Assessment objectives

Take note

Try to find out the assessment objectives for each unit you're taking, and the weighting each objective has. For example, in the A2 synoptic module (Unit 6), you might find that AO3ii accounts for as much as 50% of the total marks.

Assessment objectives (**AOs**) identify the skills and knowledge you're expected to acquire during the course. Each module usually assesses a combination of four or five objectives. Overall the objectives have a fairly equal weighting, but within individual modules the objectives will have varying degrees of importance.

It is helpful for you to know and understand the assessment objectives for the course – you are more likely to pick up marks if you know what the examiner is looking for.

Listed below are the eight assessment objectives for English Language and Literature, with a brief explanation of what each one means. Unless indicated, they are tested at both AS and A2; the difference is that at A2 a higher standard is expected.

AO1

Communicate clearly the knowledge, understanding and insights gained from the combination of literary and linguistic study, using appropriate terminology and accurate written expression.

This objective highlights your own writing skills (you need to *communicate clearly*), and also the need to know and use effectively relevant technical terms.

Links

For more on what is meant by **literary and non-literary texts**, see pages 140–141.

AO2i (AS only)

In responding to literary and non-literary texts, distinguish, describe and interpret variation in meaning and form.

This objective indicates that you will study a range of literary and non-literary texts and that you will be tested on your ability to understand their meaning and their overall structure and organisation.

AO2ii (A2 only)

Respond with knowledge and understanding to texts of different types and from different periods, exploring and commenting on relationships and comparisons between them.

This is similar to AO2i, but takes it further by referring specifically to texts from the past (*from different periods*), and by saying you need to show an ability to compare texts.

AO3i (AS only)

Respond to and analyse texts, using literary and linguistic concepts and approaches.

This means that you need to analyse texts from both *literary* and *linguistic* perspectives. Looking at characters and examining themes are examples of literary approaches. Linguistic approaches include, for example, the analysis of lexis and grammar.

AO3ii (A2 only)

Use and evaluate different literary and linguistic approaches to the study of written and spoken language, showing how these approaches inform their reading.

This extends AO3i by saying that at A2 you also need to explain and comment on your own methods of analysis.

AO4

Show understanding of the ways contextual variation and choices of form, style and vocabulary shape the meanings of texts.

This objective focuses on the various influences on the meaning of a text, including the context (which involves looking at elements such as genre and audience) and the way language is used.

AO5

Identify and consider the ways attitudes and values are created in speech and writing.

This objective refers to particular aspects of a text's meaning: the *attitudes and values* that are expressed within it. Attitudes are essentially views and opinions; values are more to do with what is considered important in life, and judgements about what is morally right or wrong.

AO6

Demonstrate expertise and accuracy in writing for a variety of specific purposes and audiences, drawing on knowledge of literary texts and features of language to explain and comment on the choices made.

You need to show that you can write a variety of texts, and comment analytically on your own writing.

Take note

You are likely to compare texts at AS as well, but the ability to compare texts analytically is tested more rigorously at A2.

Links

For a fuller discussion of **context**, see page 171.

Take note

The attitudes and values might be those of the author, or those given to characters in a literary text such as a play or novel.

Take note

As this objective indicates, whenever you write a text you need a clear sense of your **audience** and **purpose**. See page 155.

Terminology checklist

Here is a checklist of terms it would be useful for you to know, arranged into categories such as lexis, grammar, phonology etc. These terms are all explained elsewhere in the book (use the **Index** to find the relevant pages), and many are also in the **Glossary** that begins on page 188.

Examiner's secrets

It is one thing to know these terms, but another to get the credit you deserve for knowing them. Remember the only way to make the examiner aware of your knowledge is to **use** the relevant terms in your answers.

Take note

Although it is important to know and use these terms, remember that references to literary and linguistic features should always be accompanied by **examples** (usually in the form of **quotations**) and by **comment** on the **effects** that the features have.

Lexis		
Word classes	Noun	Proper noun
Common noun	Concrete noun	Abstract noun
Collective noun	Adjective	Comparative
Superlative	Verb	Dynamic verb
Stative verb	Active verb	Passive verb
Adverb	Pronoun	Conjunction
Preposition	Determiner	Intensifier
Denotation	Connotation	Figurative language
Metaphor	Simile	Personification
Pathetic fallacy	Imagery	Visual imagery
Auditory imagery	Gustatory imagery	Olfactory imagery
Tactile imagery	Semantic field	Field-specific lexis
Hypernym	Hyponym	Synonym
Antonym	Contrast	Antithesis
Formal	Informal	Complex
Simple	Polysyllabic	Monosyllabic
Colloquial	Dialect vocabulary	Irony
Ambiguity	Pun	Oxymoron
Emotive	Taboo language	Euphemism
Pathos	Bathos	Jargon
Archaism	Neologism	Borrowing
Contraction	Elision	Deictic expression
Modes of address	Hyperbole	

Grammar		
Simple sentence	Compound sentence	Complex sentence
Subordinate clause	Ellipsis	Minor sentence
Declarative sentence	Interrogative sentence	Imperative sentence
Exclamatory sentence	Rhetorical question	Main verb
Auxiliary verb	Syntax	Phrase
Clause	Noun phrase	Head word
Modifier	Pre-modifier	Post-modifier
Adverbial	Foregrounding	End-focus
Inverted syntax	Parallelism	Tripling
Syndetic listing	Asyndetic listing	First person
Second person	Third person	Tense
Inflection	Non-standard grammar	Dialect grammar

Phonology		
Onomatopoeia	Rhyme	Sibilance
Dissonance	Alliteration	Half-rhyme
Assonance		

Discourse structure		
Cohesion	Anaphoric reference	Cataphoric reference
Non-linear text	Exophoric reference	Intertextual reference
Linear text		

Spoken language		
Utterance	Referential utterance	Expressive utterance
Phatic utterance	Directive utterance	Monologue
Dialogue	Disjointed construction	False start
Non-fluency features	Filler	Filled pause
Unvoiced pause	Prosodic features	Intonation
Pitch	Pace	Liaison
Juncture	Pause	Volume
Stress	Oral signal	Accent
RP accent	Transactional exchange	Interactional exchange
Adjacency pair	Three-part exchange	Topic marker
Topic shift	Topic loop	Repair
Feedback	Turn-taking	

Drama		
Plot	Sub-plot	Exposition
Complication	Resolution	Denouement
Props	Soliloquy	Dramatic irony
Aside	Naturalistic dialogue	Stylised dialogue
Hero	Protagonist	

Fiction		
Narrative viewpoint	Narrative voice	First-person narrator
Third-person narrator	Omniscient narrator	Unreliable narrator
Intrusive narrator	Unintrusive narrator	Multiple narrators
Direct speech thought	Indirect speech thought	Free direct speech
Free indirect speech		

Poetry		
Stanza	Quatrain	Refrain
Lyric poetry	Sonnet	Ode
Elegy	Narrative poetry	Epic
Ballad	Persona	Rhyme scheme
Half-rhyme	Internal rhyme	Couplet
Heroic couplet	Metre	Iambic pentameter
Blank verse	Trochaic metre	Dactylic metre
Anapaestic metre	Spondaic metre	Enjambement
Caesura		

Other terms		
Standard English	Register	Dialect
Sociolect	Idiolect	Context
Rhetorical features	Genre	Symbolism
Allegory	Old English	Middle English
Early Modern English	Late Modern English	

Tips for success

Here are some final tips to help you achieve exam success.

Know what you have to do

Try to make sure that from the outset of the course you have a clear idea of what lies ahead of you. You need to know which examining board specification you're taking, how many exams you'll be sitting and when you'll be taking them, whether you'll be doing coursework, what set texts you'll be studying and so on. Your teacher will probably give you much of this information; make sure you keep it in your file and remember where it is for future reference. The complete specification can usually be downloaded free of charge from the relevant examining board website.

Combining language and literature

You also need to grasp from quite early on that the course is very different from GCSE English. In particular, the way you write about literary texts (such as novels and plays) demands new skills. You need to analyse the **language** of texts much more closely, and use relevant terminology when you are doing this. This is often the big mistake made by students who are not as successful as they should be: when they write about literary texts they focus on characters and themes and do not pay enough attention to language.

How to analyse

As has been mentioned earlier in the book, a standard analytical point has three parts to it (the three elements do not always have to be in this order):

→ Identification of a literary or linguistic feature (often this will involve the use of **terminology**).
→ Supporting **evidence**, usually in the form of one or more **quotations**.
→ **Comment** on the effect that a feature has, or the reason it is there.

When students lose marks it is often because one of these elements is missing. They might write an answer that does not make enough use of terminology, or include enough quotations. Or they might identify features without commenting on their effects (this is known as feature-spotting, and is very common).

Studying set texts

When you are studying a set text for an exam, you need to know whether it is for an **open book** or a **closed book** exam. 'Open book' means you can take the book into the exam with you, 'closed book' means you can't.

If it is an open book exam, you are usually allowed to annotate the book with handwritten notes. Be careful here. The examining boards usually stipulate that annotation should be brief, and notes rather than

Take note

The examining boards all have publications departments which can supply copies of past exam papers. You can telephone them for more details or order from their online catalogues. Past exam papers are extremely useful, but they can take a week or so to arrive so you shouldn't leave it to the last minute before ordering them.

Links

See pages 184–185 for a *Terminology checklist*.

continuous prose. In any case, excessive annotation can lead to confusion in the exam itself. You should have a detailed set of notes that you use for revision purposes, and the book then only needs to contain key words, highlighted passages etc. to remind you of these more detailed arguments.

If it is a closed book exam, part of your revision will involve memorising key quotations. When you learn the quotation, always revise at the same time the point that the quotation illustrates. Quotations that can be used to illustrate several different points are especially worth knowing.

Coursework

There should be no excuse for students under-achieving on coursework modules, though many do. The reason is often that the work has been completed in a rush and as a result does not reflect the student's true ability. You need to give yourself plenty of time to complete the assignment, and it is important to keep to deadlines. The deadline for the first draft is often the most crucial. Meeting this gives your teacher time to look at your work, and you time to act on your teacher's advice.

Exam revision

Many books have been written about revision techniques, and you will certainly be given advice at your school or college. Most experts would agree that you should do the following:

→ Start early.
→ Be organised. Work out what you're going to revise and when you're going to revise it.
→ Don't draw up a revision schedule that's over-ambitious. Allow for breaks and days off.
→ Find a revision method that works for you (this might involve a bit of experimentation!).

Exam technique

As part of your preparation for the exam you should familiarise yourself with the format of the exam paper. Even so, in the real exam it is still important to **look over the paper carefully**, checking how many questions you need to answer and how many marks are allocated to each question (the way you divide your time in the exam should reflect this). You should also **read the questions very carefully**. Underline key words and make sure you know exactly what the question wants you to do. There may be valuable advice on how to approach the question. Often questions also contain important background information about unseen texts.

Above all, **be positive**: if you've prepared well, you should be able to look forward to the exam as an opportunity to impress the examiner with the depth of your knowledge and understanding. Good luck!

Take note

In an open book exam you should be careful to avoid the temptation to include overlong quotations, and should not copy out passages from any critical material (such as an introduction) provided in the book itself (examiners can always spot this). Although you will have the book with you, you still need to know it thoroughly. You do not want to waste time in the exam hunting down quotations.

Take note

Grade A students have not always achieved the top grade in every exam. Instead, through conscientious effort, they have gained a very high coursework mark and this has offset lower marks in one or more of the examination modules. On the other hand, if you get a low coursework mark you will be facing an uphill battle to achieve a high overall grade when you sit the exams.

Glossary

adjacency pair

In conversation, a two-part exchange (e.g. a question followed by an answer).

adjective

A word used to describe a noun.

adverb

Usually a word that gives more information about a verb. Many adverbs end in *-ly* (e.g. *slowly, carefully*).

adverbial

An element in a sentence that usually indicates when, where or how something happened.

alliteration

When two or more words begin with the same sound.

ambiguity

Having more than one possible meaning.

anaphoric reference

A reference back to something mentioned earlier in a text.

antithesis

When words, ideas etc. are directly opposite in meaning.

archaism

A word or expression that has fallen out of use.

assonance

The rhyming of vowel sounds within two or more words.

asyndetic listing

A list that does not use conjunctions.

auxiliary verb

A 'helping' verb placed in front of a main verb (e.g. I <u>will</u> see you).

blank verse

Unrhymed poetry based on the iambic pentameter.

cataphoric reference

A reference forward to something mentioned later in a text.

cohesion

The techniques used to link together different parts of a text.

comparative

An adjective that makes a comparison, such as *bigger, worse, better.*

complex sentence

A sentence with a main clause and one or more subordinate clauses.

compound sentence

Two simple sentences combined to form a single sentence by the use of a co-ordinating conjunction (*and, but* or *so*).

conjunction

A word that joins together parts of a sentence (e.g. *and, but*).

connotations

The associations that a word has.

contraction

A shortened word form such as *can't, she's* etc.

couplet

A pair of rhymed lines.

declarative sentence

A sentence that makes a statement or gives information.

deixis

'Pointing' words (**deictic expressions**), often referring to place (e.g. *over there*) or time (e.g. *yesterday*).

denotation

The straightforward, objective dictionary meaning of a word.

determiner

A word placed in front of a noun to indicate quantity or identify the noun in some way. The most common determiners are *a, an* and *the*.

dialect

A form of language with distinctive features of vocabulary, grammar etc. Usually the term refers to **regional dialect** (e.g. Geordie, Cockney).

discourse marker

Words that indicate links or divisions between parts of (usually spoken) discourse (e.g. *well, anyway*).

dramatic irony

In drama, when something said by a character has an additional meaning or significance, apparent to the audience but not to the character.

elision

The omission of a sound or syllable (e.g. *o'er* instead of *over*).

ellipsis

When elements are missing from a clause or a sentence.

emotive language

Language intended to produce an emotional response in the reader or listener.

enjambement

In poetry, when the sense of one line continues into the next, and the end of the first line has no punctuation mark.

exclamatory sentence

An emphatic sentence ending in an exclamation mark.

false start

In speech, a change from one grammatical construction to another.

field-specific lexis

Words associated with a particular topic or field.

filled pause

A voiced hesitation (e.g. *um, er*).

filler

A word or expression with little meaning inserted into speech (e.g. *like, you know*).

first person

Use of first person pronouns such as *I, me, we, us*.

foregrounding

Using word order to highlight part of a sentence.

genre

A type of text (e.g. short story, newspaper article).

hyperbole

Intentional exaggeration.

iambic pentameter

A poetic metre in which a line has five pairs of syllables, with the stress falling on the second syllable in each pair.

idiolect

The way language is used by a particular individual.

imagery

Any aspect of a text that appeals to the reader's senses. Also used more specifically to refer to the use in literature of similes and metaphors.

imperative sentence

A sentence that gives a command or instruction.

intensifier

A word that increases or decreases the strength of another word (e.g. *very, scarcely*).

interrogative sentence

A sentence that asks a question.

intonation

Tone of voice.

irony

Saying the opposite of what is meant. Can also refer to an event having consequences that are the opposite of those expected or intended. See also **dramatic irony**.

metaphor

A comparison that is not literally true because it refers to something as if it were something else.

monologue

An extended utterance spoken by one person.

monosyllabic

Having one syllable.

neologism

A new word or expression.

non-fluency features

Features that interrupt the flow of a person's speech.

noun

A word that names an object, person, feeling etc.

omniscient narrator

In prose fiction, an 'all seeing, all knowing' narrator.

onomatopoeia

When words imitate the sounds they describe (e.g. *splash, buzz*).

oral signal

An expressive sound such as *mmm* or a laugh, sigh etc.

parallelism

When parts of sentences (or complete sentences) have a similar pattern or structure.

passive voice

Using a verb in a way that emphasises the object of an action rather than the person or thing performing the action (e.g. *The man was questioned by the police* instead of *The police questioned the man*).

pathetic fallacy

A literary technique that uses natural elements (such as the weather) to reflect human moods and emotions.

persona

In a literary work, a narrator who is a character created by the author.

personification

When something not human is described as if it were.

phatic utterances

'Small talk' – utterances that mean little but serve a social purpose.

polysyllabic

Having three or more syllables.

post-modifiers

Words that follow other words or phrases, giving us more information (e.g. *the house across the road*).

pre-modifiers

Words placed in front of other words or phrases, giving us more information (e.g. *the bright red door*).

preposition

A word that indicates how one thing is related to something else (e.g. *The book is on the table*).

pronoun

A word that takes the place of a noun (e.g. *he, it*).

prosodic features

Phonological aspects of speech such as intonation, pitch and volume.

pun

A humorous play on words, dependent on a word or phrase having a double meaning.

Received Pronunciation (RP)

The accent associated with upper-class speakers of English.

register

The form of language appropriate to a particular situation.

repair

An utterance that resolves a problem in a conversation (e.g. a speaker correcting themselves).

rhetorical features

Traditional devices and techniques used to make speech or writing more powerful and persuasive.

rhetorical question

A question that does not require an answer.

second person

Use of second person pronouns such as *you* and *your*.

semantic field

A group of words with linked or associated meanings.

sibilance

The repetition of *s*, soft *c*, *sh* and *z* sounds.

simile

A comparison that uses the words *like* or *as*.

simple sentence

A sentence that has one clause.

soliloquy

In drama, an extended speech by a character, heard by the audience but not by the other characters.

sonnet

A poem of 14 lines, usually with a traditional rhyme scheme and a rhythm based on the iambic pentameter.

Standard English

The 'standard', formally correct variety of English, used in most written texts and taught in schools.

subordinate clause

A clause in a sentence that is of less importance than the main clause, and which cannot stand on its own and make sense.

sub-plot

A secondary plot running alongside the main plot of a play or a novel.

superlative

An adjective meaning 'the most' of something (e.g. *biggest, worst, best*).

syndetic listing

A list with one or more conjunctions.

syntax

An aspect of grammar, referring to the ways in which words are put together to form sentences.

taboo language

Words that are avoided because they are considered offensive or obscene.

tag question

A question attached to the end of a statement (e.g. *It's hot, isn't it?*).

third person

Grammatical constructions that do not use the **first** or **second person**. This may involve nouns (e.g. *The house is a ruin*) or third person pronouns (e.g. *It is a ruin*).

topic

In spoken language, the subject being talked about. A **topic marker** is an utterance introducing a topic. A **topic shift** is a change of topic. A **topic loop** occurs when there is a return to an earlier topic.

unvoiced pause

A silent pause.

verb

A word that refers to a physical or mental action (e.g. *run, think*) or to a 'state' (e.g. *seems, is*).

Index